JOURNAL FOR THE STUDY OF THE OLD TESTAMENT SUPPLEMENT SERIES
174

JSOT Press
Sheffield

'The Book of the Covenant'
A Literary Approach

Joe M. Sprinkle

Journal for the Study of the Old Testament
Supplement Series 174

Copyright © 1994 Sheffield Academic Press

Published by JSOT Press
JSOT Press is an imprint of
Sheffield Academic Press Ltd
343 Fulwood Road
Sheffield S10 3BP
England

Typeset by Sheffield Academic Press
and
Printed on acid-free paper in Great Britain
by Bookcraft
Midsomer Norton, Somerset

British Library Cataloguing in Publication Data

A catalogue record for this book is available
from the British Library

ISBN 1-85075-467-5

CONTENTS

PREFACE

This book is a shortened version of my dissertation 'A Literary Approach to Biblical Law: Exodus 20.22–23.19' (Hebrew Union College–Jewish Institute of Religion, 1990), written under the supervision of H.C. Brichto and S. Greengus. I am grateful to them for sparking my interest in biblical and cuneiform law, for their patience in guiding me in my research, and for their many helpful suggestions, not always adequately footnoted, which have been incorporated into this work. I am also grateful to the Directors of Sheffield Academic Press for accepting the manuscript for publication, and for the careful editorial work of Andrew Kirk, Senior Editor at Sheffield Academic Press. Naturally, I am responsible for any shortcomings that remain.

My dissertation was completed before the monograph by Ludger Schwienhorst-Schönberger (*Das Bundesbuch [Ex 20,22-23,33]* [Berlin: de Gruyter, 1990]) became available to me. Time demands related to my daughter's leukemia, space considerations, and publication deadlines have allowed but limited reference to this important work in the present revision of my dissertation, but the interested reader will enjoy comparing his old-fashioned source-critical study that, as one reviewer put it, is 'preoccupied with speculative issues of development' (W. Brueggemann, *JBL* 111 [1992], p. 128) with the 'literary approach' of this book.

ABBREVIATIONS

AfO	*Archiv für Orientforschung*
ANET	J.B. Pritchard (ed.), *Ancient Near Eastern Texts Relating to the Old Testament*
AnOr	Analecta Orientalia
AOS	American Oriental Studies
ArOr	*Archiv orientální*
BA	*Biblical Archaeologist*
BARev	*Biblical Archaeology Review*
BDB	F. Brown, S.R. Driver, and C.A. Briggs, *A Hebrew and English Lexicon of the Old Testament*
Bib	*Biblica*
BSac	*Bibliotheca Sacra*
BT	*The Bible Translator*
BZ	*Biblische Zeitschrift*
BZAW	Beihefte zur *ZAW*
CAD	*Chicago Assyrian Dictionary*
CBQ	*Catholic Biblical Quarterly*
GKC	*Gesenius' Hebrew Grammar*, ed. E. Kautzsch, and trans. A.E. Cowley
HAT	Handbuch zum Alten Testament
HUCA	*Hebrew Union College Annual*
IDB	*Interpreter's Dictionary of the Bible*
IDBSup	*Supplementary Volume of the Interpreter's Dictionary of the Bible*
JANESCU	*Journal of the Near Eastern Society of Columbia University*
JBL	*Journal of Biblical Literature*
JETS	*Journal of the Evangelical Theological Society*
JJS	*Journal of Jewish Studies*
JNES	*Journal of Near Eastern Studies*
JPS	Jewish Publication Society
JSOT	*Journal for the Study of the Old Testament*
JSOTSup	*Journal for the Study of the Old Testament*, Supplement Series
JSS	*Journal of Semitic Studies*
JTS	*Journal of Theological Studies*
LE	Laws of Eshnunna
LH	Laws of Hammurapi

MAL	Middle Assyrian Laws
NCB	New Century Bible
NICOT	New International Commentary on the Old Testament
OTL	Old Testament Library
OTS	*Oudtestamentische Studiën*
RB	*Revue Biblique*
SBLDS	SBL Dissertation Series
Tanakh	A new Jewish translation of the Hebrew Bible (Philadelphia: Jewish Publication Society, 1985)
TDOT	*Theological Dictionary of the Old Testament*, ed. G.J. Botterweck and H. Ringgren
TOTC	Tyndale Old Testament Commentaries
TynBul	*Tyndale Bulletin*
TZ	*Theologische Zeitschrift*
UF	*Ugarit-Forschungen*
VT	*Vetus Testamentun*
VTSup	*Vetus Testamentum*, Supplements
WBC	Word Biblical Commentary
WTJ	*Westminster Theological Journal*
ZAW	*Zeitschrift für die alttestamentliche Wissenschaft*

INTRODUCTION

This book seeks to determine whether a synchronic 'literary approach' to biblical law might not be superior to the heavily source-oriented methodologies that in modern times have dominated the study of biblical law. Source-oriented inquiry, which is at the heart of all historical-critical methodologies (e.g. source criticism and form criticism), is defined by Meir Sternberg as follows:

> Source-oriented inquiry addresses itself to the biblical world as it really was, usually to some specific dimension thereof. The theologian, qua theologian, dreams of piecing together a full picture of ancient Israelite religion, mutations and conflicts included. The historian wants to know what happened in Israelite history, the linguist what the language system (phonology, grammar, semantics) underlying the Bible was like. And the geneticist concentrates on the real-life processes that generated and shaped the biblical text: the origins and features of the material (documents, traditions) that went into the Bible, the passage from oral to written transmission, the identity of the writers or schools, the modes of editorial work, the tampering by way of interpolation, scribal misadventure, etc. In each case, then, interest focuses on some object behind the text—on a state of affairs or development which operated at the time as a source (material, antecedent, enabling condition) of biblical writing and which biblical writing now reflects.[1]

Source-oriented approaches are diachronic and genetic in orientation, being directed, above all, towards defining and dating the 'sources' (oral or written) used by the biblical authors as the first step in evaluating their historical value. Source-oriented critics regularly explain incongruities in the text on the basis of textual corruptions or disordering by rearrangements or secondary insertions. Moreover, source-oriented critics are highly influenced by the hypothetical sources that they posit to have been used by the editors of a text, for

---

1. M. Sternberg, *Poetics of Biblical Narrative* (Bloomington: Indiana University Press, 1985), p. 15.

they deem the discernment of such sources essential to correct interpretation.

Source-oriented scholars[1] have posed many questions regarding Exod. 20.22–23.33. Among them: Is there any basis for isolating this unit and calling it the 'book of the covenant'? Did it, or parts of it, exist independently before being incorporated into its present literary format? Regardless of this, were there sources to which the framers of Exod. 20.22–23.33 had recourse, and is it possible to isolate these sources and determine with any confidence the date and provenance of each source? Is it possible to recover the process of growth and development, if any, by which this unit was formulated? When and where can we locate its final redaction? How did it come to be a part of the surrounding Sinaitic narrative? Can the different literary 'forms' used in this collection (apodictic, casuistic, etc.) be used to ascertain the pre-literary origins of these laws? What is the real historical setting or settings (as opposed to the literary setting at Sinai specified by the narrative), if any can be ascertained in the laws of Exod. 20.22–23.33? In connection with these last questions, can we speculate as to the audience to whom these regulations were addressed? For example, was it a literate population at large; or a population which was not literate, but to whom the laws could be read; or a projected or existing magistracy? If to a local magistracy, when and where, if at all, were these regulations ever enforced as law?

The 'literary approach' to be adopted here,[2] in contrast, looks at the

---

1. For a review of source-oriented scholarship on Exod. 20.22–23.33, see O. Eissfeldt, *The Old Testament: An Introduction* (trans. P.R. Ackroyd; New York: Harper & Row, 1965), pp. 212-19; J. Halbe, *Das Privilegrecht Jahwes: Ex 34, 10-26* (Göttingen: Vandenhoeck & Ruprecht, 1975), pp. 391-413; H.J. Boecker, *Law and the Administration of Justice in the Old Testament and the Ancient East* (Minneapolis: Augsburg, 1980), pp. 135-75; D. Patrick, *Old Testament Law* (Atlanta: John Knox, 1985), pp. 63-96; and L. Schwienhorst-Schönberger, *Das Bundesbuch (Ex 20, 22–23-33)* (BZAW, 188; Berlin: de Gruyter, 1990), pp. 1-37 and *passim*.

2. There are, to be sure, other kinds of 'literary approaches'. My approach is in contrast with structuralist, reader-oriented, feminist, and deconstructionist approaches. These approaches sometimes agree together with the kind of literary approach adopted here against source-oriented approaches. However, D.M. Gunn ('New Directions in the Study of Biblical Hebrew Narrative', *JSOT* 39 [1987], p. 69) rightly foresaw conflict between reader-oriented and deconstructionist critics

text in a synchronic rather than a diachronic way. This approach, used increasingly in recent years,[1] is associated with such names as R. Alter, A. Berlin, H.C. Brichto, and Meir Sternberg. It is akin to the approach to literature called New Criticism, traceable to the 1920s, that centers on a 'close reading' of the text itself, with an eye to its inner coherence, rather than its historical development or production. Others have (less happily) used the term rhetorical criticism for this approach.[2] Sternberg labels this approach 'discourse-oriented analysis' and provides a good contrast with source-oriented criticism.

> Discourse-oriented analysis, on the other hand, sets out to understand not the realities behind the text but the text itself as a pattern of meaning and effect. What does this piece of language—metaphor, epigram, dialogue, tale, cycle, book—signify in context? What are the rules governing the transaction between storyteller or poet and reader? Are the operative rules, for instance, those of prose or verse, parable or chronicle, omniscience or realistic limitation, historical or fictional writing? What image of a world does the narrative project? Why does it unfold the action in this particular order and from this particular viewpoint? What is the part played by the omissions, redundancies, ambiguities, alternations between scene and summary or elevated and colloquial language? How does the work hang together? And, in general, in what relationship does part stand to whole and form to function? The thrust here remains determinate and stable

on the one hand, and text-centered readers on the other, between those for whom the 'reader's experience and commitment' are central, and those like myself who pursue the original setting and intention. Cf. the contrasting analysis of Genesis 34 by feminist critics D.N. Fewell and D. Gunn ('Tipping the Balance: Sternberg's Reader and the Rape of Dinah', *JBL* 110 [1991], pp. 193-212), and that by M. Sternberg ('Biblical Poetics and Sexual Politics: From Reading to Counterreading', *JBL* 111 [1992], pp. 463-88).

1.   Cf. J.M. Sprinkle, 'Literary Approaches to the Old Testament: A Survey of Recent Scholarship', *JETS* 32 (1989), pp. 299-310.

2.   The term 'rhetorical criticism' was coined by J. Muilenburg ('Form Criticism and Beyond', *JBL* 88 [1969], pp. 1-18), though his inadequate definition of rhetorical criticism as a methodology has allowed various interpretations. M. Kessler ('A Methodological Setting for Rhetorical Criticism', in *Art and Meaning* [JSOTSup 19; ed. D.J.A. Clines *et al.*; Sheffield: JSOT Press, 1982], pp. 1-2) sought to define the 'rhetoric' of rhetorical criticism in the broadest sense, including the analysis of literary units and themes within the Bible as a whole. Furthermore, he wanted to limit rhetorical criticism to 'synchronic criticism' in contrast with the geneticism of form criticism (pp. 13-14). So defined, rhetorical criticism is identical with the literary approach used here. However, the classical usage of 'rhetoric' for the art of persuasive speech weighs against adopting such a broad definition.

under wide terminological, even conceptual variations. To pursue this line of questioning is to make sense of the discourse in terms of communication, always goal-directed on the speaker's part and always requiring interpretive activity on the addressee's.[1]

A critic adopting this approach, when faced with an incongruity in the text, attempts to find authorial purpose where source critics tend to find scribal misadventure, seams between sources, disorder, contradiction, or corruption. The setting for such a critic is not a *Sitz im Leben* deduced by historical scholarship, but the world created by the literary artistry of the biblical author, a literary world that is 'real' whether or not it was historical.

This kind of 'literary approach' has been frequently applied to biblical narratives, but rarely applied to law. D. Patrick is largely correct in suggesting that Moshe Greenberg's approach to law which assumes the text to express a coherent conceptual system, 'is comparable for this genre [law] to the poetics of narrative and poetic literature'.[2] Greenberg's approach is in fact by and large discourse-oriented. However, my approach differs from Greenberg's in seeking to interpret the text without any recourse to source-oriented explanations. Greenberg, on the other hand, combines source-oriented and discourse-oriented explanations.

My approach draws upon and accepts some of the techniques of the comparative-legal approach to biblical law.[3] It differs, however, from that approach in that the text is viewed not so much as law, but as literature. That is to say, the issues are not so much the technical ones of jurisprudence as they are of rhetorical technique. Furthermore, it does not depend primarily on the availability of similar materials from cognate cultures, although that kind of material and the use of it will be more than welcome. Rather, it focuses on the unique and idiosyncratic biblical formulation, not only with a view to the substantive judicial or regulative principle, but also to why that principle

---

1.   Sternberg, *Poetics*, p. 15.

2.   D. Patrick, 'Studying Biblical Law as a Humanities', *Semeia* 45 (1989), p. 30. Cf. M. Greenberg, 'Some Postulates of Biblical Criminal Law', in *Yezekhel Kaufmann Jubilee Volume* (ed. M. Haran; Jerusalem: Detus Goldberg, 1960), pp. 3-28. Greenberg has been followed to some degree by S. Paul and J.J. Finkelstein in this 'underlying principles' approach.

3.   For example, the works of D. Daube, A. Phillips, B.S. Jackson, and R. Westbrook, among others.

is formulated as it is. To put it differently, the literary approach is not concerned with the values of Israelite or Mesopotamian societies as they actually existed, but with the values (perhaps unconsciously betrayed) in the cuneiform legal corpora and with the values expressed by the biblical authors in the form of narrative containing legal and moral prescription.

In principle, the choice between discourse-oriented analysis and source-oriented analysis does not have to be a matter of either/or. Rather, each is asking different kinds of questions of the text, aiming at different goals. Nor are the two approaches totally independent of each other since answers to discourse-oriented questions may involve genetic solutions, and answers to source-oriented questions must begin by understanding the text as it stands first, which is the realm of discourse analysis. I wish to state emphatically that I am not opposed in principle to geneticism. Nonetheless, this work will attempt to show that many scholars in practice, having developed a source-oriented mind-set, are too quick to adopt source-oriented explanations for the phenomena found in the text, and tend to overlook equally if not more convincing discourse-oriented explanations. Further, it will attempt to show that an approach which avoids source-oriented explanations altogether is both possible and generally superior to heavily source-oriented exegesis.

To justify or discredit this thesis, I will attempt a detailed interpretation of the text of Exod. 20.22–23.19 as it now stands exclusively along the lines of a synchronic, discourse-oriented analysis. I will assume, as part of the thesis to be tested, that Exod. 20.22–23.19 is an artfully crafted unity, well integrated both internally and in relation to the Pentateuch of which it is a part. No speculation will be offered as to its 'prehistory', and reference to no longer extant sources will be avoided as much as possible. My concern is not with 'original' historical settings of various laws, but with their literary setting as God's address to Moses.

If the author(s) of Exodus and the Pentateuch welded the constituent parts into a meaningful whole, one would expect a discernible relationship between the narratives and the legal text embedded in the narratives. Similarly, it would follow that even the individual laws have been formulated or edited in such a way as to fulfill the purpose of the literary work as a whole. Thus, I will assume that, whatever the hypothetical, or (as in one case) demonstrably available extrabiblical sources which the author(s) may have used, the final product is more likely to appear as an integrated unity rather than a confused conflation. Moreover, I will assume that the collection of legal and moral literature, which is the narrower focus of my discussion, reflects in itself and its relationship with the surrounding Exodus narrative, the purposes of the author or authors who put together the Pentateuch in the form which we now have.

The vindication of this approach depends first and foremost on the degree to which a plausible exegesis of the text as it stands can be given that does not require recourse to source-oriented explanations. My procedure will be to investigate the relationship of Exod. 20.22–23.33, the so-called 'book of the covenant', with the surrounding narrative to see if it has been purposefully positioned. I will go on to treat the regulatory portion of that unit, namely Exod. 20.22–23.19, with a view to the exegesis of the provisions in themselves, their collocation vis-à-vis one another, including the alternation among options in formulation such as casuistic versus apodictic, second person versus third person, and the like. I will, in the process, seek the organizing principles of these so-called 'laws', and the relationship of these 'laws' to similar texts and themes in other books of the Pentateuch.

The vindication of this approach depends secondarily, however, on the frequency of the persuasive exegetical solutions that it offers as compared with the source-oriented explanations that have been proposed. Consequently, critical asides must appear here and there to compare conclusions based on source-oriented methodologies with those of this literary approach, and to inquire which method has produced the more convincing explanations.

Where this literary approach should fail, in that it raises significant problems which it cannot answer, I will compare the implications of such failures for methodological evaluation with the kind of failures of other critical approaches to answer satisfactorily the questions they raise. The final chapter evaluates the degree to which the literary approach has been successful in this regard.

It is my hope that my investigation will justify this synchronic approach to biblical 'law' as an approach in no way inferior to the source-oriented emphasis common in the recent past.

Chapter 1

THE NARRATIVE FRAMEWORK OF EXODUS 20.22–23.33

Exod. 20.22–23.33 has been placed in the midst of the narrative of YHWH's theophany on Sinai and the making of the covenant with Israel in Exodus 19–24. What is the relationship between Exod. 20.22–23.33 and the surrounding narrative framework? If Exod. 20.22–23.33 is a well-crafted unity, artfully placed in the book of Exodus, as the thesis being tested here assumes, it implies an intelligent and purposeful placement of Exod. 20.22–23.33 in its narrative framework as opposed to its being a literarily awkward insertion of this material into the Sinaitic narrative, a view not uncommon among source-oriented scholars. It will be the purpose of this chapter to investigate the relationship of Exod. 20.22–23.33 as a whole with the narrative which surrounds it to see if this thesis is plausible given the evidence of the text as it stands.

This task has been made easier by the publication of an article by Chirichigno[1] that anticipated some of the conclusions that I had already reached concerning the use of resumptive repetition in this passage.

The Intertwining of Narrative and Regulations in Exodus

Exodus 19–24 exhibits an alteration of narrative and regulatory sections; that is, to borrow from rabbinic terminology, an alternation of haggadic and halachic sections.[2] Exodus 19 is essentially narrative (haggadah), presenting YHWH's offer of a covenant and preparing the people for the theophany. There are instructions in this section, to be sure, but they mostly apply to the specific situation in the narrative rather than intending long-range regulation. Next, Exod. 20.1-18

---

1. G.C. Chirichigno, 'The Narrative Structure of Exod. 19–24', *Bib* 68 (1987), pp. 457-79.
2. Chirichigno, 'Narrative Structure', p. 472 n. 33.

presents the regulations of the Decalogue (halachah). Exod. 20.18-21 returns to a narrative (haggadah) describing the people's fear at the theophany at Sinai, then the text returns to the regulations of Exod. 20.22–23.33 (halachah), followed by the narrative of the consummation of the covenant in Exodus 24 (haggadah). Taking Exodus 19–24 as a whole, however, everything in a sense is haggadah or narrative since even the halachic or regulatory sections are put in the mouth of YHWH in the context of the narrative.

This intertwining of narrative and regulations is not unique, but is common not only in Exodus (e.g. Passover and Tabernacle regulations are surrounded by narratives), but also in Leviticus and Numbers.[1] This pattern is not random, but seems to be a consistent stylistic feature of Exodus through Numbers. This is an important preliminary observation to make before attempting to explain the particular purpose of this juxtaposition in Exodus 19–24.

The Chronological Sequence of Exodus 19–24

It is difficult to follow the chronology of the events at Sinai, a difficulty that has led to much source-oriented speculation. One difficulty is the awkward movements of Moses up and down the mountain.[2] Another difficulty is the fact that the Decalogue and Exod. 20.22–23.33 seem to disrupt the narratives (19.18-25; 20.18-21; 24.1-18) which (it is said) would flow more smoothly without them. This leads many source-oriented scholars to speculate that 20.22–23.33 is a secondary addition to a narrative that once existed without it, and that disruptions in the narrative were made to accommodate it.[3] Some even consider the Decalogue itself to be secondary to the narrative, and that it originally followed 20.18-21.[4]

But even if one omits the Decalogue, there remain problems with the narrative's chronology. In 19.21-24 Moses is told to go down,

1.   There is little narrative in Leviticus, but see the consecration of Aaron and his sons in Lev. 8–9, and the Nadab and Abihu narrative in Lev. 10 (cf. 16.1). G.J. Wenham (*Numbers* [Downers Grove: Inter-Varsity, 1981], pp. 14-18) discusses the juxtaposition of law and narrative in Numbers.

2.   D.C. Arichea, 'The Ups and Downs of Moses: Locating Moses in Exodus 19–33', *BT* 40 (1989), pp. 244-46.

3.   Eissfeldt, *Old Testament*, pp. 213-19; Boecker, *Law*, p. 136.

4.   M. Noth, *Exodus: A Commentary* (OTL; Philadelphia: Westminster, 1962), p. 154; J.P. Hyatt, *Exodus* (NCB: London: Oliphants, 1971), p. 197.

warn the people not to go up the mountain, and return with Aaron; and the text records that he went down and spoke to the people. Skipping the Decalogue, Moses in 20.18-21, far from needing to instruct the people to stay away from the mountain, finds that they in terror of the theophany had removed themselves at a distance from it and has to encourage them not to be so afraid; almost the opposite of the message he was told to deliver. And instead of returning with Aaron as directed in 19.24, Moses ascends the mountain in 20.21 alone. Only later, after all the regulations of the 'book of the covenant' have been given and written and read to the people does Moses return with Aaron, as God had instructed him (24.9; cf. 24.1-8). Why this delay, if delay it is? Positing a later insertion of the Decalogue resolves nothing since it merely leads to further speculations as to how the narrative got to be a mess.

The resolution to this awkward sequence of events involves the recognition of a literary technique used frequently by biblical narrators called synoptic/resumptive (or synoptic/resumptive-expansive) repetition in which the narrator treats one event two times. The use of this technique has been observed, for example, by Brichto in Jon. 3.4-5/3.6-9; 3.10–4.4/4.5-11; Exodus 32–34; 2 Kgs 2.1/2.2,[1] and Woudstra in Joshua 2–5.[2]

The essence of this technique is that the narrator tells a story once, then picks up the story again somewhere in the chronological sequence and retells it, often expanding the story or telling it from a different point of view. An example of this is the Abrahamic Covenant of Genesis 15.[3] If the chapter is read as an ordinary sequence, problems occur: in v. 5 God shows Abram the stars, implying it is night, but in v. 12, apparently the same day, the sun has not yet set. Moreover, in v. 6 Abram's doubts about the promise seem to have been resolved when he is said to have believed God, but in v. 8 Abram seems to be full of doubts again. Had Abram regressed? The problem is not in the narrative, but in the reader's trying to read these two sections as a

---

1. H.C. Brichto, *Toward a Grammar of Biblical Poetics* (New York: Oxford University Press, 1992), pp. 86, 118, 165.

2. M.H. Woudstra, *The Book of Joshua* (NICOT; Grand Rapids: Eerdmans, 1981), p. 78.

3. Discussed by J.P. Fokkelman, 'Genesis', in *The Literary Guide to the Bible* (ed. R. Alter and F. Kermode; Cambridge, MA: Harvard University Press, 1987), pp. 48-49.

chronological sequence when in fact it is an example of resumptive repetition. A better reading takes vv. 1-6 as one version of the story and vv. 7-21 as a retelling of the same story from another perspective. The first telling (vv. 1-6) emphasizes the 'offspring' promise, while the second (vv. 7-21) emphasizes the 'land' promise. Verse 7 resumes the appearance of deity in v. 1 and should be translated as a flashback. Hence there is one event, told in two episodes. This reading resolves all the chronological difficulties.

The same sort of technique of resumptive repetition also occurs in Exodus 19–24, and once this is recognized the chronological difficulties evaporate. On this reading, 19.16-25 gives the synopsis of the story, and all the sections that follow—the Decalogue (20.1-17), the people's fear (20.18-21), the further instructions (20.22–23.33)— occur simultaneously with the actions of 19.16-25, expanding the previously given story. Exod. 24.1-3a repeats the end of ch. 19 with more detail, preparing the reader for subsequent actions. Only with 24.3b does the chronology advance beyond the end of ch. 19.

It is necessary to defend this understanding of the narrative sequence. I begin with 19.16-19 since it will be seen to have striking parallels with 20.18-21.

> (16) And it came about on the third day when it was morning that there were thunder [קֹלֹת] and lightning and heavy smoke upon the mountain, and the exceedingly loud sound of the ram's horn, so that all the people in the camp trembled. (17) But Moses brought forth the people from the camp to meet deity so that they stood at the base of the mountain. (18) Now the whole of Mount Sinai was smoking because YHWH had descended upon it in fire. Its smoke went up like the smoke of a furnace and the whole mountain quaked violently. (19) While the sound of the ram's horn became louder and louder, Moses was talking and deity answered him with a crack of thunder [קֹל].

The narrative goes on to call Moses towards the summit of the mountain (v. 20), then he is told to go back down and warn the people not to come too close to the mountain. Not even those destined to be priests were allowed near (vv. 21-22).[1] Moses protests that there is no

---

1.   Reference to 'priests' seems strange in this context since the Aaronic priesthood was not yet established. Source-oriented commentators tend to see an anachronism here due to a secondary insertion of 19.20-25 (e.g. A.H. McNeile, *The Book of Exodus* (Westminster Commentaries; London: Methuen, 3rd edn, 1931), p. lxvi; B.S. Childs *The Book of Exodus: A Critical, Theological Commentary* (OTL;

problem since boundaries were set (v. 23). God goes on to ask Moses to go down and bring Aaron back up with him, and so he descends (vv. 24-25).

For the moment passing over the Decalogue, one comes to the narrative of Exod. 20.18-21:

> (18) When all the people were perceiving the thunder [קוֹלֹת] and the lightning and the sound of the ram's horn and the smoking mountain, upon seeing the people trembled and stood at a distance. (19) They said to Moses, 'You speak to us and we will listen, but let not deity speak with us lest we die.' (20) But Moses responded to the people, 'Do not be terrorized, for deity has come in order to test you, so that reverence of him might be present with you that you should not sin.' (21) So the people stood at a distance while Moses approached the thick cloud where deity was.

This section begins with a circumstantial clause using a participle [וְכָל־הָעָם רֹאִים אֶת־הַקּוֹלֹת] to convey simultaneous action,[1] rather than the waw-consecutive and finite verb that one would expect for subsequent action. And the circumstance described is that of 19.16-19, the wording being repeated almost verbatim. It is not the circumstance of 19.21-25. In other words, the narrator is going back into the story saying, in effect, 'Now this is how the people reacted when they first experienced the preliminary signs of the theophany that I have just described to you.' The narrator has gone back in time *before* Moses

Philadelphia: Westminster, 1974), p. 375). A traditional resolution of this problem is to understand the 'priests' to refer to the firstborn sons of every family who were specially dedicated to God (Exod. 13.2, 22.28) for whom the Levites were subsequently chosen as substitutes (Num. 3.12-13; cf. Exod. 32.25-29). According to this view, the 'young men' who offer sacrifice in 24.5 are the first born (so Rashi; Cassuto). Others (W.H. Gispen, *Exodus* [Bible Student's Commentary; Grand Rapids: Zondervan, 1982]), p. 184; C.F. Keil, *The Pentateuch* [Biblical Commentary; ed. C.F. Keil and F. Delitzsch; Grand Rapids: Eerdmans, 1978 (1864)], p. ii.103) suppose that Israel, like the other nations, already had priests, though these were not the firstborn. I propose that reference to 'priests' is proleptic, i.e., is a reference to those destined to become priests, the Levitical priests (represented later in the narrative by Nadab and Abiju; cf. 24.1) even though they are not yet officially priests. If so, this is an instance of 'free direct discourse' in which the narrator has given not the exact words of what a character (in this case God) has said, but the gist of it, to emphasize for the narrator's audience that even the Levites (whom the reader knows to be priests) had to keep their distance.

1. Cf. R.J. Williams, *Hebrew Syntax: An Outline* (Toronto: University of Toronto Press, 1976), §§219, 494.

first ascended the mountain, but after Moses had brought them out of the camp, to tell us that the people were so terrified by the theophany that they preferred to have Moses mediate for them with God rather than to hear God directly.

After Moses reassures the people, he goes up towards the dark cloud while the people stand at a good distance (20.21). This is not an ascent in addition to 19.20, 'And so YHWH descended onto Mount Sinai at the head of the mountain, and YHWH called Moses up to the head of the mountain, and Moses went up.' These verses record exactly the same event in resumptive repetition to prepare for the further revelation of 20.22–23.33 that follows.

Passing over 20.22–23.33 for the moment, we find the narrative picks up again in 24.1-3a:

> (24.1) Now unto Moses he had said, 'Go up unto YHWH, you and Aaron, Nadab and Abihu and seventy of the elders of Israel that you (pl.) may worship at a distance, (2) but Moses alone may draw near to YHWH, and as for them, they will not draw near, nor will the people go up with them'. (3) So Moses came and recounted to the people all the words of YHWH, and all the norms. [There follows, in 24.9-18 the fulfillment of this command].

Exod. 24.1-3a is very similar to the last part of Exodus 19, Exod. 19.21-25:

> (21) Then YHWH spoke to Moses, 'Go down, warn the people, lest they break through to YHWH to gaze and many of them perish. (22) Even the priests who normally come near to YHWH must keep themselves separate, lest YHWH break out against them...' (24) The Lord further said to him, 'Go down and come up again, you and Aaron with you; but do not let the priests and the people break through to come to YHWH, lest he break forth upon them.' (25) And so Moses went down to the people and talked to them.

The similarities are striking. In both accounts. Moses is told to fetch Aaron and bring him up the mountain. Both warn that the people should not be allowed to draw near God. In 19.22 and 24 the priests are to be told to keep their distance, and in 24.1 two who would eventually become priests, Nadab and Abihu, are not allowed to draw as near as Moses can, but must remain at a distance.

Again, this can be understood as a case of resumptive repetition. 19.24-25 had marked the temporary end of the narrative that 24.1ff. resumes and continues. The resumed version adds additional information to the earlier version, that Nadab, Abihu, and the seventy elders were to accompany Aaron, but this does not seriously damage the case for resumptive repetition since resumptive repetition need not be worded exactly as the clause that it resumes,[1] and in general the resumptive clause is usually longer and expansive.[2]

It remains to determine when the Decalogue and 20.22–23.33 occur chronologically. The Decalogue (20.1-17) cannot have been spoken between Moses' going down to warn the people (19.24-25) and the request for mediation (20.18-21), because, as has been shown, the events of 19.21-24 are simultaneous with 24.1-3a at the end of Moses' stay on the mountain, after he had received YHWH's 'words and norms' (24.3a). Rather, the Decalogue itself is an example of synoptic/resumptive, going back to somewhere in the events of 19.18-20, but before the command to come down from the mountain in v. 21. Moses was speaking to God, and God was answering him with the clap of thunder (v. 19), and God summoned Moses up the mountain (v. 20). The Decalogue (20.1-17) gives some of what God was telling Moses during these conversations.

It is impossible to pin down the chronology of the Decalogue much more precisely. It is quite plausible to understand the Decalogue to be part of the 'thunder' that the people hear—they heard it as thunder, but Moses heard the Decalogue[3]—before they requested for Moses to mediate (20.18-21). The positioning of the Decalogue before the request could be considered support for this view. Or it could be contemporaneous with the request for mediation. In that case, the juxtaposition of the Decalogue and the request for mediation would be the author's way of portraying simultaneous action.[4] The Decalogue could also have been given on the mountain after Moses ascended in 19.20, which is after the request for mediation from the people, but before the command to descend in 19.21. This view would require an explanation as to why the request for Moses' mediation is placed after the Decalogue. One explanation: the author desired to separate and clearly demarcate the general stipulations of the Decalogue from the

---

1. Chirichigno, 'Narrative Structure', p. 476. See, for example, Gen. 37.36 which is resumed in 39.1.

2. Brichto, *Poetics*, pp. 13-14.

3. S.R. Driver (*The Book of Exodus* [Cambridge: Cambridge University Press, 1911], p. 177) takes this position.

4. Chirichigno, 'Narrative Structure', pp. 470-71.

more specific ones of 20.22–23.33, and therefore abandoned chronological arrangement. Still another view, which I find attractive, is that
the giving of the Decalogue overlaps with two or more of these
periods: before, during, and after the request for mediation. The exact
chronology does not seem very important to the narrator at this point.
Whenever it occurred, this is the sort of thing that God was saying
during the theophany at Sinai, and the people's reaction to it was dread.

This leaves Exod. 20.22–23.33. Being placed after 20.21 where
Moses, having acquiesced to mediate for the people, ascends the
mountain, it is to be regarded as material delivered by God to Moses
on the mountain after he ascends (19.20 = 20.21), but before the
request to go down to warn the people and fetch Aaron, etc. (19.21-25
= 24.1-3a).

In summary, the story line, rearranged chronologically, begins with
Moses bringing the people to the mountain where the theophany is
occurring. Moses calls to God and God answers him with a clap of
thunder, or so it sounds to the people (19.16-19, cf. 20.18), though
the real message includes at least part of the words of the Decalogue
(20.1-17). While all this is occurring, the people are overwhelmed
with terror, falling back away from the mountain and asking Moses to
mediate for them (20.18-19). Moses tries to reassure them, but
ultimately ascends the mountain at the call of God alone as their mediator with God (19.20, 20.20-21). There he receives the remainder of
God's revelation for Israel pertaining to the establishing of the
covenant (remainder of Decalogue and 20.22–23.33). At the end of
his stay on the mountain, Moses is told to descend from the mountain
to warn the people and the priests again not to approach the mountain,
but he is to ascend again up the mountain with Aaron and others
(19.21-25, 24.1-3b). The warning is necessary because sufficient time
has passed for the initial terror of 20.18-21 to wear off while Moses
was alone on the mountain, and because Moses would later be
returning part way with Aaron and others, an act that might embolden
some to attempt the ascent on their own.

This reading resolves the chronological difficulties without any
appeal to hypothetical insertions or sources.

Rationale for the Non-Chronological Arrangement

Why does the author of Exodus 19–24 choose to arrange story and
regulations here in a non-chronological way? What is the literary

purpose of this arrangement? Authors may have no single reason for writing the way they do. Moreover, they might not even be able to articulate why they write in a certain way, so that any explanation offered here is both tentative and speculative. Nonetheless, the following reasons seem plausible in explaining the present arrangement.

First, the use of resumptive repetition is a technique for showing simultaneous actions, as discussed above. The author wished to indicate contemporaneous action and the technique was available to use.

Secondly, non-chronological arrangement isolates material for didactic purposes that in a chronological arrangement would get jumbled together.[1] The giving of the Decalogue, it is argued above, is contemporaneous with the events of 19.16-20, perhaps covering a period of time before, during and after the people's request for mediation. If it were so portrayed, its presentation would lose much of its force and majesty, and would be more difficult to study for didactic purposes. This goes along with the general tendency in Exodus mentioned above for the author to separate regulatory material from narrative.

It is probable that the giving of the Decalogue also overlaps with the giving of the regulations of 20.22–23.33. Separation allows the general stipulations of 20.1-17 to be distinct from the more specific regulations of 20.22–23.33, just as Deuteronomy separates its general stipulations (chs. 4–11) from its more specific ones (chs. 12–26). The separation of the Decalogue from the detailed stipulations of Exod. 20.22–23.33 prevents the summary principles of the covenant, the Decalogue, from being buried in a sea of particular applications of them.

The Decalogue and the regulations of 20.22–23.33 are also, I think, a case of synoptic/resumptive. If so, the Decalogue and 20.22–23.33 are not two independent collections, but two ways of summarizing what God said. The former is a 'synopsis', a summary statement, a 'bottom line' of the minimum principles of the covenant, while 20.22–23.33 is 'expansive', telling in more detail how some (not necessarily all) of those principles can be worked out in daily life.

There are a number of parallels in content and/or subject matter that can be taken as evidence in support of the idea that the Decalogue is synoptic, while Exod. 20.22–23.33 is resumptive and expansive: 'No other gods' (20.3) finds echo in 22.19; 23.13, 24, 32. The

1. Chirichigno, 'Narrative Structure', pp. 472-75.

prohibition against images (20.4) is repeated in 20.23. Not taking the name of YHWH in vain (20.7) is backdrop to the YHWH-oath of 22.7, 10. The Sabbath command (20.8) is repeated and expanded in 23.10-12. The duty to honor parents (20.12) is assumed in two crimes of children against parents (21.15, 17), the wording of the one (v. 17a) being the exact antithesis of it; this duty is also assumed in giving the father right of approval in his daughter's marriage (22.15-16). The prohibition of homicide (20.13) is implicit in 21.12-14, 20, 23, 29 and 22.2. Although the prohibition against adultery (20.14) is not repeated, the case of the seduction of a maiden (22.15-16) is another aspect of marriage law. Laws concerning theft of animals (21.37; 22.2b-3), attempted theft (22.1-2a), accusation of theft (22.6-8), rustling of an animal (22.9), and stealing a man (21.16) all expand on the command 'Do not steal' (20.15). The prohibition of false testimony (20.16) is repeated and expanded (23.1-3, 7). The prohibition of coveting (20.17) is implicit in the regulation concerning the safekeeping of a neighbor's money, goods, or livestock (22.6-12).

If the relationship of the Decalogue and Exod. 20.22–23.33 is that of synoptic/resumptive-expansive technique, then the words of the Decalogue can be regarded as 'free direct discourse' in which the author has given the gist of what a character said, or more or less what a character said, or what a character would have said rather than an exact quotation. This technique is not uncommon in biblical dialogues.[1]

Thirdly, the non-chronological arrangement allows for the separation of differing points of view. Chapter 19 presents the events from the objective point of view of the narrator who gives the summary of the theophany. In Exod. 19.16-19 the narrator says that the people trembled but does not elaborate why, but 20.18-21 focuses on the viewpoint of the people as to why they were afraid.[2] The resumptive repetition facilitates this change from the narrator's to the character's point of view.

Fourthly, the juxtaposition of the statement of the Decalogue and the people's fearful reaction is meant to provoke the reader to reflect on the awesomeness of God's Torah, to which the reader's reaction ought also to be the 'fear' which leads to obedience.

Fifthly, by placing the reaction of the people in between the

---

1. For a discussion of 'free direct discourse' see Brichto, *Poetics*, pp. 12-13.
2. Chirichigno, 'Narrative Structure', p. 471.

Decalogue and 20.22–23.33, the author has formed a chiastic structure for his account of the establishment of the covenant as follows:

Exodus 19–24

A Narrative, the Covenant offered (ch. 19)
  B General regulations, the Decalogue (20.1-17)
    C Narrative, people's fear of God (20.18-21)
  B′ Specific regulations (20.22–23.33)
A′ Narrative, the Covenant consummated (ch. 24)

Within this structure, the emphasis is on the first and last units that deal with the establishment of the covenant. The two units of regulations represent the stipulations that the people must follow to be in compliance with the covenant. The central narrative accentuates the operating principle of the covenant, namely, the 'fear of God'. It is the proper fear of God, awe not terror, that operates within that covenant to inspire the people to obedience rather than sin. The obedience that 'the fear of God' produces is central to the idea of a covenant with God (cf. 19.5-6; 24.7), and accordingly the section portraying and redirecting the people's 'fear of God' has been placed at the center of the account of the establishing of the covenant.

'The Book of the Covenant' (Exodus 24.7)

Biblical scholars have generally used the term 'book of the covenant' or sometimes 'covenant code' to designate Exod. 20.22–23.33, though some would use these terms only for the hypothetical 'original' form of that corpus.[1] The term 'book of the covenant' comes from Exod. 24.7 where the 'book of the covenant' refers to the words of YHWH that Moses wrote down and read to the people.

The term 'covenant code' reflects the source-oriented assumption that at least part of 20.22–23.33 was a portion of an independent legal collection or law code before being incorporated into the Bible. This terminology, however, is falling into disuse since a law code is a systematic statement of law, but the so-called 'codes' in the Bible are neither individually nor as a whole comprehensive enough to justify this designation.

---

1.   E.g. S. Paul (*Studies in the Book of the Covenant in the Light of Cuneiform and Biblical Law* [VTSup 18; Leiden: Brill, 1970], p. 43) who limits the 'formal legal corpus' of the book of the covenant to 21.2–22.16.

The other term used by scholars for Exod. 20.22–23.33, namely 'the book of the covenant', has an advantage over the term 'covenant code' in that it is derived from the biblical text itself and does not have to assume a speculative theory concerning the origin of the laws. The expression occurs in 24.7 in the context of God's theophany and revelation on Sinai. At issue is whether or not this expression was intended by the author of chs. 19–24 to be equated with 20.22–23.33 (or some portion therefore) the way it has frequently been used by biblical scholars.

It would be helpful to quote Exod. 24.3-8 in full before beginning the discussion.

> (24.3) Moses came and recounted to the people all the words of YHWH (דברי יהוה) and all the norms (משפטים). The people responded in unison, 'Everything that YHWH has said we will do.' (4) And Moses wrote all the words of YHWH (דברי יהוה) and arose early in the morning and built an altar at the base of the mountain along with twelve pillars for the twelve tribes of Israel. (5) Then he sent Israelite young men who offered up עולות and sacrificed שלמים bulls to YHWH. (6) Moses took half of the blood and put it in basins, and half the blood he sprinkled over the altar. (7) He then took the book of the covenant (ספר הברית) and read it in the hearing of the people who said, 'All that YHWH has spoken we will do and heed.' (8) So Moses took the blood and sprinkled it over the people while saying, 'Behold the blood of the covenant that YHWH has made with you [pl.] on the basis of all these words (כל־הדברים האלה).'

Is the 'book of the covenant' (v. 7) exactly equivalent to 20.22–23.33 or some portion thereof? Evidence in favor of the term 'book of the covenant' at least including much of 20.22–23.33 comes from v. 3 where it is said that Moses recounted all the 'norms' (משפטים) that YHWH had related to him. The term משפטים sounds like an echo of 21.1, 'These are the norms (משפטים) that you are to set before them', the heading which precedes the bulk of the regulations of 20.22–23.33. It is reasonable to think that what Moses writes in v. 4 is the same as what he spoke in v. 3, which would then be expected to include the משפטים of Exodus 21–23. Moreover, 24.3-8 is probably another example of synoptic/resumptive technique in which v. 3 is a synopsis of events that are told in greater detail in vv. 4-8. If so, the inclusion of the laws of the משפטים in the 'book of the covenant' is virtually certain.

So, the 'book of the covenant' of 24.7 seems to include Exod. 20.22–23.33. On the other hand, there is not sufficient reason to limit the 'book of the covenant' to 20.22–23.33. The terms 'words of YHWH (דברי יהוה) in vv. 3-4 and 'all these words' (כל־הדברים האלה) in v. 8 echo the prologue to the Decalogue, 'And deity spoke all these words (כל־הדברים האלה)' (20.1). This implies that 'book of the covenant' includes the Decalogue. Cassuto has argued that to be the book of the *'covenant'*, what Moses read would have to include not only ordinances, but also the essence of the covenant, Exod. 19.5-6 ('…if you obey my voice…you will be my special possession among all the peoples…a kingdom of priests and a holy nation…') and the Decalogue.[1]

If, as argued above, the Decalogue is a synopsis of what God told Moses given in free direct discourse and Exod. 20.22–23.33 is resumptive and expansive, then there is even less reason to separate the Decalogue from 'the book of the covenant' in Exod. 24.7. Indeed, since the Decalogue provides the essence of norms expanded in 20.22–23.33, it alone could suffice to express 'all the words of YHWH' and thus be in itself 'the book of the covenant' of 24.7.

In sum, the context is not sufficiently clear to determine precisely what the author means by 'the book of the covenant' in Exod. 24.7. The expression is never used again in the Pentateuch to help clarify its meaning, and as it stands, it could refer to some or all of Exod. 20.22–23.33, the Decalogue, and Exod. 19.5-6. In any case, there is insufficient evidence to limit 'the book of the covenant' to 20.22–23.33. Accordingly, I will not use the technical term 'book of the covenant' in the sense of 20.22–23.33 except in so far as I cite scholars who use this terminology.

Exodus 20.22–23.33 and the Surrounding Narrative

Before leaving the topic of Exod. 20.22–23.33 and its narrative framework, it is well to examine some more obvious links between 20.22–23.33 and its surrounding narrative. Exod. 20.22–23.33 begins:

(20.22) YHWH said to Moses, 'Address the children of Israel as follows. "You yourselves have seen how from the sky I have spoken with you [pl.]."'

---

1.   U. Cassuto, *A Commentary on the Book of Exodus* (trans. I. Abrahams; Jerusalem: Magnes, 1967), p. 312.

There follow cultic regulations concerning idolatry and altars (20.23-26). This verse connects what follows into the previous narrative structure and its characters. The third person narrator introduces the first character, YHWH himself, who addresses Moses who has just ascended onto Mount Sinai after the people, terrified by what they had seen and heard on Sinai, took their stand afar off (20.18-21). Moses in turn is to address a third 'character', the people, for Moses is now mediating God's laws to them as a result of the people's retreat from the base of the mountain. Moreover, Moses' message to Israel begins by reminding them of the theophany they have just experienced: God's speaking from the sky. But ultimately, the narrator is using this dialogue to speak to his readers who likewise are to accept these divine instructions as their own (cf. Deut. 5.3, 'Not with our fathers did YHWH make this covenant with us, but with all of us here alive this day').

Noth, like many source-oriented critics, sees a discrepancy between 20.22 and the preceding narrative:

> The speech of Yahweh from heaven which supposes heaven to be the divine realm is surprising after the previous narrative both according to the J version, which has Yahweh descending on Sinai (19.18, 20), and still more according to the E version in which God is present on the mountain itself in the thick cloud (19.17; 20.21b). We evidently have here an idea which is independent of these narratives.[1]

The implication of Noth's explanation, if true, is that the author or editor responsible for combining 20.22 with the previous narrative was clumsy and incompetent. Otherwise, he would have either changed the earlier account or conformed his new one to harmonize with what had gone before.

Despite Noth, it is not difficult to read the Sinai story and this verse in a coherent, harmonious way. First, one must observe that the point of view described in 20.22 is that of the people. From the people's perspective, God 'spoke from heaven'. According to ch. 19, the people had gathered at the base of the mountain, though a boundary was set to keep them from going on the mountain itself, and God descended in fire to the top of the mountain (Exod. 19.18, 20). They would have to look straight upwards to see the dreadful atmospheric

---

1.   Noth, *Exodus*, pp. 175-76. Cf. Schwienhorst-Schönberger, *Bundesbuch*, p. 417, who attributes 20.22aßb to a priestly redaction at the stage when the Decalogue was introduced from Deut. 5.

phenomena at the top of the summit that was covered with a thick cloud now filling the surrounding sky. Out of that cloud they heard the voice of God, and being unable to see the summit, they might just as easily have said that the voice came from the sky as say that it came from the mountain. And since people commonly believed that the heavens were the abode of the gods, it is especially appropriate for God to remind the people of their personal experience of the divine by expressing the matter in this way. There need be no contradiction, and hence no necessity of positing a source division.

A second link between Exod. 20.22–23.33 and the surrounding narrative is found in Exod. 21.1.

> (21.1) These are the norms (מִשְׁפָּטִים, *mishpaṭim*) that you [sing.] are to set before them.

Again YHWH is addressing Moses as mediator with a message for the people ('them'). This new introduction repeats and thereby emphasizes the claim of 20.22 that the regulations that follow, presumably 21.2–23.19, are the words of YHWH meant for the people. Exod. 21.1 thereby connects all these regulations with the narrative framework.

Many source-oriented scholars view this verse quite differently. According to them, the reason for the new heading of 21.1 is that all or part of 21.2–22.16 was originally a part of a preexisting casuistic case law collection which had been used in Israelite, or possibly Canaanite law courts before being incorporated into its present context. According to this view, the regulations of 20.22-26 are not under the *mishpaṭim* heading because מִשְׁפָּטִים means 'case laws' whereas 20.22-26 is 'cultic law', and because 20.22-26 formed no part of that original case-law collection, being rather a later addition.[1] Attempts have been made to distinguish, on the basis of Exod. 24.3 between מִשְׁפָּטִים (secular 'case laws') and דְּבָרִים ('words'), the latter being identified with cultic and moral laws such as those in the Decalogue.[2] Others have tried to identify חֻקִּים (and sometimes מִצְוֹת and תּוֹרוֹת) as non-case laws, such as participial or apodictic formulations that are also distinct from מִשְׁפָּטִים.[3] On this basis, regulations following 21.1

1.   Eissfeldt, *Introduction*, pp. 213-15.

2.   B. Bäntsch, *Das Bundesbuch: Ex. xx 22–xxiii 33* (Halle: Max Neimeyer, 1892), pp. 28-34. Cf. Childs, *Exodus*, p. 452.

3.   C.A. Briggs, *The Higher Criticism of the Hexateuch* (New York: Charles Scribner's Sons, 1897); J. Morgenstern, 'The Book of the Covenant, Part II',

that are not secular case laws must therefore reflect later additions.

The lexical basis for distinguishing between חֻקִּים, דְּבָרִים, מִשְׁפָּטִים, מִצְוֹת and תּוֹרוֹת has been recognized to be inadequate; each of these denotes the legal corpus as a whole.[1] דָּבָר is used as a term for a case in the so-called case laws (Exod. 22.8; cf. 23.7-8).[2] As for מִשְׁפָּטִים in Exod. 21.1, not all the regulations that follow can be regarded as 'case laws'. There is a lengthy series of moral, ethical and cultic injunctions at the end of this so-called book of the covenant, namely 22.20–23.19, that is not separated by a new heading or any other device so as to indicate that these regulations are no longer מִשְׁפָּטִים.[3] In addition, there are regulations that differ in form from 'normal' case laws by being introduced by a participle rather than כִּי or אִם (21.12, 21.15-17; 22.18-19). Source-oriented scholars typically exclude these from the hypothetical original מִשְׁפָּטִים as well.[4] Furthermore, the form of the first regulation after this heading, the case of the 'Hebrew slave' (21.2-6), does not follow a 'casuistic' impersonal form, but addresses the owner as 'you': 'If *you* [sing.] acquire an עֶבֶד עִבְרִי'. Since the use of the second person personal pronoun contradicts their definition of מִשְׁפָּטִים as impersonal casuistic laws, many source-oriented scholars have attempted either to emend the use of the second person singular formulation to third person[5] or else eliminate 21.2-11 entirely as a later addition since it shares more in spirit with the later ethical-religious regulations than the case laws.[6] Such actions are based on the

---

HUCA 7 (1930), pp. 19-27; G. Liedke, *Gestalt formgeschichtlisch-terminologische Studie* (WMANT 39; Neukirchen–Vluyn: Neukirchener Verlag, 1971), p. 185.

1. H. Ringgren, 'חקק', *TDOT*, V, pp. 142-45.

2. Schwienhorst-Schönberger, *Bundesbuch*, p. 300.

3. Patrick (*Law*, p. 85) suggests that the religious/moral regulations are set apart from the מִשְׁפָּטִים by a 'shift in mood, style and subject matter'. It is to some extent true that such a shift occurs at the end of Exod. 20.22–23.33, but this is not proof that these regulations are not מִשְׁפָּטִים. They could be מִשְׁפָּטִים collected together here because of their similar mood, style, and subject matter.

4. For example, A. Alt, 'The Origins of Israelite Law', in *Essays in Old Testament History and Religion* (trans. R.A. Wilson; Garden City, NY: Doubleday, 1967), pp. 140-46.

5. A. Jepsen, *Untersuchungen zum Bundesbuch* (BWANT 5; Stuttgart: Kohlhammer, 1927), p. 56; Alt, 'Origins', p. 119 n. 28; N.P. Lemche, 'The "Hebrew Slave"', *VT* 25 (1975), p. 135.

6. J. van der Ploeg, 'Studies in Hebrew Law: III', *CBQ* 13 (1951), pp. 28-29.

unwarranted premise that the denotation of משפטים is limited to impersonal case law.

A simpler explanation is to say that משפטים in context does not mean 'case laws'. משפט has a variety of senses[1] and the context of Exod. 21.1 suggests some sense which includes legal, moral, and cultic regulations, not just impersonal case laws. A general rendering for משפטים, such as 'norms'[2] seems best suited to the kind of material that actually comes under the heading of 21.1 if one accepts the text as it stands without indulging in source-oriented gymnastics.

If the new heading of 21.1 does not introduce a collection of secular case laws, why is there a new heading? Why are regulations prohibiting the making of images and concerning the altar (20.23-26) not included under the same heading as the regulations following 21.1? One possible explanation is that the cultic regulations of 20.23-26 have an earlier heading in order to underscore them, to set them apart. Exod. 20.22-26 introduces cultic regulations dealing directly with the people's relationship with God (idolatry, altars). The people's relationship with God is, in fact, the essence of the covenant. Nothing else is so important. It is not unreasonable, then, for an author to emphasize them this way.

A third link between 20.22–23.33 and the narrative framework is the frequent use of the first person and second person pronoun in this corpus, the 'I' being God, and the 'you' being Israel.[3] This use of pronouns makes the corpus as a whole a personal rather than an impersonal group of regulations in the context of the narrative, as will be seen in my discussion of individual passages. I reserve for later a

---

1.   The word משפט can be translated in a variety of ways depending on the context. BDB lists these definitions for משפט:

> 1. Judgment (act of deciding, place of deciding, process of deciding, a case to be decided, decision which has been made, execution of judgment, time of judgment). 2. Justice. 3. Ordinance. 4. Decision. 5. Right, privilege, or claim. 6a. Proper, fitting measure. 6b. Custom. 6c. Manner. 6d. Plan.

See especially such passages as Judg. 13.12; 1 Sam. 8.9, 11; 27.11; 1 Kgs 18.28, etc. where משפט has the nuance 'manner of life' or the like.

2.   *The Torah: The Five Books of Moses* (Philadelphia: Jewish Publication Society, 1962). The revision of this translation, Tanakh, has reverted back to the less satisfactory 'rules'.

3.   D. Patrick, 'I and Thou in the Covenant Code', in *SBL Seminar Papers 1978* (Missoula: Scholars Press, 1978), pp. 78-86.

discussion of this phenomenon and the lack of personal language in the
central core of regulations in Exod. 21.15–22.16.

Finally, Exod. 23.20-33 serves to tie the regulations to the
surrounding narrative framework. It contains YHWH's admonition to
obey his 'angel' along with the promise that blessings follow from
such obedience, and states that the angel would bring Israel to the land
and that with God's help they would win the land and defeat the
various peoples living there by gradual conquest (23.20-33). Although
there is no new heading here, and its prohibition of worshipping other
gods (23.24) is reminiscent of 22.19, nonetheless, this section differs
from what goes before both in content and in form, and so should be
regarded as a separate unit. It is more 'sermonic' or 'paranetic' than
the regulations of 21.2–23.19, more an exhortation for the Israelites
in the immediate situation of leaving Sinai and pressing toward the
promised land than the earlier norms that ought to be established
more or less permanently when Israel would settle in the land. The
instructions in this 'epilogue' would become antiquated once the land
was fully taken.

The mention of the 'angel' anticipates Exod. 32.34 and 33.2-3 in the
Golden Calf story where Moses is again told that God's angel would
go ahead of Israel to aid in conquering the land; 33.12-16 where
Moses requests God's Presence rather than the intermediation of an
angel; and ch. 34 where the metaphor of Moses' shining face indicates
that Moses himself is the angel (or 'agent') who leads the people and
who indirectly reflects the Presence of God in their midst.[1] The end of
20.22–23.33 continues to place itself in the context of the Exodus story
for which the next event should have been, had Israel's subsequent
disobedience not delayed it, the conquest of the land.

Similar 'epilogues' with concluding warnings and promises follow
other regulatory corpora of the Pentateuch: Deuteronomy 27 and 28
follow the regulations of Deuteronomy 12–26, and Lev. 26.3-46
follows the regulations of Lev. 17–26.2.[2]

---

1.   Brichto, *Poetics*, pp. 110-11.

2.   It can be compared also, though the parallels are weaker, to the epilogues of
cuneiform law collections. Cf. Paul, *Studies*, pp. 34-38.

Chapter 2

ON IMAGES AND ALTARS: EXODUS 20.22-26

This chapter begins a section-by-section analysis of Exod. 20.22–23.19. Each section begins with my own translation, followed by a discussion that emphasizes matters of structure, style, genre, relationship with other passages, problems of interpretation, as well as comparisons and contrasts with source-oriented analysis.

Cultic Regulations: On Images and Altars: Exodus 20.22-26

(22) YHWH said to Moses, 'Address the children of Israel as follows: "You yourselves have seen how from the sky I have spoken with you [pl.]. (23) You [pl.] are not to make in my case (אתי)[1] either a god of silver, nor even a god of gold are you permitted to make for yourselves. (24) You [sing.] may make an altar of earth (אדמה) in order to offer your burnt offerings and your שׁלמים-offerings, your flock and your herd.[2] In each and every place in which I will cause my name to be mentioned, I will come to you [sing.] to bless you. (25) Now if you [sing.] should choose to make an altar consisting of stones, you are not to make it of

---

1. Most translators seem to take אתי to mean 'with me' in a sense similar to על-פני ('beside me', 'in my presence') in Exod. 20.3; that is, in reference to other gods who would be 'with' YHWH as rivals. However, אלהים probably refers to images of YHWH himself (as this chapter will argue). N. Leibowitz (*Studies in Shemot* [Jerusalem: World Zionist Organization, 1976], pp. 352-60) notes a variation on the MT division: R. Nathan in the *Mekilta* divided the verse with the MT, but read אתי as if the vocalization were אוֹתִי, making God the object of the verb: 'You shall not make Me'. The view adopted here (cf. H. Cazelles, *Études sur le code de l'alliance* [Paris: Letouzey & Ané, 1946], pp. 39-40) takes אתי to mean 'in close connection with me', 'in my case'.

2. Samaritan reads מן: '*from* your flock and your herd'. The MT's 'your flock and your herd' must be taken as synecdoche meaning 'animals taken for sacrifice from your flock and herd', giving the same sense.

hewn stone, for you have wielded your instrument upon it thereby rendering it profane. (26) Nor are you [sing.] to go up on stairs above my altar which is not intended for any such revealing of your nakedness."'

Exodus 20.22-26 and Structure

Exod. 20.22 is a historical prologue that connects the regulations that follow with the preceding narrative, followed by the cultic matters of vv. 23-26. The following structure can be discerned:

I. Historical Prologue: 'You yourselves have seen... (Exod. 20.22)
II. Cultic Regulations: (Exod. 20.23-26)
   A Iconoplasm prohibited (v. 23)
      B Altars of earth (אדמה) permitted (v. 24a)
         X Promise: God's presence and blessing
            at [sacrificial] worship (v. 24b)
      B´ Altars of hewn stone (גזית) prohibited (v. 25)
   A´ Steps prohibited for altars (v. 26)

Why should an author choose to introduce the regulations of Exod. 20.22–23.19 with this kind of material? Durham sees little purpose in the structure of the 'laws' generally. He remarks on v. 23:

So obvious a summary of the first two commandments may have been placed at the beginning of the Book of the Covenant precisely because it was such a loosely organized miscellany.[1]

Childs observes how many scholars ignore the present literary context of Exod. 20.22-26:

the overwhelming number of critical commentaries (Bäntsch, Noth, Te Stroete, etc.) judge vv. 22-23 to be a later redactional framework and therefore without exegetical significance. Their interest focuses exclusively on the history of religions implications to be found in the original ancient [altar] law itself.[2]

But the suggestion that these verses are 'without exegetical significance' ignores the text that we have in favor of a hypothetical one that may never have existed. Whatever the prehistory of this collection, our author, if competent, would not leave a 'loosely organized

---

1. J. Durham, *Exodus* (WBC; Waco, TX: Word, 1987), p. 319.
2. Childs, *Exodus*, p. 465. Cf. Schwienhorst-Schönberger (*Bundesbuch*, pp. 287-99, 417), for more recent opinions; he sees v. 22aßb as priestly, v. 23 as 'dtr', but vv. 24-26 as proto-dtr.

miscellany' but is likely to have had a purpose in introducing the regulations of 20.22–23.19 with 20.22-26.

In the light of the narrative, it is, in fact, quite natural for Exod. 20.22–23.33 to begin with cultic matters. The central purpose of chs. 19–24 is to describe the establishment of a covenant relationship between YHWH and Israel. Fundamental in a relationship with a god is how the god is to be worshipped. Consequently, both 20.22–23.19 and the Decalogue, being the stipulations of this covenant, begin with cultic matters. Moreover, 20.22–23.19 also concludes with cultic matters (23.10-19, sabbaths and holidays). Other legal corpora in the Bible likewise exhibit inclusios in which cultic matters envelope mostly non-cultic regulations: the Laws of Holiness (Leviticus 17–26) and of Deuteronomy (chs. 12–26).[1] All this emphasizes the religious rather than the secular aim of all these corpora as they stand. Cuneiform law collections, in contrast, are overwhelmingly secular and non-cultic in nature.[2] Given the theological nature of the covenant of which the regulations of 20.22–23.19 form a part, it is, if anything, less difficult to explain the presence of the cultic laws in the narrative than it is the non-cultic.

Exod. 20.22–23.19, like the Decalogue which it resumes and expands (cf. ch. 1) is introduced by a historical prologue (20.22; cf. 20.2), followed by a prohibition of images of deity or iconoplasm (20.23; cf. 20.4).

A logical connection exists between v. 22 and the prohibition of v. 23. In v. 22, the author chose to describe Israel as 'seeing' (in the sense of 'perceiving', cf. 20.18) that the voice of God came 'from the sky'. The choice of 'sky' rather than 'the cloud' or 'the mountain', and 'see' rather than 'hear' is intended to produce a contrast between 'heaven' in v. 22 and 'earth' in vv. 23-26 for which the expression 'from the mountain' or 'from the cloud' would be inappropriate. Israel 'saw' (ראיתם) that God spoke and they 'saw' cosmic phenomena associated with that, but they did not see God nor hear with complete understanding. The manner in which God spoke was not without significance. By speaking as an invisible voice from the sky, he was indicating that no earthly image is appropriate for him.[3] An altar

1. Paul, *Studies*, p. 34.
2. Paul, *Studies*, pp. 8-9.
3. G. Beer, *Exodus* (Tübingen: Mohr, 1939); G. Bush, *Notes on the Book of Exodus* (New York: Newman & Ivison, 1852), p. 290; Cassuto, *Exodus*, p. 255.

of the earth may be appropriate (20.24), but no earthly image is. Deut. 4.15-16 gives a similar explanation of our verse:

> You must be exceedingly cautious for yourselves, for you did not see any form when God spoke to you on Horeb from the midst of the fire lest you should act corruptly and make a carved image of any likeness whatsoever, whether it be male or female.

This reading of the text depends on taking אלהים in v. 23 as a reference to YHWH rather than 'gods'. Support for this interpretation is in Exod. 32.31 which echoes 20.23: 'This people have sinned greatly; they have made for themselves אלהי זהב. Whereas many versions translate the last phrase 'gods of gold', in context only one golden calf is in view. Hence, the אלהים that Aaron made in ch. 32, along with the associated plural verbs (vv. 4, 8), are to be understood as plurals of majesty in reference to YHWH. Likewise, אלהים in Exod. 20.23 is a plural of majesty for 'images of God'.

Exod. 20.24-26 is sometimes called 'The Law of the Altar'. Verses 24a and 25 have to do with materials that can and cannot be used in the building of altars: altars of earth permitted, hewn stones not permitted. The 'altar of stones' (v. 25) is a sub-category of the altar of אדמה in which wood or a natural outcrop of rock would be other possible sub-categories. Verse 26 has to do with an architectural feature, namely a stairway, that is prohibited for altars.

Exod. 20.24-26 advances the discussion that begins in v. 23. Verse 23 said that the people may not make a god of silver or gold to represent YHWH. Verse 24 states what they may do: namely, make an altar of אדמה ('earth') to offer sacrifices to God. אדמה ('earth') continues the heaven-earth polarity begun in the previous verses. God had spoken from the sky (מן־השמים, v. 22), and therefore no earthly thing should represent him (v. 23). But sacrifice on an 'earthly' altar (v. 24) is permitted (not commanded).[1]

Verse 24b is a parenthetical remark in which God promises his presence and his blessing at worship. This statement breaks the flow between 24a, the kind of altar materials permitted, and 24b, the kind of altar materials prohibited. Predictably, some source-oriented scholars

---

1.   The mood is not imperative ('you shall'), but permissive ('you may'). J. Milgrom (*Studies in Cultic Theology and Terminology* [Leiden: Brill, 1983], pp. 119-21) observes that sacrifice of עולות or שלמים זבח outside of the official central sanctuary was strictly voluntary for laymen according to the so-called Priestly Code; hence, Jer. 7.22 is not in conflict with the Priestly writings.

suggest a secondary, and by implication clumsy, insertion of 20.24b here, perhaps as an anti-Jerusalem cult polemic.[1]

Whether or not v. 24b is secondary is irrelevant for our synchronic analysis, but the implication that 24b is a *clumsy* insertion contradicts our thesis that Exod. 20.22–23.19 is a well integrated unity. As a matter of fact, the enveloping of seemingly irrelevant material is a consistent, hence probably deliberate, stylistic feature in 20.22–23.19.[2] To test this thesis at this point, one should ask, 'Why would an intelligent author (assuming that he is such) choose the present placement of v. 24b?'

An answer to this question can be deduced from a close examination of the outline given above. The regulatory portion of 20.22-26, namely, vv. 23-26, is semi-chiastic in structure with v. 24b (element X) at the center of the chiasm. Although element A (the prohibition of iconoplasm) is not strongly parallel with element A* (the prohibition of stairs), nonetheless, elements B (where altars of earth are permitted) and B* (where altars of hewn stone are prohibited) are strongly parallel, and there is a balancing of two cultic regulations before 24b and two cultic regulations after 24b. Given this structure, v. 24b can be understood, not as a clumsy insertion, but as a parenthetical remark placed at the center of these regulations in order to express a fundamental, central principle: The goal of worship, for which the rules of worship are enabling conditions, is to meet with God and to find his blessing.

The principle of v. 24b conceptually undergirds the particular regulations that surround it, preventing a reader from forgetting the purpose of worship, and indeed the relational purpose of the covenant of which these regulations are a part. A similar bracketing of a more general cultic principle with more specific cultic regulations will be seen in the discussion of Exod. 23.10-19.

Pronouns, Style, and Other Rhetorical Features

There is a change from second person plural to second person singular in Exod. 20.22-26. Frequently scholars interpret this change from second person plural to second person singular in v. 24 as a change of

---

1. Boecker, *Law*, p. 147, following D. Conrad, *Studien zum Altargesetz: Ex 20.24-26* (Marburg: H. Kombächer, 1968), pp. 11-13. Cf. Schwienhorst-Schönberger, *Bundesbuch*, pp. 296-98.

2. See Exod. 21.16; 21.22-25; 21.33-34; 22.1-2b; 22.8; 23.4-5; 23.13.

sources.[1] Hence, they argue that vv. 24-26 originally had nothing to do with vv. 22-23. Although possible, this is not a necessary conclusion. The change from second person plural to second person singular could further a rhetorical purpose rather than being an indication of a change of sources.

The use of second person plural in vv. 22-23 reflects the situation in the story at Sinai and so helps to connect the regulations with the narrative context. Moreover, the plurals of vv. 22-23 perhaps serve to underscore or 'intensify' this basic covenant requirement on images applicable to every Israelite in his or her relationship with God. Note the changes from singular to plural in 22.20-26, 22.28-30, 23.9, 23.13, 23.15, several of which can be explained as plurals of intensification for admonitions directed to every listener.[2]

The switch to the singular possibly has to do with the fact that unlike the making and possessing of images which would be a temptation for most Isralites, building an altar was a less common activity, and less likely to involve every individual. Hence, the collective 'you [singular]' for Israel as a totality,[3] rather than 'you [plural]' stressing individual Israelites, was employed. The only explicit application of v. 23, namely Deuteronomy 27.5-7 that commands an altar to be built, and Joshua 8.30-31 where it is built on Mount Ebal in accord with our regulation, was a corporate and official activity rather than an individual one.

Verse 23 can be understood to exhibit an almost poetic style that is unusual for regulatory material. The most likely renderings see balance and artful flow in this verse. Most translators divide the verse after אלהי כסף ('god/gods of silver'), thus making it the object of the first verb, and אלהי זהב ('god/gods of gold') the object of the second. Yet it is difficult to break up the pair 'silver and gold' that are so frequently coupled as to be almost idiomatic. Hess[4] proposes that the entire phrase אלהי כסף ואלהי זהב is the object of both verbs simultaneously. The division of the Masoretic accents that divide this verse

---

1. E.g., Conrad, *Studien zum Altargesetz*, pp. 9ff.

2. See R. Sonsino, *Motive Clauses in Hebrew Law* (SBLDS 45; Chico, CA: Scholars Press, 1980), p. 197.

3. D. Patrick 'I and Thou in the Covenant Code', pp. 71-86, shows that 'thou' in Exod. 20.22-23.33 is Israel, God's people.

4. R.S. Hess, 'The Structure of the Covenant Code' (ThM Thesis, Trinity Evangelical Divinity School [Deerfield, IL], 1980), p. 34 n. 1.

after אתי, demanding a translation, 'You will not make with me [at all]!...' seems less likely because it is too abrupt and provides no object for the verb.

The progression from silver to gold is from the less valuable to the more valuable. Silver and gold forms a merismus representing precious materials of whatever sort regardless of value.[1] The wording precludes the notion that a more valuable image might be acceptable where a less valuable one was not. Type of material makes no difference.

Exod. 20.24-25 imparts symbolic value to making an 'altar of the earth (אדמה)', putting this in contrast with making one from 'hewn stones (גזית)'. It is not easy to pin down the symbolism. E. Robertson[2] argues that the expression מזבח אדמה refers to a 'natural' altar, אדמה being used in lieu of a better term in biblical Hebrew to express the sense 'natural'. In other words, those who build altars must use material from the ground as it left the hand of the Creator rather than any humanly manufactured material. He argues that this meaning for אדמה can be seen elsewhere in 2 Chron. 26.10 in which Uzziah is said to be 'a lover of nature (אוֹהב אדמה)'. It must be said that 2 Chron. 26.10 is not itself unambiguous, though the general interpretation merits consideration in a context where the altar of אדמה is in contrast with one of hewn stone (גזית).

Although Robertson's view of מזבח אדמה is not without difficulty, other views are each less likely. The view that מזבח אדמה means an altar of loose earth or soil[3] symbolizing the earth's receiving back the blood of the sacrificial victim fails because altars are almost universally made of hard materials such as stone or metal or wood, not loose dirt. Dirt and clay may fill such an altar, as it did the Israelite altar at Arad,[4] but the 'earth' would be below the hard surface. Moreover, although classical and especially Latin sources refer to altars of turf, this kind of turf is practically non-existent in the stony soil of Palestine and therefore is unlikely to be the meaning of מזבח אדמה.[5]

---

1. R.A. Cole, *Exodus* (TOTC; Downers Grove: Inter-Varsity, 1973), p. 163.
2. E. Robertson, 'The Altar of Earth', *JJS* 1 (1948), pp. 18-21.
3. Cazelles, *Études*, p. 40.
4. Z. Herzog, M. Aharoni and A. Rainey, 'Arad—Ancient Israelite Fortress with a Temple to Yahweh', *BARev* 13.2 (Mar./Apr. 1987), p. 33.
5. Robertson, 'Altar of Earth', pp. 18-19.

The view that מזבח אדמה refers to an altar of sun-dried mud bricks,[1] though supported by archaeological finds (Megiddo, Shechem, Lachish, Alalakh) of what can be interpreted as mud-brick altars, fails to explain why the Hebrew term for 'brick' (לבנים) is not used.[2] Noth[3] understood אדמה to be the cultivated soil of free, agricultural land away from settlements, as opposed to fixed settlements and to mountainous land where stones would form natural altars. However, one is never far away from stones in Palestine. An altar made primarily of stones could be made almost anywhere, and stones are generally more suitable than cultivatable soil as building material for an altar.

Conrad rejects Robertson's view because it interprets vv. 24 and 25 as a unity. Conrad denies the unity of these verses on source-critical grounds.[4] But even if, as Conrad claims and Robertson admits, various elements of originally diverse origins have been brought together in these verses, a thesis beyond proof or disproof, it does not preclude the possibility that the one who brought these diverse elements together had in mind a unified concept which he wished to convey by arranging them in the manner that he did. That vv. 24-25 can be read together as a unity is consistent with the thesis that the author/editor had a unified concept in mind.

Exodus 20.22-26 and Other Altar Laws

An important issue for this study is the relationship between Exod. 20.22-26 and two other passages: Deuteronomy 12 that speaks of the 'central sanctuary' and Exodus 27 that speaks of the bronze altar to be built for the Tabernacle.

Deuteronomy 12 seeks to establish a central sanctuary only at the place God chooses. Source-oriented scholars since Wellhausen[5] regularly take this as a veiled reference to Jerusalem's sanctuary in contradiction with the permission of multiple altars in Exod. 20.23. Most source critics, moreover, suppose the description of the bronze altar in Exodus 27 (which they assign to P) to be in contradiction with Exod. 20.24-26 that prohibits manufactured altars.

1. Conrad, *Studien zum Altargesetz*, pp. 26-31.
2. Childs, *Exodus*, p. 466.
3. Noth, *Exodus*, p. 176.
4. Conrad, *Studien zum Altargesetz*, p. 25.
5. J. Wellhausen, *Prolegomena to the History of Ancient Israel* (Gloucester, MA: Peter Smith, 1983), pp. 29-34.

Is it possible to read these three passages without concluding that they are in contradiction? Insofar as a harmonious reading proves impossible, to that extent our thesis that the author/editor(s) of the Pentateuch produced a well-crafted unity will have turned out to be ill-founded.

The fact that the editor of the final form of Exodus left these laws in their present form in the same book suggests that he did not perceive any contradiction between the altar laws of chs. 20 and 27. Moreover, the editor of Deuteronomy seems to have perceived no contradiction between the altar law of Exodus 20 and the central sanctuary at the place which YHWH chooses in Deuteronomy 12, since the same book (Deut. 27) commands the making of a stone altar patterned after the description of Exod. 20.25, and the Deuteronomistic History records the fulfillment of that command not at Jerusalem but at Mount Ebal (Josh. 8.30-32).

It will not do to say that Deuteronomy 27 is a late addition, because Joshua 8 records the continuation of the story at Ebal. Such a double 'insertion' shows careful, deliberate editing. If such editing occurred, the person adding this material could be expected to delete the contradictory material in Deuteronomy 12 if he considered it contradictory. Furthermore, subsequent editors, if they wanted to stress the Jerusalem sanctuary, would be expected to eliminate these embarrassing additions. The fact that it was not deleted implies either that the person adding this material (along with any editor who followed him) was so incompetent that he did not notice or correct the contradictions between the texts, or else that the contradiction is in our minds rather than in the minds of the transmitters of the tradition.

How might the biblical author(s) have resolved the discrepancy which modern readers perceive? Cassuto tries to resolve the discrepancy by limiting Exod. 20.24-26 to 'lay' altars built in the Tabernacle's courtyard.[1] It is true that additional altars would have been necessary to accommodate the large number of worshippers during festivals who would otherwise overwhelm a single altar;[2] however, Cassuto's approach does not go far enough. It fails, for example, to account for the explicit application of these verses on Mount Ebal (Josh. 8.30-34), evidently outside of the Tabernacle. Moreover, other altars outside of the central sanctuary are not uncommon in biblical narrative, and

1.   Cassuto, *Exodus*, p. 256.
2.   Mentioned by Robertson, 'Altar of Earth', p. 15.

there is no hint of illegitimacy even in the Deuteronomistic History (Exod. 24.4; Judg. 6.24; 13.15-20; 1 Sam. 7.17; 14.35; 2 Sam. 24.18ff.; 1 Kgs 18.30; 19.10, 14 [note the plural]).

Additional altars were in principle necessary because cultic laws require the slaughter of animals even for food to be a sacrifice in which the blood was to be poured out on an altar to acknowledge before deity that it is only by divine permission that animal life can be taken (cf. Gen. 9.1-4).[1] To eat flesh without pouring out the blood to God on an altar is to 'eat the blood', an offense against deity (cf. 1 Sam. 14.31-35).[2] Additional altars were therefore required for the slaughter of domestic animals for food (the שלמים-offerings of Exod. 20.24) in cases where distance made the use of the Tabernacle impractical, and provision also had to be made for the slaughter of wild game (cf. Deut. 12.15-16, 20-25).

Perhaps a holistic reading is possible along the following lines: the altar law of Exodus 20 applies to all sacrifice outside the official bronze altar of the Tabernacle but not to the bronze altar itself which is distinguished from all other legitimate altars by being a work of skilled craftsmanship, not by human choice, but by divine direction.

Deuteronomy 12 describes the ideal of a central, pre-eminent sanctuary, but not an exclusive one. Deuteronomy tacitly allows lesser altars (so McConville):[3] 27.5ff. commands the building of an altar of stone and 16.21 prohibits planting a tree as an Asherah beside 'the altar of YHWH your God which you [sing.] shall make'. McConville understands the emphasis on the central sanctuary in ch. 12 to be an expression of an ideal of religious unity rather than being 'legislation' prohibiting altars of the type described in Exod. 20.24-26. This same ideal also leads the writer of Deuteronomy to play down tribal distinctions. To emphasize this ideal of unity, the author of Deuteronomy exalts the role of the central sanctuary by down-playing not only the existence but also the sanctity of secondary altars. Hence, whereas only the ceremonially clean eat food from the Tabernacle's altar, both the clean and unclean may eat food from these altars (Deut. 12.15, 22). Nevertheless, Deuteronomy acknowledges their legitimate existence.

---

1. H.C. Brichto, 'On Slaughter and Sacrifice, Blood and Atonement', *HUCA* 47 (1976), pp. 19-55; Milgrom, *Studies*, pp. 104-108.

2. Brichto, 'On Slaughter and Sacrifice', pp. 21-22.

3. J.G. McConville, *Law and Theology in Deuteronomy* (JSOTSup 33; Sheffield: JSOT Press, 1984), pp. 21-38.

This interpretation is in contrast with the source-oriented view of J. Milgrom[1] who argues that Deuteronomy not only reduces the sanctity of slaughter outside of the central sanctuary, but has made it completely profane; hence, Deuteronomy 12 contradicts the priestly law of Lev. 17.3-7 (H). Read holistically apart from hypothetical sources, however, Lev. 17.3-7 merely demands that in the wilderness the 'camp' stationed around the Tabernacle must slaughter meat at the Tabernacle's altar. This was the only one available in the context of the narrative. It does not contradict Deuteronomy 12's regulations for those after the conquest who would live far from the Tabernacle (cf. Ibn Ezra). Moreover, Deut. 12.15, 21 uses זבח ('sacrifice') as its term for slaughter. Milgrom himself demonstrates that זבח in its 127 other occurrences never means profane slaughter. Deut. 12.15 and 21 give no exception: sacrifice, not merely slaughter is intended.

The book of Exodus, like Deuteronomy, highlights the Tabernacle as a central sanctuary, describing it in detail in chs. 25-31. Chapter 27 emphasizes the Tabernacle's bronze altar without excluding the possibility of the lesser altars as allowed previously in 20.24-26. However, the prohibition of altars of hewn stone served to prevent the construction of a finely crafted altar that might rival the Tabernacle's altar, thus maintaining the bronze altar's preeminence.

Exodus 20.22-26: Law, Religion, or Morality?

The present regulations cannot be considered, strictly speaking, laws. Unlike law, there are no legal consequences or penalties, either from God or man, specified for their violation. Rather, the passage is one of instruction as to what kinds of worship YHWH finds acceptable and what kinds are unacceptable, along with a promise of God's presence in acceptable worship. Even the acceptable worship is more a matter of permission than command: no one has to make an altar or bring a sacrifice. Anyone so doing, however, is to comply with these guidelines.

These regulations make a number of religious-theological points. The central one is in 20.24b, the promise of God's presence and blessing when the Israelite rightly worships him. Although the general thrust of this promise is clear, there are some exegetical difficulties in fully explicating this promise to which I now turn.

The expression in 24b 'I will cause my name to be mentioned' is

---

1. J. Milgrom, 'Profane Slaughter and a Formulaic Key to the Composition of Deuteronomy', *HUCA* 47 (1976), pp. 1-17.

difficult. Childs[1] understands the expression הזכיר את השם to mean simply 'to proclaim the name' as in Isa. 12.4, 26.13 and Ps. 45.18. This is possible. But how is it that God proclaims his own name? The more expected reading would be second person, 'where *you* proclaim my name', which is what the Syriac version actually does read. Is the text corrupt? Such a source-oriented view is plausible here.

There is also, however, a plausible literary explanation for the use of the first person that requires no emendation. The author might be playing on our expectation of a second person verb in order to underscore the divine election in worship. The verse could be rendered, 'In every place where I will move you to worship me, I will manifest my presence to you and bless you.' The sense is thus: 'When you choose to offer me sacrificial worship and call upon my name, it is not simply you who have chosen to worship me, but rather I who have chosen you, reaching out to you, making myself available to you, giving you a sense of my Presence, granting you permission to worship me.' In short, this is a promise of continued divine Presence after Israel leaves Sinai.

An alternative view is offered by Robertson. Robertson understands המקום ('the place') to mean not just any place, but an altar site legitimized by revelation as in Gen. 28.11.[2] Thus he understands the meaning as 'in any/every sanctuary I will cause my name to be remembered'.[3]

It is true that many of the altars built in the Bible occur after some sort of numinous experience (Gen. 12.7; 13.4; 26.23-25; 35.1), and these often became permanent cult sites. According to this view, only those places in which God has previously revealed himself are appropriate for the building of altars, for only there has he 'caused his name to be remembered', an expression equivalent to a 'place that God chooses' (Deut. 12.5).[4] Consequently, only in such places does God promise to come and grant blessings in the future. This leads

---

1. Childs, *Exodus*, p. 447; following J.J. Stamm, 'Zum Altargesetz im Bundesbuch', *TZ* 1 (1945), pp. 304-306.

2. Robertson, 'Altar of Earth', pp. 15-16. *GKC* §126r, p. 407 interprets המקום in Gen. 28.11 similarly.

3. Robertson, 'Altar of Earth', p. 20. Cf. the Aramaic Targum. BDB, p. 880 claims that מקום means 'sanctuary' in Gen. 12.6; 13.3-4; 22.3-4, 9, 14; 28.11, 19; Deut. 12.2-3, Ezek. 6.13 and 2 Chron. 33.19.

4. Robertson, 'Altar of Earth', p. 16.

Robertson to the conclusion that only official rather than lay altars are in view here.[1]

Although there is much to be said for this alternative view, I doubt that the altar described here is limited to official altars. The simplicity of the materials speaks against it. In the examples cited from Genesis, altars were built by individuals before the sites became 'official'. A theophany could certainly lead someone to build an altar, but so could practical considerations such as the distance to existing altars. The point is not, I think, that altars are permitted only where theophanies have occurred. It says rather that altars are places where God's name is remembered or proclaimed; such remembrance is not only permitted by God, but has been initiated by him and prompted by him; and in each and every place of this kind where true praise occurs, God promises his presence and blessing.

Another difficulty in the theological promise of v. 24b is the expression בכל־המקום which I translate 'in each and every place'. The article before מקום suggests to some interpreters that the intended meaning cannot be 'in every place' but must be understood to mean 'the entirety of the place'[2] in reference to the central sanctuary, the article 'ה' representing a scribal addition to avoid the original implication of multiple altars being authorized instead of one central sanctuary.[3] This source-oriented explanation is not necessary, however. Not only does the Tabernacle lack an altar of earth, there are good linguistic grounds for taking בכל־המקום to mean 'in a totality of places' or 'in each and every place'. See Deut. 11.24 where 'כל־המקום that the sole of your foot treads' must mean 'each and every place' and Gen. 20.13 and Exod. 1.22 where a similar construction, כל־הבן, must mean 'each and every boy'.[4]

---

1. Robertson, 'Altar of Earth', p. 20. Compare הזכיר את שמי ('to cause my name to be mentioned') with the similar expression לקרוא את שמי על־ ('to call my name upon [something]', cf. Jer. 7.10). The latter expresses ownership, and in the case of temples authorization for worship. Likewise the expression לשכם שמו שם 'to make his name dwell there' (Deut. 12.11) seems to mean that God associates his name with a place.

2. Conrad, *Studien zum Altargesetz*, p. 5.

3. *GKC* §127e, p. 410. Support for viewing the article as a late addition is found in the Samaritan Pentateuch which omits כל though it retains the article, which might be regarded as an alternate scribal solution to an original בכל־מקום.

4. Childs, *Exodus*, p. 447; E. König cited by Conrad, *Studien zum Altargesetz*, p. 6.

Other religious and moral points can be observed: the religious point of v. 23 (which states that YHWH worship is not to be perverted by images) and v. 24a (which grants permission to make an altar of earth) has already been sufficiently discussed. What needs more discussion is the religious motivation behind the prohibitions of altars of 'hewn stone (גזית)' in v. 25. This verse states that using any kind of an instrument upon a stone renders it profane. It must instead be unhewn, 'natural', without human manufacture or decoration. Why is this so?

As already suggested, the lack of decoration set these altars apart from the 'manufactured' bronze altar of the central sanctuary. There is no contradiction, as some source-oriented scholars are prone to see, between the 'elaborate, excessively luxurious' altars of the official cult and the simple stone altar described here since such an explanation fails to address adequately the reason the author/editor(s) combined this instruction with the more elaborate Tabernacle altar regulation of Exodus 27 (cf. the discussion above). Rather, the prohibition of גזית ('hewn stone') served other purposes. It clearly prevented secondary altars from rivaling the bronze altar of the Tabernacle which, unlike any others, was to be of skilled craftsmanship according to divine instruction. It perhaps also excluded the possibility of engravings and decorations to prevent any altar from becoming an idolatrous object of worship.[1] Finally, the exclusion of hewn stone probably expresses symbolically the idea that all human effort or improvement is unacceptable as a means of approaching God. God instead prefers simpler means of approach, on his own terms, without human ingenuity or effort, using God's own materials as can be found naturally on the ground to make offerings to him. If stones be used, which by necessity require some assemblage, the human part is to be limited. One may assemble them, but one may not hew them.[2]

1.   E.B. Smick, *Theological Wordbook of the Old Testament* (gen. ed. R.L. Harris; Chicago: Moody, 1980), p. 157, s.v. 'גזית'. Similarly R. Samuel b. Meir. Note, however, that Deut. 27.5-8 and Josh. 8.30-32 do allow the engraving of 'all the words of this law' on the unhewn stones of this kind of altar built on Mount Ebal.

2.   That unhewn stones were believed to have a 'special numinous quality' (K. Galling, 'Altar', *IDB*, I, p. 97) is mere speculation. Conrad sees the prohibition of גזית as anti-Canaanite in intent, prohibiting גזית not in the sense of 'hewn stone', but rather as forbidding ostentation by means of a particular treatment of the surface of the altar involving the chiselling out of so-called bowl-holes for libations in the Canaanite pattern known from archaeology (Conrad, *Studien zum Altargesetz*,

Finally, the moral or religious intent of v. 26, 'Nor should you go up on stairs above my altar that is not intended for any such revealing of your nakedness', can be considered. Conrad omits the second half of this verse on speculative, source-critical grounds and argues that the 'original' motivation for prohibiting steps is its connection with Near Eastern 'high god' cults'.[1] Many scholars speculate that the thrust of this law is anti-Canaanite since Canaanite altars known from archaeology often had steps, and Canaanite worship is believed to have included sexual elements.

The only motivation against steps in the text itself, however, is to avoid exposure of the genitals. The text seems to be making a moral and religious statement about the relationship between worship and sexuality. No sexual act was permitted as a means of worshipping YHWH, nor was any hint of sexual impropriety allowed (contrast Canaanite worship, Hos. 4.13-14). A similar sort of call for sexual purity is seen in the call for the people to prepare for their encounter with YHWH at Sinai by abstaining from sexual relations (Exod. 19.15), and the requirement that priests, unlike the ordinary Israelite, wear breeches (Exod. 28.42-43). The laws of purity and impurity indicate that sexual discharges rendered a person 'unclean' and therefore prohibited persons from approaching that which is holy (cf. Lev. 15). Hence, those who serve God's altar must be modest, without even a hint of sexual impropriety.

The command to avoid an altar design that would result in indecent exposure applied especially to 'lay' altars. It could be ignored at altars served by official priests who (as noted) wore breeches over their loins. Hence Ezek. 43.17 could conceive of having steps leading to the altar in its visionary Jerusalem Temple. It is possible that Solomon's Temple altar also had steps (cf. 2 Chron. 4.1), but since priests avoided indecent exposure by wearing breeches, such an altar would in no way contradict the spirit of the altar law of Exod. 20.26.

---

pp. 43-50; cf. Boecker, *Law*, p. 148). However, as Conrad admits (p. 39), גזית in late biblical Hebrew (1 Chron. 22.2) clearly means 'hewn stone' in the sense of a squared ashlar. His case that גזית has a different meaning at Exod. 20.25 is not strong.

1.   Conrad, *Studien zum Altargesetz*, pp. 123-25.

Chapter 3

THE QUESTION OF SERVITUDE AND FREEDOM: EXODUS 21.2-11

Although Exod. 20.22-26 might be excluded from the designation 'law' because of its cultic character, the unit of Exod. 21.2–22.16 is clearly more 'legal' in character as reflected by the many parallels between these regulations and cuneiform laws. S. Paul, whose interest focuses on these parallels, therefore limits his annotations to Exod. 21.2–22.16 which he calls the 'formal legal corpus'.[1]

These regulations provide an opportunity to test the degree to which biblical law is literary in character. If a literary approach can be successfully applied to this 'formal legal corpus', that is, to the material that most resembles Near Eastern legal parallels, then great strides will have been made in establishing that the material here is best treated as an essentially literary phenomenon rather than as an essentially historical or legal one.

Exod. 21.2-11 consists of two cases: the 'Hebrew' bondsman (vv. 2-6) and the 'slave-wife' (vv. 7-11).

Concerning Servitude: Exodus 21.2-11
Case A: The 'Hebrew' Bondsman

(2) Should you [sing.] acquire a 'Hebrew' bondsman (עבד עברי), he may serve you for six years, but in the seventh year he must be allowed to go forth as a free man without payment of redemption money. (3) If he came into servitude by himself, then he may leave by himself. If he came in married, then his wife must be allowed to leave with him. (4) If his master granted him a woman to bear him sons and daughters, the woman along with her children remain in the custody of the master, though he is permitted to leave by himself. (5) But if the bondsman insists, 'I prefer my master, my woman, and my children. I do not wish to go free', (6) then

---

1. Paul, *Studies*, p. 43.

his master must bring him near to האלהים, even to the door or the door-post to bore his ear with a boring-instrument and so he will be in his service for life.

Case B: The Slave-Wife

(7) If, on the other hand, someone sells his daughter as a slave-wife (אמה), she does not go free in the manner of bondsmen. (8) If her master, who has not designated her to marriage [for anyone] (Qere: designated her to marry himself), is displeased with her, then he should have her redeemed. He may not arrogate in his treachery against her to sell her to an outside clan (עם נכרי). (9) Now if he designated her to marry his son, he should deal with her in accordance with the custom regarding freeborn daughters-in-law (בנות). (10) If he takes another wife for himself, he may not withhold her meat [שארה], her (fine?) clothing, and her ענתה (cosmetics?). (11) If he is unwilling to do these three things for her, then she should be permitted to leave freely without payment of redemption money.

Exodus 21.2-11 and Structure

Case A and Case B balance each other: Case A has to do with the servitude and release of a bondsman while case B is one example of the servitude and potential release of a bondwoman where sale was for the purpose of marriage.

אמה (*'amah*) here seems to have the limited sense of slave-wife rather than simply a bondwoman.[1] This is but one kind of female servitude. Where sexual favors are not involved a bondwoman would go free at the same time as a bondsman in accord with Deut. 15.12-18 and LH §117. Some have seen a contradiction between Deut. 15.12-18 and Exod. 21.2-11,[2] but this is unnecessary. It is the element of marriage that causes the אמה not to be released in the manner of the 'Hebrew' bondsman. Where marriage plays no role in a woman's servitude, the bondwoman differs little from the bondsman of Exod.

---

1.   F.C. Fensham ('The Son of a Handmaid in Northwest Semitic', *VT* 19 [1969], pp. 312-21) observes that אמה often refers to a 'second wife' even in tomb inscriptions; A. Jepsen ('אמה and שפחה', *VT* 8 [1958], pp. 293-97) defines אמה as, 'an unfree woman as well as the second wife of a free man and also an unfree woman of an unfree man, a slave'. In Genesis every woman called an אמה was also a concubine: the concubines of Abimelech (20.17), Hagar (21.10, 12, 13), Bilhah (30.3), Bilhah and Zilpah (31.33).

2.   E.g., Patrick, *Law*, p. 113; Durham, *Exodus*, p. 321.

21.2-6, and the principles of 21.2-6 rather than that of Exod. 21.7 could then be thought to apply. The author of Deut. 15.12-18 included the female עבריה in his discussion because he recognized the limited nature of Exod. 21.7-11, not because he was contradicting Exod. 21.7.

The laws in Exodus regularly mention female slaves along with the male when this social class is treated: cf. 20.10, 20.17, 21.20, 21.26-27, 21.32 (the exception בן־אמתך in 23.12 probably representing members of the slave class regardless of sex). There is perhaps more than simple balance at Exod. 21.2-11, however. Turnbam makes a good case for seeing a chiastic structure in Exod. 21.2-11.[1] This chiasm is characterized by the movement from freedom to servitude in Case A and from servitude to freedom in Case B. His chiasm can be summarized as follows:

A Freedom (יצא) for the עבד apart from redemption money
    (חנם) guaranteed (21.2)
      B Complications due to marital status, including an
          introduction of an outside woman when the master
          grants a wife (21.3-4)
            C Freedom not chosen by the עבד (21.5-6)
            C′ Freedom not allowed the אמה (21.7)
      B′ Complications due to marital status, including an
          introduction of an outside woman when the master
          takes another wife (21.8-10)
A′ Freedom (תצא) for the אמה apart from redemption money
    (חנם) guaranteed (21.11)

This conceptual parallelism is supported by a more formal balance in that both Case A and Case B consist of an introductory כי clause followed by four related אם clauses. The first כי clause limits servitude to no more than seven years (v. 2). The four אם clauses (vv. 3-6) refine this general statement by giving cases where the general rule does or does not apply.

The second unit introduced by וכי[2] (v. 7) states that the אמה (slave-

---

1.   T.J. Turnbam, 'Male and Female Slaves in the Sabbath Year Laws of Exodus 21.1-11', in *SBL Seminar Papers 1987* (Decatur: Scholars Press, 1987), pp. 545-49.

2.   Schwienhorst-Schönberger (*Bundesbuch*, p. 304) takes the ו in וכי as designating a 'contrasting case' (*Gegenfall*) with 21.2-6. Likewise ואם in vv. 5 and 11 are in contrast with אם clauses of vv. 4 and 10 respectively. This rule often

wife) does not receive her freedom in the same way as (male) servants. The remainder of the case is organized around three stipulations introduced with אם where she does obtain freedom, followed by an overall conclusion also expressed by אם.

1.   If the master has not yet designated her for marriage (Qere: has designated her for himself) and is displeased with her he must have her redeemed and not sell her to an עם נכרי, the last term perhaps having the sense of someone outside of the circle of her biological, extended family (v. 8).[1]

2.   But if (ואם) the אמה marries a son, that is, a freeborn member of the household, she must be treated like a daughter-in-law rather than a slave (v. 9).

3.   Even if her husband takes another wife, he must not withhold from the slave-wife three items: שְׁאֵר, כסות, and ענתה (v. 10). I take שאר, normally translated 'flesh', as not just 'food'—any slave would be fed—but butcher meat (cf. Ps. 78.20, 27; Mic. 3.3 for this sense for שאר), which for the ancient diet was a delicacy, a 'choice food'. If שאר is metonymy for 'choice food', it followed that כסות ('covering') should imply more than mere clothes (which would again be provided any slave), but rather 'fineries', clothes as befits a master's wife.

---

works (here and 21.23, 29; 22.11), but it is difficult to apply it consistently for ו with כי and אם elsewhere. All the 'case laws' of 21.2-36 begin with וכי (21.18, 20, 22, 26, 28, 33, 35; cf. 22.14, 15), but not all seem strongly adversitive. Nor does ואם seem to be strongly adversitive at 21.27. אם without the ו seems to be strongly contrastive at 22.2.

1.   Although עם נכרי could mean 'a foreign people', the rendering 'an unfamiliar/ unknown clan' or the like seems more appropriate in this context. The אמה in the present case has been purchased, not simply to be a slave, but for marriage. If the master is displeased and refuses to marry her himself or to have her married to another member of the family, then he has violated the original marriage agreement, in which case she should be returned to her original family. To sell her as a slave to another clan would be a breaking of the agreement (cf. ב.ג.ד. in v. 8). עם frequently refers to the people of a nation, but it can refer to smaller units: cf. Jer. 37.12; 39.14; and 40.6 where people probably refers to Jeremiah's kinsmen, and עם II: 'kinsman (on father's side)' and passages such as Gen. 25.8 where Abraham is 'gathered to his kin (עמיו)' in which עם (with a plural of majesty?) is limited to that kinship group which shares a common burial site (cf. BDB, p. 769). נכרי can have the sense of 'unknown, unfamiliar, strange' (cf. Isa. 28.21; Ps. 69.9 [8]; Job 19.15; Prov. 20.16; 27.2, 16).

The third item, the hapax legomena עֹנָתָהּ, is uncertain in meaning, but 'cosmetics', is an attractive guess.[1]

4.   A fourth clause introduced by וְאִם (v. 11) probably forms a contrast with the other clauses introduced by אִם or וְאִם. It can be understood to say that if the master is unwilling to fulfill these three requirements—to redeem her to her own clan if displeasing, to treat her like a freeborn daughter-in-law if she marries a freeborn member of the family, or to continue to give her full support if there is another wife—then she is to obtain freedom in what amounts to a divorce without redemption price.[2]

This conceptual parallelism and formal balance between 21.2-6 and 21.7-11 shows artful crafting of the two cases. Turnbam sees the emphasis in the chiasm as its center: that the text encourages the bondsman to remain in the master's care, to choose family and servitude over freedom. In contrast, I prefer to see the emphasis in this case of chiasmus not in its center (servitude), but in its beginning and the end (freedom). Rather than encouraging servitude, the text could be understood (and was in Rabbinic tradition)[3] as frowning upon the choice of servitude by requiring a 'punitive' measure, namely, ear piercing, against the עֶבֶד who chooses it over freedom.

---

1.   The interpretation 'cosmetics' builds on the view of S. Paul, 'Exod. 21.10, A Threefold Maintenance Clause', *JNES* 28 (1969), pp. 48-53, which argues that the עֹנָה refers to 'oil, ointments'. He bases his view on passages such as Hos. 2.7, Eccl. 9.7-8 as well as cuneiform parallels where oil is listed with food and clothing as a staple commodity. Keeping in mind that two reasons for using oil were for perfume and maintaining the skin's beauty against the sun, I propose the translation 'delicacies, fineries, and cosmetics' for the sense of these three items.

Other proposals for עֹנָה include 'conjugal rights' (*Mekilta*; LXX; A. Deem, 'The Goddess Anath and Some Hebrew Cruces', *JSS* 23 [1978], p. 28); 'quarters' (Cassuto, *Exodus*, p. 269; cf. Rashbam), and 'right of parenthood' (R. North, 'Flesh, Covering, and Repose, Ex. xxi 10', *VT* 5 [1955], pp. 204-206).

2.   Another plausible view is that 'these three' refer to the three items in v. 10—flesh, clothing, and עֹנָה. Taking 'these three' as the three conditional clauses is slightly preferable because it allows a more tightly unified reading of Case B. On the other hand, if the referent is the three items of v. 10, then the fourth אִם clause of both Case A and Case B would be more closely parallel with each other since each would be tied to the third אִם clause of each case respectively.

3.   *Mekilta* on Exod. 21.6, and *b. Qid* 22a.

Examples of Literary Artistry in Exodus 21.2-11

The piercing of the bondsman's ear illustrates the literary artistry of the author of Exod. 21.2-6. The piercing of the bondsman's ear is more than a utilitarian function to make a hole in the ear for a tag or ring as a mark of slavery. If that were the sole purpose, there would be no practical need to specify the use of the 'door or doorpost' as the backstop for the piercing. Common sense dictates that one use a backstop to keep an earlobe from tearing during piercing with an awl or boring device; there is no need to legislate its use. Moreover, any backstop would do. Why specify a particular backstop, a door or doorpost, rather than a tree or a table or a plank? The answer is that boring the ear in this particular way expresses a particular symbolism.

The ear is the organ of 'hearing' and 'hearing' in Hebrew is commonly used in the sense of 'obedience'. Ps. 40.7(6) states that 'you have dug ears for me' in the sense of allowing the psalmist to hear and obey God's Torah (cf. vv. 8-9). A similar motif in Babylonia with regard to slaves occurs in LH §282 where a slave who says to his master 'You are not my master' has his ear cut off, symbolic of his lack of hearing/obedience. This motif of the ear as the organ of obedience seems to be found elsewhere in Exod. 29.20 where the priests are consecrated by placing blood on their ears, thumbs, and big toes ('hearing/obeying' with ears, 'doing' with hands and 'goings' with feet) and 32.2-3 that ironically stresses that the golden rings used for making the Golden Calf come not from the fingers, wrists, necks or noses of the people, but from their ears: the symbol of obedience being used for disobedience.[1] So here, the ear of the bondsman plays a role in this ritual because he must henceforth hear/obey his master.

The door or doorpost by metonymy represents the master's house to which this organ of obedience at the moment of piercing is fixed. The other option is that the door or doorpost is that of a sanctuary,[2] but this is based on evidence that is geographically, religiously, and

---

1. H.C. Brichto, 'The Worship of the Golden Calf', *HUCA* 54 (1983), p. 5.

2. F.C. Fensham, 'New Light on Exodus 21.6 and 22.7 from the Laws of Eshnunna', *JBL* 78 (1959), pp. 160-61, and O. Loretz, 'Ex 21, 6; 22, 8 und angebliche Nuzi-Parallelen', *Bib* 41 (1960), pp. 167-75. Fensham and Loretz note that LE §§36-37 reads: 'The owner of the house shall swear for him an oath at the gate (Akk. *babu*) of the temple of Tishpak.' The reference to 'gate' is taken as parallel with the use of 'door' in Exod. 21.6, suggesting the entire ceremony in Exod. 21.6 was at a sanctuary as well.

chronologically remote from the regulations of Exodus 21–23, and produces a less fitting symbolism: the bondsman is not being attached to a sanctuary. In the narrative context, the only sanctuary is the Tabernacle that, though it might be said to have doorposts (1 Sam. 1.9), does not have any door (דֶּלֶת). The parallel in Deut. 15.17 makes no mention of 'drawing near to deity', nor does it in any way hint at a locale in or around any sanctuary, suggesting that the writer of Deuteronomy also understood Exod. 21.6 to be referring to the door or doorpost of the master's house not a sanctuary.[1]

The piercing of the bondsman's ear at the master's house conveys an elaborate symbolism. On the negative side, the organ of obedience (the ear) might be thought of as 'punished' for not choosing freedom, perhaps because the bondsman would no longer be free to obey God alone. On the positive side, it pictures the bondsman now with the security of being permanently attached to the household and promising his obedience to the head of that household. He is no longer an outsider, a mere worker, but has become attached to the house as a member of the household.

Part of this symbolic ceremony involves drawing near to האלהים, but the meaning of that symbolism hinges on the interpretation of האלהים. A wide range of interpretations has been offered for האלהים: (i) God,[2] (ii) judges,[3] (iii) the place of the court,[4] (iv) gods,[5] and (v) teraphim.[6]

The translation of האלהים as 'the gods' takes this term as a primitive polytheistic element. However, the context of Exodus 19–24 excludes this view as highly improbable. The Decalogue condemns the worship of other gods, as does 20.23, 22.19, 23.13, 23.32-33 within the literary unit of 20.22–23.33. If the author(s) and/or editor(s) of Exodus 19–24 had any notion of consistency at all, the meaning cannot be 'the

1.   Schwienhorst-Schönberger (Bundesbuch, p. 308) speculates that Exod. 21.6 originally referred to a holy place, but that Deut. 15.17 has relocated the ritual to the master's house. Deut. 15.17 may actually be the original meaning, however, and in any case, it represents the meaning of the final redactors.

2.   E.g., the RSV, Tanakh.

3.   E.g., Targum Onqelos, King James Version.

4.   Cassuto, Exodus, p. 267.

5.   C.H. Gordon, 'אלהים in its Reputed Meaning of "Rulers, Judges"', JBL 54 (1935), pp. 139-44; A.E. Draffkorn, 'Ilâni/ELOHIM', JBL 76 (1957), pp. 216-24.

6.   H.C. Brichto, 'Kin, Cult, Land and Afterlife—A Biblical Complex', HUCA 44 (1973), pp. 46-47; K. van der Toorn, 'The Nature of the Biblical Teraphim in the Light of the Cuneiform Evidence', CBQ 52 (1990), pp. 208-10.

gods' in the context of instruction from the mouth of YHWH.

The renderings of 'judges' and 'place of the court' also seem unlikely for האלהים. The number of instances in the Bible where the translation 'judges' has been suggested for אלהים is small, and the interpretation is dubious in every case.[1] But even if the meaning 'judges' for אלהים were incontestably established, that meaning is inappropriate here for the simple reason that the circumstances described provide no case for judges or a court to decide.[2] At most, the 'judges' would serve as witnesses, but there seems little reason why the witnesses of this event should have to be judges and the location have to be at a court.

More plausible is the view that האלהים means 'God, Deity'. This is, of course, a common meaning for אלהים elsewhere. The bringing near to האלהים and to the door and doorpost would probably then represent a hendiadys in which the bondsman's attention is drawn to God in a ceremony at the door of the master's house. Against this view, however, is lack of linguistic support for taking 'drawing near God' in this metaphorical sense. Possibly 1 Sam. 14.36, 'Let us approach God here', has this sense since no sanctuary is mentioned, though use of an ephod representing God as in 1 Sam. 14.18ff. is likely.[3] Josh. 24.1, that refers to a presentation 'before האלהים' at Shechem, could mean metaphorically a public convocation, though the presence of the Tabernacle or Shechem's altar (Josh. 8.30-35) may be the reference instead. There are no unambiguous examples.

The most likely view of האלהים in Exod. 21.6 is that האלהים refers to teraphim in the sense of 'figurines representing the ancestors'. Defense of this view requires (1) demonstrating that אלהים can refer to

1. BDB translates אלהים as 'judges' at Exod. 21.6, and Exod. 22.7, 8, and considers this rendering doubtful at Exod. 22.27, 1 Sam. 2.25, Judg. 5.8, Pss. 82.1, 6, and 138.1. Interpretation along the lines of 'judges' has been suggested for Pss. 45.7 and 58.2. That אלהים means 'judges' at Exod. 21.6 goes back as far as the *Targum Onqelos* which translates it דיניא, 'judges', probably because it found the rendering 'God' offensive. Cf. the LXX, πρὸς τὸ κριτήριον τοῦ θεοῦ, 'towards the judgment seat of God'. H.C. Gordon, 'אלהים', pp. 139-44, argues אלהים never means 'judges'.

2. J.R. Vannoy, 'The Use of the Word האלהים in Ex. 21.6 and 22.7, 8', in *The Law and the Prophets* (ed. J.H. Skilton; Philadelphia: Presbyterian and Reformed, 1974), p. 231.

3. P.K. McCarter, Jr, *I Samuel* (Anchor Bible; Garden City, NY: Doubleday, 1980), p. 249.

teraphim, (2) giving evidence that the term teraphim could refer to 'figurines representing ancestors' rather than 'household gods' and (3) answering the objection that אלהים cannot refer to teraphim here since these objects are prohibited by the law as idolatrous.

Teraphim are mentioned in the following passages: Gen. 31.19, 34, 35; Judg. 17.5–18.30; 1 Sam. 15.23; 19.13-16; 2 Kgs 23.24; Hos. 3.4; Ezek. 21.26; and Zech. 10.2. They are mentioned pejoratively in 1 Sam. 15.23 in connection with sin (און) and 2 Kgs 23.24 in connection with idolatry (גִּלֻּלִים). There is no question that אלהים can be used as a term for teraphim: teraphim are called אלהים in Gen. 31.30 and Judg. 18.24, and the term אלהים may mask reference to teraphim elsewhere, e.g., Jacob's burial of אלהים at the oak near Shechem in Gen. 35.2, 4.[1]

The fact that the term אלהים can be used for teraphim is often used, in conjunction with Hittite etymology and Near Eastern conceptual parallels, to support the view that teraphim refer to 'household gods' or the like. However, another view is that teraphim refer to ancestor figurines rather than household gods. This view has recently been given thorough and able defense by van der Toorn.[2]

אלהים need not be a term for deity. אלהים has the meaning of 'spirit(s) of the dead' in 1 Sam. 28.13 where the medium of Endor uses the term to designate the ghost of Samuel. Likewise, Isa. 8.19, 'Should not a people consult their אלהים, the dead on behalf of the living?' suggests the meaning 'ancestral spirits' or 'departed spirits' for אלהים.[3] A plausible reconstruction for the reason why teraphim could be called

---

1. Brichto, 'Kin, Cult, Land and Afterlife', p. 46; van der Toorn, 'Biblical Teraphim', pp. 210-11.

2. Van der Toorn, 'Biblical Teraphim', pp. 203-22. Brichto, 'Kin, Cult, Land and Afterlife', pp. 28-29, 46-48 reached much the same conclusion earlier.

3. Brichto, 'Kin, Cult, Land and Afterlife', p. 28; R.E. Clements, *Isaiah 1–39* (Grand Rapids: Eerdmans, 1980), p. 102; H. Ringgren, אלהים', *TDOT* I, p. 282. The Akkadian term *eṭemmu* ('spirit of the dead, ghost') is used in parallel with *ilâni*, as noted by Draffkorn, '*Ilâni*/ELOHIM', p. 221, and *CAD* E, s.v. *eṭemmu*, pp. 397-400. Van der Toorn ('Biblical Teraphim', pp. 219-21) argues that the *eṭemmu* where these parallels occur refer to ancestor figurines, placing the care of them in the home on the same level as care of the *ilâni*. The *eṭemmu* relate to ancestor worship. According to van der Toorn, the best parallel with teraphim in Mesopotamia is *eṭemmu* rather than *ilâni*. Note the older etymology which related תרפים with רפאים ('shades, ghosts'), cited as dubious by BDB, p. 1076.

אלהים is that they were the images of the departed dead who could be regarded as spiritual beings.[1]

That teraphim were (or at least could be) anthropoid in appearance is supported from 1 Sam. 19.8-17 where Michal places teraphim (perhaps here a plural of majesty for a single, large figurine) in David's bed to make Saul's men suppose that he was still there. These teraphim are associated with the home, particularly the bedroom. Teraphim were in Laban's house (Gen. 31), and those of Judg. 17.5 appear in a household shrine, perhaps at a 'family altar'. Hence, these figurines could be found in an Israelite's home rather than exclusively in sanctuaries in the public cult.

Teraphim were in use during all periods of the Hebrew Bible: patriarchs, judges, early and late monarchy, and the post-exilic period (Zech. 10.2). But how could they have been a common feature of Israelite homes, given the condemnation of them elsewhere in the Bible? If teraphim are ancestor figurines, the condemnation of them may be connected with the magical use of these objects rather than the objects themselves. It is the use of them for purposes of divination or necromancy that is condemned in 1 Sam. 15.23, 2 Kgs. 23.24, Ezek. 21.26, and Zech. 10.2. However, a use of them that is neither idolatrous, nor connected with divination, nor related to ancestor worship could be viewed with indifference. This explains why a nearly life-size teraphim can be mentioned as a part of David's and Michal's house in 1 Sam. 19.13-16 without the biblical author feeling constrained to add a condemnatory aside. Such a use might include the remembering and enshrining—as family portraits do today—of past members of the family.

Acceptance that האלהים of Exod. 21.6 refer to ancestor figurines allows a compelling interpretation of the ceremony described there consistent with the symbolism already suggested above. I have argued that the ear is used metaphorically for 'obedience', and that the piercing of the bondsman's ear both discourages the choice of servitude and symbolizes the permanent attachment of the bondsman to the household. If this occurs before the האלהים in the sense of the family's ancestor figurines, the ceremony would then be in the symbolic presence of the family's ancestors (represented by teraphim). The implication is that in attaching the bondsman to the house, the family's ancestors are now considered his ancestors. Their heritage is his

1. Van der Toorn, 'Biblical Teraphim', p. 211.

heritage. He has been adopted into the family.

If this interpretation of Exod. 21.5-6 is correct, the author has shown himself to be a consummate literary genius. He has conveyed through this symbolism with elegance and succinctness complicated ideals concerning the position of this slave in the Israelite household. Implicit is the notion that this bondsman is not to be regarded as chattel but as a member of the extended family sharing the family's ancestral heritage (symbolized by the presence of האלהים), this having profound (though not immediately elaborated) significance for how he is to be treated.

Another possible example of literary artistry is found in Case B in a possible word play in v. 8. The MT preserves two versions of this verse. The Ketiv reads '[her master] has not designated her' (לא יעדה). This reading is possible even though Driver found it grammatically difficult.[1] The Ketiv implies that the אמה lived with the family unbetrothed in a manner similar to the traditional Chinese custom of buying a slave-girl as a wife for a son in days to come.[2] This custom in Chinese cultures allowed the family to obtain a wife at a price less than the bride-price for a free woman, and allowed them to rear the future wife within the family for a time to insure that she would 'fit in' before the commitment of marriage was made. Under such conditions, if the master concludes that she is not a suitable bride for any of the family members, the woman ought not remain in her maidservant status: she is to be returned to freedom.

The Qere reads '[her master] has designated her for himself (לו יעדה, in which לו (lo, 'for himself') has replaced its homonym לא (lo', 'not'). This reading makes v. 8 parallel with v. 9 where 'If for his son (לבנו) he designates her' places לבנו in the same sentence position as לא or לו in v. 8. The Qere implies that the master of the house himself intended to marry the אמה, but no longer wants her. In this case also, if she is not to be a wife, she cannot remain an unmarried slave or be sold. Rather she must be 'redeemed' and returned to freedom.

Source-oriented scholars feel they must decide whether the Qere or the Ketiv is the 'original' reading. However, it is possible to see a bit

---

1.   Driver, *Exodus*, *ad. loc.*, states that י.ע.ד does not mean 'espouse' absolutely, but means 'designate'. The meaning 'espouse' only becomes possible with the addition of preposition ל, to 'designate (a woman) for' hence 'espouse'. He and the majority of commentators reject the Ketiv.

2.   Cole, *Exodus*, p. 166.

of literary artistry here in which the author intends a double entendre. Whether לֹא or לֹו were written, when this verse was read aloud two possible interpretations would be possible to the hearer. Similar play on homophony occurs at 2 Kgs 8.10 that is deliberately ambiguous[1] and at Job 13.15. The MT's Qere/Ketiv at all three texts may reflect an awareness of a double entendre.

Exodus 21.2-11 in its Narrative Context

Attention to literary context explains several features in the text. For instance, it explains the personal formulation of Exod. 21.2 which begins, 'If *you* [sing.] acquire a "Hebrew" bondsman'. The second person pronoun troubles some source-oriented scholars in that Exod. 21.2-11 is (according to them) casuistic law. However, in cuneiform legal collections as well as in other casuistic formulations in Exod. 20.2–22.19, laws are regularly stated impersonally in third person. Hence, they speculate that the law was originally expressed impersonally ('If someone acquires a slave'), but an editor or some scribe, in order to make a better transition between the laws and the prologue to the laws (20.22-26, and 21.1), has secondarily changed the text to read 'you').[2]

Regardless of whether there was an original version of Exod. 21.2 that was impersonally formulated, in the present literary context the more personal second person formulation is appropriate. The 'you' here refers to 'Israel' as represented by a typical, individual Israelite, as often in 20.22–23.19. The personal language of 21.2 connects these cases to the narrative framework in which God is addressing Israel through Moses (cf. Exod. 21.1).

The more difficult question is why, having introduced the personal style in v. 2, the text chooses to switch back to an impersonal formulation in vv. 4-11. Perhaps the reason lies in the fact that the kind of legal and semi-legal material that 21.2-11 represents is normally expressed impersonally. The author, wanting to make these regulations personal, chose the second person for the introductory clause in Exod. 21.2. Nonetheless, he felt no need to continue the second person formulation since having introduced Case A (the 'Hebrew' bondsman) with a personal formulation, he conveyed the effect both to Case A

1. Brichto, *Poetics*, pp. 218-19.
2. Jepsen, *Untersuchungen*, p. 56. Cf. Alt, 'Origins', p. 119 n. 28 who suggests a more complicated history of emendation.

and to the related Case B (the slave-wife) even without continuing the second person formulation. Hence he could revert to the impersonal formulation more typical for this genre without compromising his desire to personalize these two cases as a whole.

The narrative context also helps to explain why these two 'slave laws' introduce the regulations of Exod. 21.2–23.19 under the new heading of 21.1. Phillips remarks that these cases of the 'Hebrew' bondsman and the slave-wife by their humanitarian interest, the lack of prescription of penalty for non-compliance, and the use of the second person 'you' in Exod. 21.2 resemble most closely the mixture of humanitarian and cultic injunctions at the end of the unit (22.20–23.19). *Prima facie*, he says, this section might have seemed more appropriately placed there.[1] Why then has the author chosen to place this regulation concerning the 'Hebrew' bondsman at the head of the 'legal' regulations rather than with the regulations that it most resembles?

The topic of 'servitude' does not introduce the other ancient Near East 'legal' collections. The Laws of Hammurapi end rather than begin with slavery, though various laws deal with slaves (§§7, 15-20, 117-19, 146-47, 170-71, 175-76, 199, 205, 223, 226-27, 231, 252, 278-82). Likewise, the Laws of Eshnunna, though they mention slaves throughout (§§15-16, 22-23, 31, 33-35, 40, 49-52, 55, 57), place the laws dealing most substantially with servitude at the end (§§49-52). The Middle Assyrian Laws rarely mention slaves (MAL A §§4, 40, 54, MAL C §§1, 3). Why, then, do Exodus's civil regulations feature servitude at the beginning?

An answer lies in the narrative context: Exodus 21 begins with servitude, just as does the prologue to the Decalogue in 20.2, in order to develop the central theme of the book of Exodus, deliverance from bondage.[2]

The modifying term 'Hebrew' is of relevance to this theme of deliverance from bondage. The exact meaning of the term עברי is debated. It has traditionally been understood to be an ethnic term, 'Hebrew', derived from Eber (Gen. 11.14), the great-great-great-great grandfather of Abraham. However, many scholars since the decipherment of Akkadian have concluded that עברי is derived from

---

1.   A. Phillips, 'The Laws of Slavery: Exodus 21.2-11', *JSOT* 30 (1984), p. 52.

2.   Observed by Cassuto, *Exodus*, p. 266; Paul, *Studies*, p. 107.

the Akkadian *ḫap/biru* that occurs in cuneiform literature as early as the third millennium BCE down to near the end of the second millennium in widely dispersed locations (Ur, Isin, Larsa, Babylon, Mari, Nuzi, Harran, Boghazköi, Alalah, Ugarit, Phoenicia, Joppa, Palestine, Egypt).[1] Most scholars of Akkadian have come to understand *ḫap/biru* as designating a class of individuals rather than an ethnic group,[2] the class consisting of 'immigrants'[3] or more generally 'indigent, property-less foreigners/migrants', as well as 'vagrant and uprooted elements regardless of ethnic origin'.[4] On the assumption that עברי and *ḫap/biru* are cognate terms, עברי then might not mean explicitly an 'Israelite', but refer to a member of the lower class susceptible to being forced into debt slavery by the social conditions that he faced as a member of this group.[5] Others deny that עברי is cognate with *ḫap/biru*.[6] Lipiński

1.   M. Greenberg, *The Ḫab/piru* (AOS 39; New Haven: American Oriental Society, 1955), p. 85 provides documentation for the occurrence of this term.

2.   M.P. Gray, 'The Ḫabiru-Hebrew Problem in the Light of the Source Material Available at Present', *HUCA* 29 (1958), p. 167; Greenberg, *The Ḫab/piru*, p. 87. It is difficult to understand *ḫap/biru* as an ethnic identification, though they are often identified as foreigners, since they come from many different lands, have Akkadian, West-semitic and Hurrian names, and there is no homeland or town attested for anyone called *ḫap/biru*. Note, however, R. de Vaux, *The Early History of Israel* (trans. D. Smith; Philadelphia: Westminster, 1978), pp. 110-12, which argues that expressions such as 'gods of the Habiru', and the mentioning of *ḫabiru* along with other people groups (Lulahhu, Suteans, Shasu, Tayaru) is evidence that *ḫabiru* is an ethnic term.

3.   Gray, 'The Ḫabiru-Hebrew Problem', p. 60. She derives עברי from ע.ב.ר ('to cross a boundary').

4.   Greenberg, *The Ḫab/piru*, p. 88. I omit discussion of the less likely rendering of *ḫapiru* as 'outlaw', proposed by Lemche, 'The "Hebrew Slave"', p. 144.

5.   Gray, 'The Ḫabiru-Hebrew Problem', pp. 173-88 makes a thorough case for this interpretation. Along the lines of this argument, Brichto, *Poetics*, p. 70, suggests that even in Jon. 1.9, in which Jonah identifies himself as a עברי, Jonah is not telling his ethnic heritage, but is answering the question in Jon. 1.8, 'What is your occupation?', to which he replies 'I am a vassal/subordinate (עברי)' of YHWH.

6.   Greenberg, *The Ḫab/piru*, pp. 91-96 points to philological evidence which suggests that the Akkadian pronunciation is more likely *ḫapiru* than *ḫabiru*, which makes a connection of *ḫapiru* with /p/ with עברי with /b/ more difficult. Of the five phonemes in *ḫa-pi-ru*, only two (' and *r*) occur in עברי. Moreover, *ḫap/biru* is a verbal adjective while עברי can be taken as a gentilic or adjectival form with a final 'i'. Note, however, that the 'i' ending need not be 'gentilic' since it can also be used for adjectival formations: e.g. שלישי ('third') and נכרי ('foreign') (cf. *GKC* §86k). Gray ('The Ḫabiru-Hebrew Problem', pp. 169-73) defends the connection with

interprets עברי without reference to ḥap/biru and yet concludes that it is a sociological term for an Israelite underclass rather than an ethnic term.[1]

The decision as to whether עברי is a sociological term or an ethnic term need not be made here. What is of significance for our purposes is that by designating the bondsman as a 'Hebrew', the author has used a term associated with Israel's servitude in and deliverance from Egypt. The Israelites, who were called 'Hebrews' by the Egyptians, were reduced to servitude by them (ch. 1). Moses was a 'Hebrew' (2.6). 'The God of the "Hebrews"' demanded through Moses and Aaron that Pharaoh 'let My people go' (3.18; 5.3; 7.16; 9.1, 13; 10.3) as a part of an overall plan to deliver the Israelites from servitude entirely.

The roots ע.ב.ד ('serve') and י.צ.א ('go out') of Exod. 21.2 are also related to the exodus theme. י.צ.א is the verb used to describe the exodus or 'going out' from Egypt associated with release from Egyptian bondage: 'I YHWH am causing you go out [H stem of י.צ.א] from the burdens of the Egyptians and I will deliver you from subjection to them (מֵעֲבֹדָתָם)' (6.6). Moses told the people on the occasion of the first Passover, 'Remember this day on which you went forth (י.צ.א) from Egypt, from a house of bondage' (בית עבדים, lit. 'house of bondsmen', 13.3), and 'It was with a mighty hand that YHWH brought us out [H stem of י.צ.א] from Egypt, from a house of bondage' (13.4). This theme of deliverance from servitude continues in the prologue to the Decalogue that begins 'I YHWH am your God who brought you out [H stem of י.צ.א] of the land of Egypt, out of a house of bondage' (20.2). It is not unfair to summarize all of chs. 1–18 as the story of the deliverance of Israel from bondage.

A connection between 21.2-6 and the theme of the exodus finds further support in the parallel passage of Deut. 15.12-18. This passage gives a parenetic retelling of Exod. 21.2-6. In Deut. 15.15, Moses

---

ע.ב.ד. C.H. Gordon (*Ugaritic Textbook* [AnOr, 38; Rome: Pontificium Institutum Biblicum, 1965], p. 459) states, 'the phonetic discrepancies between [Ugaritic] *'apir*- and "Hebrew" might possibly be attributed to nonSem. channels of transmission.'

1.   E. Lipiński ('L' "Esclave Hébreu"', *VT* 26 [1976], pp. 121-23) argues that עברי in Exod. 21.1 applies to a class of Israelites in a condition susceptible to servitude who held a status between the full citizen who could not become a slave and foreigners who could be reduced to perpetual slavery. He terms this class 'peasants' (*manant*) or 'patricians' (*patricien*). Phillips ('The Laws of Slavery', p. 64) doubts Lipiński's implication of a rigidly stratified 'underclass' in pre-exilic Israel. Nonetheless, Lipiński's general interpretation has much to commend it.

exhorts the Israelites to show kindness to slaves at their release because 'you were slaves in Egypt'. This remark is probably part of Deuteronomy's interpretation of the Exodus passage itself in which the writer of Deuteronomy has (correctly) perceived a connection between the placement of the case of the עבד עברי at the beginning of Exod. 21.2–23.19 and Israel's experience of servitude in Egypt.

To summarize, the detailed elaboration of the civil regulations of Exodus 21 begins with the 'going out' to freedom of a 'Hebrew slave' because the whole book of Exodus up until the covenant at Sinai has centered around the 'going out' of the 'Hebrew slaves' from Egyptian bondage; hence, the civil regulations have been ordered so as to reflect this theme in the narrative. Implied in this arrangement, and made explicit in Deut. 15.15's interpretation of it, is that Israel's experience of bondage in Egypt should make their treatment of those in bondage more humane. It is noteworthy that the Exodus theme which our passage develops cuts across the Wellhausen source divisions.

That the bondsman's freedom is granted in the seventh year may also connect this passage to the narrative. Why is freedom granted in the seventh year? Why not the third or sixth or the eighth? The Laws of Hammurapi sought to limit servitude of a man, his wife or his child given as a pledge to three years (§117). Why 'seven' here?

Perhaps seven has been chosen because the number 'seven' has special significance in the Pentateuch as a whole. In the creation narrative, God rested on the seventh day (Gen. 2.3) setting a pattern for various rests: the sabbath day (Exod. 20.9-11), the land on the seventh year (Exod. 23.10-11), and the jubilee year after 7×7 years (Lev. 25). Every seven years there was to be a remission (שְׁמִטָּה) of debts (Deut. 15.1-3; 31.10). Thus, the number seven is symbolic for the period at which comes divinely sanctioned 'rest/release'. Moreover, Jacob twice served Laban seven years for the privilege of marrying his two daughters Leah and Rachel (Gen. 29). It is possible that there is also a connection between this narrative and the choice of seven years in Exod. 21.2.[1] Significantly, this theme again cuts across the source divisions postulated by the Wellhausen school, implying an integrated final product.

As for the case of the slave-wife, the desire to balance the section on male servitude with a case having to do with female servitude

---

1. Suggested independently by C.M. Carmichael, *The Origins of Biblical Law* (Ithaca, NY: Cornell University Press, 1992), p. 80.

provides a sufficient reason for including this section. However, if the 'Hebrew' bondsman relates to the narrative of the emancipation of the Israelites from bondage, perhaps the narrative provides a rationale for the case of the slave-wife as well. Is it mere coincidence that a stipulation on an אמה is included as a part of the covenant made with tribes among whom four are said to be descended from אמהות (Gen. 31.33)? Rachel's maidservant Bilhah bore Dan and Naphtali (Gen. 30.3-8), and Leah's maidservant Zilpah bore him Gad and Asher (Gen. 30.9-13). Thus, Case B like the placement of Case A and the use of 'seven' may possibly also be related to the Pentateuch's narrative.

Exodus 21.2-11: Law or Morality?

Is it fair to describe Exod. 21.2-11 as an example of case law, as it has commonly been described? There is reason to reject this categorization. I find myself in agreement with Gilmer who classifies Exod. 21.2-6 with other (according to his classification) 'humanitarian "If-You" formulations'[1] that occur both at Exod. 21.2-6; 22.20, 21-23, 25, 26-27; 23.1, 2-3, 4, 5, 6, 7, 8, 9, as well as some thirty-five instances in Leviticus and Deuteronomy. He says concerning this category, 'The prescriptions of this type are not laws in the strictly juridical sense, for they do not describe a case subject to legal action (what is), nor do they describe penalties (what shall be)'.[2] Rather, he says, this kind of regulation, far from being 'casuistic law', is a humanitarian prescription that depends not on the courts, but on persuasion for its performance, the If-You framing of the formulation being particularly well-suited for the didactic instruction and persuasion required in such regulations.[3]

One can add to Gilmer's argumentation from genre that the chiastic structure of 21.2-11, its complicated symbolism (cf. vv. 5-6), and its picking up of literary themes (deliverance from bondage, 'seven') from the narrative all suggest that this passage is more concerned with literary artfulness than legal precision.

Jer. 34.8-23 provides evidence that the enforcement of Exod. 21.2-6 as 'law' was nil. This passage provides a case where slaves were

---

1. H.W. Gilmer, *The If-You Form in Israelite Law* (SBLDS 15; Missoula, MT: Scholars Press, 1975), p. 49.

2. Gilmer, *If-You Form*, p. 46.

3. Gilmer, *If-You Form*, p. 56. He is followed in this observation by Phillips, 'Laws of Slavery', pp. 2-11.

released in accordance with Exod. 21.2-6 and Deut. 15.12-18, only to be quickly re-enslaved again. After paraphrasing the original prescription of releasing bondsmen in the seventh year, the text comments, 'but your fathers did not obey me or incline their ears' (Jer. 34.14b). In other words, abrogation of the promised release of bondsmen was by that time the norm, not the exception. In this instance, the bondsmen had been released, probably for military/ political reasons related to the Babylonian threat and to gain popular support,[1] though one understanding of the re-enslavement is that the certificates of debt had neither been burned nor *legally* declared null and void, so that when the crisis passed, the bondsmen were *legally* re-enslaved. Exod. 21.2-6 was probably never enforced as '*law*'.

As morality, Exod. 21.2-6 expresses the norm that within the Israelite covenant community a fellow Israelite should not be kept in indefinite servitude. Permission is granted to practice a strictly limited form of indentured service. Yet, in the literary context of Israel's experience as servants in Egypt (and presumably in our author's historical context, whenever that was), this regulation urges a limitation of subjugation as commonly practiced.

To demonstrate the moral point of the passage, it is helpful to compare the servitude envisioned in Exod. 21.2-6 with what is known in ancient Mesopotamia. There were several sources of slaves[2] in Babylonia. In the second millennium BCE the most common sources of slaves were extreme poverty that forced people to sell their children or themselves to avoid starvation,[3] and default on debt in which the

---

1. Kings in Mesopotamia often declared 'release from debt/manumission of slaves' (*anduraru*) early in their reigns to win popular support for their rule. Zedekiah, who became king under Babylonian auspices, may have been directly influenced by this Babylonian practice. Cf. R. North, 'דרור', *TDOT*, III, pp. 266-67.

2. Terms in Akkadian for slaves include masc. *wardu*, *qallu*; fem. *amtu*, *qallatu*. The abstract is *ardûtu* 'slavery'.

3. I. Mendelsohn, *Slavery in the Ancient Near East* (London: Oxford University Press, 1949), pp. 14-16. The *ḥap/biru* at Nuzi were similarly forced to become servile to a patron in order to obtain the basic necessities of life. Although their condition was called *wardûtum*, these *ḥap/biru* seemed to have enjoyed a status somewhat above chattel slavery: no price was paid nor any money exchanged, and they retained the use of patronymics in their names. *Ḥap/biru* were obligated to serve either for life or until a substitute could be found, providing a means of release not normally available to chattel slaves. Cf. Greenberg, *The Ḥab/piru*, pp. 65-70; B. Eichler, *Indenture at Nuzi: The Personal Tidennutu Contract and its Mesopotamian*

creditor seizes the debtor or some member of his household and sells him as a slave if payment is not made.[1] Other sources included prisoners of war, abandoned children, kidnapped children (though the LH §14 makes this a capital offense), and punishment for crime. The main source of slaves in the first millennium was the birth of the children of parents who were already slaves.[2] Hammurapi sought to limit debt servitude of a man, his wife or his child given as a pledge to three years (LH §117), though no such limitation existed in Assyrian laws, and the regulation itself is evidence that the tendency was to require longer periods of servitude. High interest rates on loans contributed to default by debtors.[3] Moreover, Babylonian slaves were the property of their owners. The fact that the Laws of Hammurapi never prohibit a master's killing his slave, and the killing of someone else's slave entailed only the payment of his price to his master (LH §116) leads some scholars to suppose that the owner could kill his slave with impunity, though actual documentation of an owner killing his slave with impunity is lacking.[4] The slave was, in any case, subject to maltreatment at the whim of the master.

It is not my purpose to do a complete study of servitude in the ancient Near East. A complete study would have to include detailed discussions of the practices related to such terms as *niputum* ('[person or animal taken as] pledge, distress'), *mazzazânûtu* ('state of being a

Analogues (Yale Near Eastern Researches 5; New Haven: Yale University Press, 1973), p. 47.

1. Cf. the Akkadian terms in *CAD* N 11, part 2, s.v.: *nepû* 'to take persons (mostly women) or animals as distress'; *nepitu* 'woman taken as distress'; *nipûtu* 'person or animal taken as distress'. A wife or child was commonly used as security for a loan. MAL C §3 gives a regulation where the person taken as distress is sold into slavery: 'An Assyrian man or an Assyrian woman [who] was taken [at the total value] may be sold into another country' (*ANET*, p. 187).

2. Mendelsohn, *Slavery*, pp. 14-16; M. Dandamaev, *Slavery in Babylonia: From Nabopolassar to Alexander the Great (626–331 BC)* (trans. V.A. Powell; ed. M.A. Powell and D.B. Weisberg; DeKalb: Northern Illinois University Press, 1984), p. 111.

3. I. Mendelsohn, 'Slavery in the Ancient Near East', *BA* 9.4 (1946), pp. 74-80. By Neo-Babylonian times debt slavery was no longer of significance according to Dandamaev, *Slavery in Babylonia*, pp. 103, 157-80. Rather, insolvent debtors were more often put in prison-workhouses where they were forced to work off their debts, or were released to their creditors to do the same, but this was not slavery, since such persons (it would seem) could not be sold to a third party.

4. Dandamaev, *Slavery in Babylonia*, pp. 79, 460-64.

pledge') and *kishshâtu* ('status of person given a distrainee for a debt'). Sufficient for my illustrative purposes is an examination of one other, usually non-permanent form of servitude existing in the ancient Near East, namely, a kind of indentured servitude practiced at Nuzu under the term *tidennûtu*.[1] In this system, a member of the debtor's family or the debtor himself was pledged as a *tidennu* to do service in lieu of interest payments on a loan,[2] a form of 'antichresis'.

Duration clauses for antichresis at Nuzi vary from the period of the harvest up to fifty years,[3] after which the borrowed capital could be returned and the *tidennu* set free.[4] The *tidennu*, it can be seen, differs from a permanent slave, yet default on the loan would leave the *tidennu*, his children, and his grandchildren permanently obliged to render service to the creditor.[5]

The institution of slavery and indenture in the Near East is in contrast with the ideal expressed in Exod. 21.2-6 which seeks to keep any Israelite[6] from ever falling into any permanent condition of slavery. The servitude described in 21.2-6 is debt servitude caused by insolvency rather than servitude as a result of war or birth as a slave. The sense of the imperfect in v. 2 is 'permissive' ('he may serve you six years'): small debts could be worked off in less than the six years. But no matter how great the original debt that might be owed, the servitude to pay off that debt must be no more than six years, after which the debt must be written off entirely and the bondsman set free. Hence, 21.2-6 prohibits involuntary, permanent debt slavery and condemns unlimited antichresis similar to *tidennûtu* service in which the pledge serves perhaps indefinitely in lieu of interest. Instead, at the

---

1.   W. von Soden, *Akkadisches Handwörterbuch* (Wiesbaden: Otto Harrassowitz, 1965–81), III, p. 1362, s.v. *'t/dit/dennûtu'*. Eichler, *Indenture at Nuzi*.

2.   Eichler, *Indenture at Nuzi*, pp. 37-47.

3.   Eichler, *Indenture at Nuzi*, pp. 20-21.

4.   Eichler, *Indenture at Nuzi*, p. 45.

5.   Eichler, *Indenture at Nuzi*, p. 45.

6.   Whether or not עברי ('Hebrew') is an ethnic term, the servant is probably an Israelite since the laws of Exod. 20.22–23.19 are specifically directed to those under the covenant. The parallel passage Deut. 15.12-18 confirms this view when it speaks of 'your brother the "Hebrew" (עברי)' (v. 15) in which 'brother' would seem to denote 'countryman'. Taking the 'Hebrew' servant as an Israelite also harmonizes this passage with Lev. 25.35-55 which says that Israelites are not to treat their countrymen as slaves, though foreigners could be reduced to permanent slavery and could, along with their children, be handed down by inheritance.

end of six years, both the principal as well as any interest are to be forgiven. All this serves to encourage the author's moral ideal that Israelite society should be made up of free men.

Verse 2 clearly has a humanitarian intent, but so do vv. 3-6, though it is less obvious. Verse 3 stipulates that if the man married before his servitude, his wife does not become a slave by her association with her husband's servitude, implying that any children born of this union are not slaves but are released when he is.[1]

If, as in v. 4, the bondsman entered into servitude unmarried, he would not be able to marry without the help of his master since, being insolvent, he would be unable to pay the bride-price (cf. Exod. 22.15). The text presents a case where a master gives to his bondsman a slave-woman, evidently of foreign origin whose children would also be slaves (cf. Lev. 25.44-46). Such an arrangement benefits the bondsman by making his servitude less lonely, and benefits the master by increasing his property through the children born from the union, and perhaps, by giving him a happier bondsman.

At the end of his servitude, the bondsman who had been given a female slave for a wife faces a difficult choice: perpetual servitude or leaving his wife and children. Nonetheless, this stipulation also has humanitarian intent. A freed bondsman who left the master's household would face an uncertain future. Conditions in ancient times could be very harsh. The bondsman's freedom if he left would be a precarious freedom, perhaps little more than freedom to be lonely or freedom to starve. Falling back into servitude again, possibly with a less congenial master, would not be unlikely. The bondsman probably has little family of his own to serve as a resource for him since no kinsman had redeemed him. It is true that Deut. 15.13 encourages the master to help give the servant a fresh start, but even so renewed debt and servitude remained definite possibilities.

This regulation, motivated by humanitarian concern for the bondsman's future, offers the bondsman the possibility of security. He may choose (which implies that the master ought to allow him to choose) to become a permanent part of a household as a slave. The corollary to this is that it is only if he so chooses can he be made a permanent slave. This stipulation, if followed, insured that a bondsman who was

---

1.   Likewise in Babylonia a free woman married to a slave is not a slave: her children are freeborn, her dowry remains hers, as well as half of her husband's possessions obtained after marriage in the event of his death (LH §§175-76).

given a wife would not simply be exploited for breeding purposes and then forced to leave. He is to be allowed the option of staying with his family in the security of the master's household as a slave if he desires.

There are, of course, other possibilities which the text does not contemplate. The master could generously choose to release the woman and children. Secondly, the bondsman, once released, could work to earn enough money to return and redeem his family. Whether this would be feasible for someone who had fallen into debt servitude is another matter. Thirdly, a bondsman could volunteer to serve for another period of time, as Jacob did for Leah and Rachel in Genesis 29, to gain release of his family. There may be other means of release: Josephus, *Antiquities* 4.28 (p. 607 in the Loeb edition) states that even this slave 'for life' and his family go free at the year of jubilee (cf. Leviticus 25) and *m. Qid* 1.2 states that the bondsman of Exod. 21.6 (and family?) is freed at the death of his master or at the year of jubilee every 49 years. The present regulation is not trying to be comprehensive, nor does it try to lay on the master unrealistic moral demands.

Incidentally, given the economic realities, the best prospects of a healthy, stable environment for the bondsman's children through the slave-wife given by the master lies in the children staying with the master rather than leaving with the bondsman. This consideration perhaps contributes to the text's not contemplating letting the wife and children leave with the bondsman.

Exod. 21.7-11, Case B, continues the humanitarian concern for those in servitude and the theme of freedom. Case B is one where a father sells his daughter as a slave-wife (אמה), perhaps because of debt or because the father is too poor to afford a dowry for his daughter's marriage. The אמה does not choose to sell herself, but her father chooses to sell her, reflecting the woman's status in biblical times as subordinated first to her father, then to her master/husband. The girl could live within the family as a כַּלָּה (designated 'bride' or 'daughter-in-law') for a period of time before the consummation of marriage. Moreover, she could be purchased as a future bride before it was definitely decided which of the males of the extended family would ultimately be the groom. Hence there is the use here of the term 'designate' (י.ע.ד) in the sense 'designate a bondwoman as a wife'.[1]

---

1. י.ע.ד may be a technical term for designating a bondwoman for marriage;

A woman under these circumstances was vulnerable to abuse. The purpose of this regulation is to encourage the humane treatment of such women.

When a אמה is sold for the purpose of marriage to a free man, if she remains a wife in good standing, then she does not become free, but neither does she remain a mere slave. Rather, when given to a younger man in the household, she is to be treated as a freeborn daughter-in-law, that is, as a בת (cf. Exod. 21.31 where בת 'daughter' could also mean 'female freeborn member of household' and our discussion *ad loc*.). And if married to the master of the household, she should be given all wifely privileges. If, on the other hand, she proves an unsuitable wife, or if she is displaced by another wife, she cannot be kept by the family as a slave. Rather, she must be granted her freedom. Ultimately, then, if this regulation were followed, her 'slavery'— whether she remains in the family, or whether she be released—turns out, like Exod. 21.2 and the 'Hebrew' bondsman, to be temporary. That Case B like Case A works towards her freedom reflects the text's humanitarian, moral concern.

א.ר.ש is used for betrothal of a free woman. Cf. E. Neufeld, *Ancient Hebrew Marriage Laws* (London: Longmans, Green, 1944), pp. 69-70.

Chapter 4

Exod. 21.12-27 can be isolated as a distinct unit in that all of these regulations deal with offenses of humans against other humans. This feature separates it as a unit from subsequent units: offenses of (animal) property against humans (21.28-32), offenses of a man's property (pit, ox) against another man's (animal) property (21.33-36), and offenses of humans against property (21.37–22.16).[1] Exod. 21.12-17 is also clearly distinct from the discussion of servitude and freedom that precedes it (21.2-11).

Exod. 21.12-27 can be divided into two parts. The first (21.12-17) consists of four offenses for which מות יומת ('he may be put to death') is the penalty clause. The second part (21.18-27) consists of four somewhat less serious offenses involving battery or mayhem.

Some מות יומת Offenses: Exodus 21.12-17
Case A—Murder

(12) He who strikes a person to death may be put to death (מות יומת). (13) Nevertheless, he who did not lie in wait, but deity put him into his hand, in that case I will establish for you [sing.] a place to where he may flee. (14) But should someone act arrogantly against his fellow to kill him deceptively [בערמה], you [sing.] may take him from my altar to kill him.

Case B—Striking Parents

(15) He who strikes his father or mother may be put to death [מות יומת].

Case C—Kidnapping

(16) He who kidnaps someone, whether he sells him or whether the person is found in his possession, may be put to death [מות יומת].

---

1.   Observed by Paul, *Studies*, pp. 107-11.

Case D—Repudiation of Parents

(17) And he who repudiates (מְקַלֵּל) his father or mother, may be put to death [מוֹת יוּמָת].

Form and Structure of Exodus 21.12-17

Exod. 21.12-17 consists of four cases that allow death as a penalty, each ending with the phrase מוֹת יוּמָת, 'he may be put to death'. Each also begins with a participle: the first two (vv. 12 and 15) with מַכֵּה ('he who strikes'), the next (v. 16) with גֹּנֵב ('the one who steals'), and the last (v. 17) with מְקַלֵּל ('the one who repudiates').

Contrary to Alt,[1] the participial form here is not 'apodictic' (that is, 'absolute' or 'unconditional'). It should be regarded as essentially casuistic ('case' or 'conditional' laws) in which the participle 'He who does X' is equivalent to '*If* one does X' of casuistic formulation, followed as in casuistic formulation with the legal outcome of that condition.[2] Hence the participial formulation מכה איש ('The one striking a man') could be reworded כי יכה איש את רעהו ('If a man strikes his neighbor'), a casuistic formulation. Likewise the qualification of this statement in v. 13, ואשר לא צדה ('But the one who did not lie in wait'), is equivalent to the 'casuistic' expression ואם לא צדה ('But *if* he did not lie in wait') introduced by אם and which modifies laws introduces by כי. The differing formulations convey the same idea.

Alt's view that vv. 13-14 should be excluded from the 'original' participial version of these laws, and that the participial laws themselves have a different origin than the laws that follow rests on a doubtful assumption that an author must slavishly adhere to a literary 'form'. This is untrue, not only for biblical laws, but also for Mesopotamian laws where forms are normally mixed, even where certain patterns predominate.[3] An author is free to change his style if

1. Alt, 'Origins', pp. 140-46.
2. W. Kornfeld, *Studien zum Heiligkeitsgesetz* (Vienna: Herder, 1952), p. 49; A. Bentzen, *Introduction to the Old Testament*, I (Copenhagen: Gad, 1952), p. 224; R. Kilian, 'Apodiktisches und kasuistisches Recht im Licht ägyptischer Analogien', *BZ* 7 (1963), p. 189; Sonsino, *Motive Clauses*, pp. 10-13. For a defense of Alt, see J.G. Williams, 'Addenda to "Concerning One of the Apodictic Formulas"', *VT* 15 (1965), pp. 113-15.
3. T.J. Meek ('The Origin of Hebrew Law', in *Hebrew Origins* [New York: Harper & Brothers, 3rd edn, 1960], p. 72) lists the following 'apodictic' formula-

it suits his purposes. The pithy, participial formulation sets these capital offenses apart from the lesser offenses that follow, and forms an inclusio with a subsequent participial series of 22.17-19 (see there, *ad loc.*).

I turn now from discussion of the 'form' of these pronouncements to their structure. The rationale of organization for these offenses is not immediately clear to a reader. Especially confusing is the separation of two offenses against parents by one condemning kidnapping. Some hold the whole of 21.13-17 to be secondary, and that the 'original' sequence read 21.12, 18, 19.[1] Daube attributes the location of the case of kidnapping between two laws on parents to the tacking on of supplementary laws onto the end of extant collections.[2] According to him, when a legal code was emended, this was typically done by adding the new regulation to the end of the appropriate existing paragraph to minimize the disruption of the existing statutes. Few follow Daube for the explanation of v. 17, but many nonetheless think there to be some sort of disruption of the original order. The LXX places v. 17 immediately after v. 15, reflecting either a differing Vorlage or its translator's perception that v. 17 was out of place. Commentators often treat vv. 15 and 17 together despite the canonical order.[3] Another source-oriented explanation for the separation of the regulations concerning parents involves the accidental reversal of vv. 16 and 17.[4]

The order of these regulations can be explained apart from source-oriented grounds, however, though some analysis of the regulations themselves is necessary first.

Case A, striking someone to death, is the most extreme case of physical violence against another. It is followed by possible exceptions to the general penalty.

tions mixed into 'casuistic' cuneiform laws: LE §§1-4, 7-8, 10-13, 15-16, 19, 51-52; LH §§36, 38-40; MAL A §§40, 57-59; MAL B §6. S. Greengus ('Law in the OT', *IDBSup*, p. 535) adds Hittite Laws §§48, 50-52, 54-56. Cf. G.J. Wenham, 'Legal Forms in the Book of the Covenant', *TynBul* 22 (1971), pp. 95-102, esp. p. 101.

1. Schwienhorst-Schönberger, *Bundesbuch*, p. 226.
2. D. Daube, *Studies in Biblical Law* (Cambridge: Cambridge University Press, 1947), p. 95.
3. Childs, *Exodus*, p. 470; Durham, *Exodus*, p. 323; Patrick, *Law*, p. 74.
4. Driver, *Exodus*, p. 217.

Less violent is Case B, striking one's father or one's mother,[1] who notably are considered equals so far as this regulation is concerned. The verb 'strike' (the H-stem of נ.כ.ה.) expresses a wide range of nuances: as mild as clapping one's hands together in an applause (2 Kgs 11.12), severe enough to be a virtual synonym for 'kill' (e.g., Exod. 2.12). Although the use of נ.כ.ה. for fatal blows is quite common, that meaning in v. 15 would add little (except moral indignation) to v. 12 where murder is already condemned. Rather, by repeating מכה from v. 12 but leaving out the words 'that he die (וָמֵת)', the author has indicated that non-fatal blows are included.

Kidnapping (Case C) is also condemned by the text with the penalty applying whether or not the kidnapper has disposed of the stolen person by selling him.[2] Since the intent is typically to reap economic gain from the person stolen (selling as a slave, using him for labor, extorting ransom from his family), there would be no intent initially to damage the 'goods' by injury. Hence, kidnapping forcibly subdues a person without intending to injure him.

Despite the first impression, the prohibition against kidnapping is in fact related to the offenses against parents that surround it. The term translated 'kidnap', literally 'steal a man', refers here to 'man' (אִישׁ) in the sense of 'person' regardless of age or sex. Kidnapping often involves stealing of a child or youth since children are physically less able to resist than adults and are more easily sold and trained as slaves. Moreover, the stealing of a son whatever his age deprives the parent of support in old age and provision for burial that the child is expected to give, just as the 'repudiation' of a parent does in v. 17. Accordingly, 'stealing a person' is typically an offense against parents.[3]

---

1. Mesopotamian law gave stiff penalties, though not death, for similar offenses against parents: LH §195, 'If a son has struck his father, they shall cut off his hand' (*ANET*, p. 174). Cf. K. van der Toorn, *Sin and Sanction in Israel and Mesopotamia* (Studia Semitica Neerlandica 22; Assen/Maastricht: Van Gorcum, 1985), pp. 13-15.

2. A. Phillips (*Ancient Israel's Criminal Law* [Oxford: Basil Blackwell, 1970], p. 131) thinks 'whether the person is found in his possession' is a secondary addition. Against Phillips is the similar formulation of the parallel passage Deut. 24.7 which in paraphrasing our verse says, 'If a man is found to have kidnapped a fellow Israelite, enslaving him or selling him, that kidnapper shall die' (Tanakh). This reading supposes two conditions in the Vorlage. In any case, the MT reading makes perfectly good sense. On the use of ו...ו for giving alternatives, see Williams, *Hebrew Syntax*, §433.

3. E. Otto (cited by Schwienhorst-Schönberger, *Bundesbuch*, p. 224), noting

Case D, 'repudiation' of a parent (v. 17), involves no physical violence at all but rather neglect of filial duties. The key exegetical issue here is the meaning of מְקַלֵּל, a D-stem participle. Traditionally, קִלֵּל has been translated 'to curse', but this has been shown by Brichto to be dubious.[1] Better translations for this word would be 'treat with disrespect, abuse, derogate, denigrate, repudiate'. According to Brichto, only in a few cases (if any) of the forty times קִלֵּל is used can it refer to imprecations.[2]

What does this word mean here? Brichto expressed well the general parameters:

> What is clearly intended is a serious breach of filial duty, so flagrant as to merit a penalty equal to that prescribed for physical violence.[3]

But the nature of this 'serious breach of filial duty' is not spelled out any more than the positive command to 'honor' one's parents is spelled out. It is necessary, then, to look to parallel messages in the Bible and the ancient Near East to try to determine the probable intended meaning.

A most suggestive passage is LH §§192-93 (*ANET*, p. 175):

> (192) If the (adopted) son of a chamberlain or the (adopted) son of a votary has said to his foster father or his foster mother, 'You are not my father', 'You are not my mother', they shall cut out his tongue. (193) If the (adopted) son of a chamberlain or the (adopted) son of a votary found out his parentage and came to hate his foster father and his foster mother and so has gone off to his parental home, they shall pluck out his eye.

Here an adoptive son is punished for repudiating his parents. The chamberlain (Akkadian *girsequ*) and votary (Akkadian *SAL ZI.IK.RU.UM = sekretu*) probably refer to a eunuch and a cloistered woman[4] without children who adopt a son for the purpose of having

---

that 21.15-17 has to do with the family, dubiously tries also to limit 21.12 to inner-family killing. But if the 'place' of v. 13 refers to the Cities of Refuge, as I argue, then the meaning in the present context anticipates murder between families where the 'avenger of blood' is involved. Note also the parallel between 21.12 (killing a citizen) and 21.18-19 (injuring a citizen) as noted below.

1.   H.C. Brichto, *The Problem of 'Curse' in the Hebrew Bible* (JBL Monograph Series 13; Philadelphia: SBL, 1963), pp. 118-99.

2.   Brichto, *'Curse'*, pp. 172-76. Cf. 2 Kgs 2.24; Deut. 23.4-5; Neh. 13.1-2; Josh. 24.9-10.

3.   Brichto, *'Curse'*, p. 134.

4.   Cf. *CAD* V, p. 96 and XV, pp. 215-17.

someone to take care of them in their old age and see to their funerary rites. The repudiation is thus viewed in the Laws of Hammurapi as both a violation of the terms of adoption and neglect of filial duty. Babylonian records of adoption usually stipulate that the beneficiary must unceasingly 'revere and honor' (*palaḫu* and *kubbutu*) the adoptive parents, which seems to imply (at minimum) providing them with clothes, food and drink in their old age.[1]

A similar expression of the duty of a son is found in the Ugaritic story of Danel, who desires a son to be:

> One who sets up the stela of his ancestral god in the shrine, the *solar-disk* (?) of his people on the earth, sends out his incense from the dust, the *soldier* (?) of his post (?) who *heaps* (?) the tablets of his *detractors* (?), expels him who would *do* (*evil*) to him, who takes his hand in drunkenness, who carries him [when] sated with wine. Who eats his ceremonial meal in the house of Baal, his [por]tion in the house of El, who plasters his roof on the day of [mu]d, who washes his clothes on the day of slime. (*KTU* 17 [= *CTA* 17, = 2 *Aqht*] I 28-33).[2]

Here 'honoring' the parent includes physical help (protection from detractors, guiding a drunken parent, plastering a roof, washing clothes), and cultic duties (setting up the stela of one's god, pouring out incense, ceremonial meals), the latter probably performed after the death of the parent that his ghost might be at peace.[3]

By analogy מקלל, involving the repudiation of one's parents, could include the rejection of the filial duty to care for one's parents in old age and death.[4] A child owes his very life to his parents; consequently, he is obligated to care for them when they no longer can do so for themselves. This filial duty is expressed in Ruth 4.15 where Ruth's son by Boaz is expected to 'sustain your old age'.

---

1. Van der Toorn, *Sin and Sanction*, p. 14. Cf. J.C. Greenfield, '*Adi Balṭu*—Care for the Elderly and its Rewards', *AfO* 19 (1982), pp. 309-16.

2. C.H. Gordon, 'Poetic Legends and Myths from Ugarit', *Berytus* 25 (1977), p. 10.

3. Van der Toorn, *Sin and Sanction*, p. 14; M. Pope, 'The Cult of the Dead at Ugarit', in *Ugarit in Retrospect* (ed. G. Young; Winona Lake: Eisenbrauns, 1981), pp. 160-61. Cf. M. Bayliss, 'The Cult of Dead Kin in Assyria and Babylon', *Iraq* 35 (1973), pp. 115-25; A. Skaist, 'The Ancestor Cult and Succession in Mesopotamia', in *Death in Mesopotamia* [= *RAI* 26 = *Mesopotamia* 8 (1980)], pp. 123-28.

4. Brichto, '*Curse*', p. 134. Cf. Brichto, 'Kin, Cult, Land and Afterlife', pp. 29-31.

Deut. 21.18-21 suggests another possible aspect of מקלל. This passage allows the parents of a 'wayward and rebellious son who does not heed the voice of his father or his mother' to be taken to the elders at the city gate and be stoned. Brichto[1] proposes that this is Deuteronomy's commentary and expansion on Exod. 21.17. A good case can be made for his interpretation. Here, as in 21.17, it is not a matter of physical violence against the parent that leads to the son's execution, but his insubordination ('wayward and rebellious', 'does not heed the voice of his father or his mother') and his disgraceful behavior ('a prodigal and a drunkard'). This habitual behavior, undeterred by repeated admonitions, is portrayed as an offense against the parents. The parents—both 'father and mother' are mentioned as in 21.17—bring their grievance as the offended party to the elders of the city who confirm the story and see to the carrying out of the sentence. If, as Brichto suggests, this offense is an expansion of 21.17, it implies that מקלל can have the sense of 'repudiation' of a parent's moral guidance, or even 'disgracing' parents by profilgate behavior. קלל elsewhere also bears the sense 'spurn, repudiate' with respect to authority figures, in the sense of 'repudiating' a king's authority and his laws and 'repudiating' God's authority by acts in disregard of the ethical standard that God expects of man.[2]

מקלל, in sum, probably involves such things as disgraceful behavior in disregard of parental admonition (as Deut. 21.18-21), and the failure to perform the filial duty of caring for an aging parent and providing for his or her funeral rites (as Ruth 4.15 and the Near East parallels).

Having examined each of these cases, a rationale for the structure can be proposed. Cases A, B, C, and D follow a descending order of physical violence: striking someone to death (Case A), striking a parent with a blow short of causing death (Case B), kidnapping which involves overpowering without intent to injure (Case C), and 'repudiating' a parent which involves neglect of filial duty rather than physical violence (Case D).

The poetic purpose is thus: though one might suppose that decreasing violence would result in decreasing penalty, according to divine justice that is not the case. The penalty for each case is the same, implying that each offense is just as bad as murder. Striking a parent

---

1. Brichto, *'Curse'*, p. 134 n. 41.
2. Brichto, *'Curse'*, pp. 137-70.

is as bad as murdering an ordinary citizen. Repudiation of a parent, though it only involves neglect rather than direct violence, is just as bad as actively beating him. Kidnapping is also a serious offense against the parents: it removes from the stolen person's parents a means of support in their old age, just as repudiation of a parent does, and is equally condemned. Thus Cases B, C, and D are fundamentally crimes against parents that are considered as serious as murder.

In addition to the explanation of the present order given above, another reason can be given for placing Case C (kidnapping) between the two directly related to parents. That reason is aesthetic: to form a pleasing parallelism that balances the four cases of the first part of Exod. 21.12-17 and the four cases of the second part. Note the parallel structure as follows:

Part I: Exod. 21.12-17	Part II: Exod. 21.18-27
Case A	Case A*
Murder of a Person	Injury of a Person
(21.12-14)	(21.18-19)
Case B	Case B*
Striking a Parent	Striking a Bondsman to Death
(21.15)	(21.20-21)
Case C	Case C*
Kidnapping	Striking a Pregnant Woman
(21.16)	(21.22-25)
Case D	Case D*
Repudiating a Parent	Injuring a Bondsman
(21.17)	(21.26-27)

Just as Cases B and D of 21.12-17 have something in common (being offenses against parents), so cases B* and D* of 21.18-27 have something in common (being offenses against bondsmen). Just as C comes in between the regulations directly related to parents, so C* comes in between the regulations directly related to bondsmen. Case A and Case A* have to do with ordinary citizens (killing and injuring them respectively), while Cases B/D and B*/D* have to do with special classes of citizens (parents and bondsmen respectively). Case C is a case indirectly related to offenses against parents (a kidnapping deprives the kidnapped person's parents of filial duties), so it will be argued below that Case C* is indirectly related to offenses against slaves (serving as a contrast for Case D*). Whereas these parallels could be coincidence, it is more likely deliberate.

Exodus 21.12-17 and Other Passages

Exod. 21.12-17 shows itself to be integrated into the Pentateuch out-side of Exod. 20.22–23.19 by what appear to be allusions in it to the Decalogue and by what seems to be an anticipation of the institution of the 'cities of refuge'.

The four cases of Exod. 21.12-17 show definite affinities with the second half of the Decalogue. The condemnation of a murderer (21.12) expands on the Decalogue's prohibition of murder (20.13). The offenses of striking and repudiating parents (21.15, 17) give the opposite side of the Decalogue's positive command to 'honor' one's father and mother (20.12). Indeed, מְקַלֵּל ('one who repudiates') in 21.17 arguably was deliberately selected here to make a contrast with the Fifth Commandment, 'Honor/show respect for (כַּבֵּד) your father and your mother' (20.12), since 'repudiate' (D stem of קלל that in G means 'to be light') is the exact antonym of 'honor' (a D stem of כבד that in G means 'to be heavy'). The condemnation of 'one who steals a man' (21.16) expands on the Decalogue's prohibition against stealing (20.15—both use גנב 'steal') and develops the theme of freedom from bondage expressed in the Decalogue's prologue (20.2) and in the bondsman regulations (21.2-11).

In terms of the unfolding of the teaching of the Pentateuch, these cases also expand on earlier regulation; namely, Gen. 9.2-6 where permission was granted to man to kill animal life for food, and for man to execute a murderer whether the culprit be man or beast.[1] Now permission is granted to take the life of certain other offenders.

Case A (Exod. 21.12-14) seems to anticipate the institution of the 'cities of refuge'. Verse 13 gives an exception to the general rule of מוֹת יוּמָת for killing a human being: If the manslayer 'did not lie in wait', i.e., showed no premeditation, 'but deity put him into his hand', which seems to refer to an accident beyond human control,[2] then God

---

1.   B.S. Jackson (*Essays in Jewish and Comparative Legal History* [Studies in Judaism in Late Antiquity 10; ed. J. Neusner; Leiden: Brill, 1975], p. 46) wants to translate באדם in Gen. 9.6 as '*for that man*, his blood will be shed' (NEB) rather than the more common rendering '*by man*'. This allows him to take God rather than man as the one who administers this punishment. However, since in v. 3 it is to man that permission is given to take animal life for food, it seems more suitable to the context to understand man as the one who administers this punishment in v. 6, even if the NEB translation were accepted. God may demand the lifeblood (v. 5), but it is man who delivers it to him, as in animal sacrifices.

2.   Childs, *Exodus*, p. 448; Cassuto, *Exodus*, p. 270. Cf. LH §266, 'If a

says 'I will establish for you a place where he may flee'. This 'place' anticipates the city of refuge.

Num. 35.6-11 commands Israel before they crossed the Jordan to establish six levitical 'cities of refuge' to which someone guilty of inadvertent (בשגנה)[1] manslaughter would be able to find asylum. Deut. 4.41-43 records how three of those cities were established in the Transjordan. Deut. 19.3, 8-10 commands that three more be established in the land proper, and that yet three more may be added as the need arises. Joshua at YHWH's direction, accordingly, designated three cities of refuge in the land proper in addition to the three in the Transjordan (Josh. 20.1-9).

The connection between Exod. 21.13 and the cities of refuge is difficult for many source-oriented scholars to accept because Wellhausen (and his school) considered the legislation concerning the 'cities of refuge' to be from the deuteronomic and the still later priestly sources (Num. 35.9-34 from P; Deut. 4.41-43, 19.1-13, and Josh. 20.1-9 from D), and never actually put in practice, whereas what is described here in the so-called 'Covenant Code' reflects earlier, actual practice. Such interpretation is based on the source-oriented theory that Deuteronomy was trying to abolish seventh-century altars, and introduced cities of refuge 'in order not to abolish the right to asylum (Exod. xxi.13, 14; 1 Kgs ii.28) along with the altars'.[2]

Wellhausen's way to avoid this connection with cities of refuge was to interpret the 'place' in v. 13 as meaning a 'sanctuary' rather than a city of refuge.[3] In that case, the 'place' of v. 13 is roughly equivalent to 'my altar' in v. 14, both having to do with sanctuaries. Another way to handle this problem is to admit that vv. 13-14 refer to cities of refuge, but to argue that they are a secondary addition to v. 12.[4]

---

visitation of a god has occurred in a sheepfold or a lion has made a kill, the shepherd shall prove himself innocent in the presence of a god' (*ANET*, p. 176).

1. On שגגה, see Milgrom, 'The Cultic שגגה and its Influence in Psalms and Job', *JQR* 58 (1967), pp. 115-25, *Cultic Theology*, pp. 122-32). According to him, שגגה results from two causes: ignorance and negligence. Either the offender knows the law but accidentally violates it, or he acts deliberately without knowing he did wrong. The translation 'unwitting' (RSV) catches only part of the meaning.

2. Wellhausen, *Prolegomena*, p. 33.

3. Wellhausen, *Prolegomena*, p. 33. Also, McNeile, *Exodus*, pp. lii, 128; Driver, *Exodus*, p. 215; R. de Vaux, *Ancient Israel*, I (New York: McGraw-Hill, 1965), pp. 160-63.

4. E.g., Noth, *Exodus*, p. 180.

Greenberg, on the other hand, resolves the difficulty by supposing that the deuteronomic and priestly legislations 'reflect the conceptions, perhaps even the custom, of the earliest age of Israel', being as ancient as the 'Book of the Covenant'.[1]

It seems clear that the altar of v. 14 is at a sanctuary. Due to the reverence bestowed upon sacred shrines, fugitives could flee to an altar to escape pursuers who might well be reluctant to desecrate a holy place and its worshippers by abducting and possibly killing a criminal there. Verse 14's reference to an altar is illustrated by the case of Joab in 1 Kgs 2.28-34: Joab, after hearing of Adonijah's execution whom he followed, fled to the horns of the altar in Jerusalem for sanctuary, and possibly also to demand a trial. Solomon (who notes Joab's murders of Abner and Amasa) responds, in effect, that he as judge has already decided his case and the sentence is death.[2] Joab was then taken from the altar and immediately executed in accordance with Exod. 21.14.

The question, then, is not whether sanctuaries could be used for refuge, but whether or not the altar of v. 14 is equivalent to the 'place' of v. 13 (both metonyms for a 'sanctuary'), or whether an 'altar' represents an additional place of refuge.

Objection has been raised to connecting Exod. 21.13 with the cities of refuge passages on the basis of grammar: the term 'place' in v. 13 is singular while the cities of refuge are six in number.[3] But מקוֹם ('place') can refer to a category or type of place rather than a particular place. The alternative interpretation—which identifies מקוֹם with the 'my altar' of v. 14—encounters the same problem with the singular מקוֹם, if that be regarded as a problem, since there were many sanctuaries, not just one. (Cf. the discussion of Exod. 20.24 above where the text contemplates many altars of YHWH in many places [בכל־המקוֹם—'in each and every place']).

The view taken here is that מקוֹם of v. 13 is in contrast with the altar of v. 14, the מקוֹם being one place of asylum, an altar of YHWH being another. There is no contradiction with the altars and cities of refuge both providing asylum. An altar is not well suited for providing a

---

1.   M. Greenberg, 'The Biblical Conception of Asylum', *JBL* 78 (1959), p. 132.

2.   H.C. Brichto, 'Law and Law-codes in the Bible—Exploding a Myth' (paper read at the World Congress of Jewish Studies, Jerusalem, 1977), p. 7.

3.   Patrick, *Law*, p. 74.

permanent refuge for a manslayer so that something like a city of refuge would be required for practical reasons even if there were many altars that could be temporary places of asylum.[1] Moreover, reading the text as it stands, the application of this prediction 'I will establish for you a place' to the cities of refuge is such a natural and compelling interpretation of the text read in the light of the Pentateuch as a whole that it seems highly probable that this is the meaning intended by the editor(s) of the final form of the text.

This interpretation is plausible on the assumption that the editors of the final form of the text were aware of these other regulations and edited in the light of them. My methodology differs from that common among source-oriented scholars who, having taken all or part of Exod. 20.22–23.19 to be a separate, earlier source, to a greater or lesser degree divorce its interpretation from other biblical laws.

Finally, I note Cassuto's interesting suggestion that Case C (kidnapping) was included in the Torah to show the reader of the Pentateuch how severe the offense committed against Joseph by his brothers was in Genesis 37, a point insufficiently stressed in the story itself.[2] Although unprovable, this kind of explanation is consistent with the assumption that the regulations of Exod. 20.22–23.19 are well integrated into the Pentateuch.

Exodus 21.12-17: Law or Morality?

The consequence of each of the offenses of Exod. 21.12-17 is, 'he may be put to death' (מוֹת יוּמַת). The form of this statement leaves many questions unanswered. Put to death by whom? By the state? By a blood relative? By a court? By local residents? The passive verb gives no answer. Put to death under all circumstances, or just sometimes? Only Case A considers the possibility of exceptions. Put to death in what way? Hanging? Stoning? Sword? The text shows no interest in answering these questions.

Case A (murder) does give further definition as to what constitutes murder, but Case B (striking a parent) does not. How severe a blow is necessary to become subject to this penalty? How old must the child be? What kind of blow counts? Who is to judge whether the line has been crossed: the parent? the community? a judge? Who prosecutes the case? Who carries out the sentence?

1.   Greenberg, 'Biblical Conception of Asylum', p. 126.
2.   Cassuto, *Exodus*, p. 271.

The lack of detail here calls into question the primary intent of this passage, whether it be legal or whether it is primarily moral in nature. Clear law gives specific details. It spells out how the court is to interpret and carry out the regulation. This text's lack of interest in the details of how and by whom it is to be enforced suggests that the main intent is less legal than moral.

What is given here is not impersonal law, but the word of YHWH, newly re-emphasized by the use of the first person pronouns ('I', 'my') in vv. 13-14 and directed to 'you', that is, the people, as a whole, the singular pronoun applying to the collective entity Israel as in the Decalogue.[1]

Here YHWH in principle gives his permission to take human life for certain heinous offenses. In the case of a murderer who has acted 'deceptively' [בערמה] in the sense of trying to disguise the murder as unintended or to hide one's involvement in it,[2] no place of asylum is allowed: Israel is granted permission to drag such murderers from YHWH's altar if need be for execution. Permission is likewise granted to inflict capital punishment on kidnappers, and those who abuse or repudiate their parents.

Paul[3] argues that מות יומת implies more than permission; he believes it to be a 'mandate' demanding that the culprit '*must* be killed'. However, Buss[4] correctly observes that grammatically the imperfect

---

1.   Cf. Exod. 20.22-26; 21.1-2, 13-14, 23; 22.17–23.19; Patrick, 'I and Thou in the Covenant Code', pp. 71-86.

2.   בערמה has been variously rendered: 'treacherously' (RSV), 'deliberately' (NIV, TEV), 'with prior intent, prudence' (Cassuto, *Exodus*, p. 270), 'by crafty plotting' (Durham, *Exodus*, p. 307). ערמה sometimes is the positive quality of 'shrewdness' (Prov. 1.4; 8.5, 12); sometimes the pejorative quality of 'guile, craftiness' (Josh. 9.4; cf. ערום of the serpent in Gen. 3.1). In Exod. 21.14, בערמה means 'with shrewd trickery, guile, deception' in which the murderer attempts to disguise his involvement in the crime or tries to make the crime appear to be an accident. It is the inverse of v. 13, being both premeditated and intentional. Brichto ('Law and Law-codes', pp. 1-3) illustrates the meaning by reference to Deut. 19.5. There the question of whether the victim fell by accident or by a deliberate act of murder parallels whether the victim fell by deity putting him into his hand or by בערמה in Exod. 21.13-14. Cassuto's connection of ערם with the Arabic *'rm* ('be vicious, strong, violent') is dubious since this meaning is not found elsewhere for ערם.

3.   Paul, *Studies*, pp. 61-62.

4.   M. Buss, 'The Distinction between Civil and Criminal Law in Ancient Israel', in *Proceedings of the Sixth World Congress of Jewish Studies 1973*, I (Jerusalem, 1977), p. 56.

verb in מוֹת יוּמָת could convey 'permission' to take human life (i.e., 'may be killed'), a reading which allows for exceptions. Moreover, מוֹת יוּמָת could be read as a hyperbole that expresses morality by condemning the offender as being worthy of death (i.e., 'he deserves to be killed') without necessarily mandating death as the outcome. Compare 2 Sam. 12.5 where a rich man who steals the poor man's ewe lamb is pronounced by David as judge to be 'a son of death', that is, 'one who deserves death' (cf. Tanakh). David's 'death sentence', however, is a hyperbole. The sanction actually prescribed by David is multiple restitution (v. 6). To the degree that the מוֹת יוּמָת cases of Exod. 21.12-17 allow exceptions, to that extent the penalty מוֹת יוּמָת is similarly hyperbolic.

That the death sentence was not always carried out is shown by 21.12-14 which gives extenuating circumstances for Case A (killing a man), making clear to the reader that the מוֹת יוּמָת of v. 12 is not universally applicable. Likewise Case B (the striking of a parent) demands exceptions to the rule: it would be absurd to apply the death sentence of Case B against an angry toddler who struck his mother. Extenuating circumstances no doubt exist for the remaining מוֹת יוּמָת cases as well. Moreover, the possibility of 'ransom' substituting for execution (see the discussion of 21.22-25 and 21.30 below) except in the case of premeditated, deliberate murder (Num. 35.31) cannot be excluded. The child who abuses or repudiates his parents might save himself by a ransom to his parents as the offended party, and the kidnapper could likewise do the same by (ironically) paying a ransom to the family of the kidnapping victim.

In sum, what is given is not a mandate to execute every one who kills a man, strikes a parent, steals a man, or repudiates a parent. Rather, though YHWH condemns these violations of morality with a 'death sentence', where there are mitigating circumstances or a willingness on the part of the offended parties to accept ransom, these death sentences need not be carried out.

The death penalty of Case B (striking a parent) is one whose implementation would undoubtedly be rare. There is, in fact, no evidence from the historical books that this regulation was ever carried out. It is inherently improbable that many parents would seek to have this rule enforced against their own child, even an abusive one.

The presumption that sons were rarely if ever executed under Case D in Israel is supported by Prov. 20.20 that says:

> As for one who 'dishonors/repudiates', (מקלל) his father or his mother,
> his lamp will go out when darkness comes [or 'in deep darkness'].

The proverb anticipates the natural outcome of imprudent behavior in which one reaps what he has sown; it is oblivious to legal consequences or the possibility of capital punishment for this offense, perhaps because it was not in fact enforced in the setting in which it was composed. Similarly Deut. 27.16, which says 'Cursed is one who dishonors [מַקְלֶה—H-stem participle of קלה, a biform of קלל] his father and his mother', places this offense under God's curse precisely because it was the sort of offense that would likely not be prosecuted and punished by human courts.

Even if some of these regulations were seldom enforced literally as law, they nonetheless retain value as 'moral admonition'. This is not to say that these regulations were completely unenforceable as law; Cases A (murder) and C (kidnapping) certainly could be enforced. It is to say that their main value here is as moral admonitions. As laws, these cases at best serve as illustrative examples. The Israelites would have to determine on their own how to administrate and how more carefully to delimit such cases. However, their value as moral admonitions is not affected by lack of legal specificity or enforceability.

As a statement of morality, Case A expresses the degree of God's outrage over murder and at the same time draws a distinction morally between intentional murder and unintentional manslaughter. Cases B and D condemn any son who would physically abuse or repudiate his parents. Case C, condemning kidnapping, underscores God's valuation of human liberty, a theme already stressed in Exod. 21.2-11, probably implying the precept that people are not to be treated as commodities.[1]

---

1.   A similar idea of 'treat as commodity' could be intended in the parallel passage of Deut. 24.7:

> If a man is found who steals a life (נפשׁ) from his kinsmen, that is, from the sons of Israel, whether (ו) he has treated him as property(?) (התעמר) or whether (ו) has sold him, that thief must die.

In this paraphrase of Exod. 21.16, 'whether he is found in his possession' becomes the term התעמר. The precise meaning of התעמר (used only here and at Deut. 21.14) is uncertain. A plausible meaning for the word is 'treat as commodity', proposed by M. David ('התעמר [Deut. XXI 14; XXIV 7]', *VT* 1 [1951], pp. 219-21) who translates 'Geschäfte abschliessen' or 'Handel treiben', and the *Targum Onqelos* which renders with the Itpaʿal of תגר which relates to trade (cf. the cognate עומר, 'omer'). If this proposal is correct Deuteronomy is expanding on the expres-

The case of stealing a man is in contrast with the case of a stolen animal. In the case of animal theft, the penalty if the animal is found in the thief's possession is less than if it has not been disposed of (21.37 and 22.3); whereas, kidnappers are subject to capital punishment regardless of whether they have disposed of their human 'goods'. This contrast reflects an ideological distinction. Even the lesser crime (stealing without selling) merits the maximum penalty when humans are involved.

LH §14 also condemns kidnapping, but seems to follow a different moral reasoning. It makes kidnapping of a minor of the *awilum* class a capital offense. In comparison with the biblical injunction, this crime is defined more specifically by age and class. Moreover, it is a continuation of laws pertaining to theft and loss of property. It thus seems to classify kidnapping as a property crime, the child being the father's property.[1] In Exod. 21.16, however, kidnapping is not among the property crimes (21.33–22.16), but is probably founded on a theologically based anthropology (e.g. Gen. 1.27) in which a sharper distinction is drawn between humans and property.

Other Offenses Involving Violence—Exodus 21.18-27
Case A—Violence Towards a Fellow Citizen*

(18) Now when men quarrel with the result that one strikes his fellow with a stone or with a fist (אגרף),[2] but he does not die yet is laid up in bed, (19) if he is able to rise and walk about on a crutch, then the offender is not culpable except for paying for his inactivity (שבתו) and he must see to his medical care.

---

sion 'found in his possession' by saying why the kidnapper is still put to death if the person kidnapped is unsold. This is because the kidnapper has demeaned the person kidnapped by treating him as merchandise rather than as a human being.

1.   Paul, *Studies*, p. 65.

2.   אגרף is either translated 'fist' (LXX, Aquila) or as some sort of instrument, 'shovel, rake, hoe' (BDB; based on Syriac and Arabic cognates). אגרף occurs elsewhere in the Bible only at Isa. 58.4, 'Behold, for contention and strife you fast, and for striking with a wicked אגרף'. Here an agricultural tool seems unlikely since agricultural tools are not normally used as weapons. That אגרף is similar in pattern to other nouns for body parts (אצבע 'finger', אזרוע 'arm') lends greater plausibility to the traditional rendering. Either rendering implies a deliberate blow.

Case B*—Killing One's Bondsman

(20) Now in the case of a man who strikes his bondsman or his bond-woman with a rod so that he dies under his hand, he must be avenged. (21) Though if he lasts a day or two, he is not to be avenged, for he is his money.

Case C*—A Pregnant Woman in a Brawl/'Lex Talionis'

(22) If men struggle with one another, and butt a pregnant woman so that the product of her womb [ילדיה] comes forth (in miscarriage), but there is no (further) serious injury [אסון] (to the woman), then one will be fined in accordance with what the woman's husband requires of him, paying by פללים. (23) But if there is serious injury [אסון], then you will pay out (according to the formula): 'Life for life, (24) eye for eye, tooth for tooth, hand for hand, foot for foot, (25) burning for burning, wound for wound, stripe for stripe'.

Case D*—Permanently Injuring One's Bondsman

(26) Should someone strike out the eye of his bondsman or bondwoman, he must send him away as a free man in exchange for (תחת) his eye. (27) Even if he should knock out but a tooth of his bondsman or his bond-woman, he must send him away as a free man in exchange for (תחת) his tooth.

Exodus 21.18-27 and Structure

The parallel structure between Exod. 21.18-27 and 21.12-17 has already been discussed above. The following discussion develops the structure and interpretation of vv. 18-27.

Case A* (injuring a fellow citizen) introduces a case that corresponds to Case A above (21.12, killing a fellow citizen). Case A concerned striking (מכה) someone to death. But such a case raises a question: what if an Israelite strikes (הכה) a fellow Israelite and causes severe injury rather than death? What is the obligation of an Israelite to the person he has injured? The present regulation answers this question.

The main clause introduced by וכי gives the premise that a quarrel between men has escalated into violence in which a man has used a 'stone' or his 'fist' to strike his fellow so that he ended up not dead, but laid up in bed. The significance of 'stone' or 'fist' is that use of either of these as a weapon proves that the blow was intentionally delivered. A stone is potentially a deadly weapon the use of which according to Num. 35.17 shows a manslayer to be an intentional murderer. The fist is also a weapon. In many cultures the clenched fist is a symbol of violence and hostile intent; in contrast, a slap with an open hand (כף) would represent insult rather than intent of physical injury. A truly unintentional injury, corresponding to the exception of Exod. 21.13-14, would not give the kind of case that the author wants to express. Accordingly, the main premise is that regardless of how the hostile act was carried out, whether with a makeshift weapon that happened to be available ('stone') or merely with one's own hands ('first'), it was an intentional attack on the person of a fellow Israelite which as a result laid him up in bed.

Following the main premise is a related clause introduced by אם. This clause states that if the injured man recovers from the blow so as to walk about on a staff, the offender is 'culpable' only for his time laid up[1] and his medical expenses. There are often several אם clauses under a כי main clause, but in this case only one is introduced, that of the wounded man rising. However, there is an implied, unstated second condition which (if expressed) would state: 'If he is *not* able to rise, but dies in bed...' The implication, in that case, is that the offender *would be* 'culpable' of the capital offense of Exod. 21.12-14. For the case as stated, the wounded man cannot demand the life of the offender on the grounds that 'he tried to kill me', but may only

---

1.   F.C. Fensham ('Exodus xxi, 18-19, in the Light of Hittite Law §10', *VT* 10 [1960], pp. 333-35) discusses four interpretations which have been offered for שבתו: (1) 'his sitting' (noun formation from יָשַׁב, 'sit') in sense of 'staying at home/loss of time', (2) 'his leisure, resting' (noun formed from the verb שׁ.ב.ת—'rest, ceasing', so perhaps LXX: ἀργεία—'idleness'), (3) 'his residence, dwelling place' (Cazelles, *Études*, pp. 53-54), and (4) 'his place or stead' (Fensham).

Cazelles' view is based on *ThBT* in Ugaritic (1 Keret 23), and on the parallel Hittite Law §10. The Ugaritic evidence is questionable: Gordon (*Ugaritic Textbook*, p. 416, §1177) does not recognize the meaning 'dwelling place' for *ThBT*. While Hittite Law §10 is clearly parallel to our passage, Cazelles' interpretation of it as requiring the offender to pay for the injured man's house has been called into question by Fensham who argues that the Hittite law calls the offender to pay not for the house but for someone to oversee the injured man's house until he recovers (cf. *ANET*, p. 189).

Fensham adopts a conjectural emendation of the text to read בשׁבתו which he interprets as 'in his place/stead', but the text as it stands makes good sense without it.

There is little difference in sense between 'his sitting' (from יָשַׁב) and 'his resting, ceasing' (from שׁ.ב.ת). Both imply paying for the time he is laid up.

demand compensation for the damages actually caused.

Case B* (killing a bondsman or bondwoman, vv. 20-21) progresses from the previous case which concerns social equals, that is, full citizens, to a case involving a social superior (master) and a social inferior (bondsman or bondwoman). Under normal circumstances, an Israelite citizen who strikes another Israelite citizen is fully culpable for what he has done, whether it be murder (Case A, 21.12-14) or mayhem (Case A*, 21.18-19), but the case of a master and a bonds- man or bondwoman different. A bondsman is the master's 'money' (v. 21). He has a monetary investment in the bondsman and deserves a return on his investment through the work that the bondsman supplies. Since the bondsman is bound to the master and cannot simply be 'fired' like a hireling if his work is inadequate, the text's אם clause, which forms an exception to the main וכי clause, concedes to the master permission to use corporal punishment to compel the bonds- man to work. Hence, unlike the case of social equals who have no general right to strike one another, the master does have the right to strike his bondsman, but only to make him work.

But despite this permission, the thrust of the regulation, as indicated by the main כי clause (v. 20), is towards the limitation of the master's power over the bondsman. The text is at pains to indicate that even if a bondsman is the master's money, the master has no power of life and death over his bondsman. If he kills his bondsman, if 'he dies under his hand', the master is culpable of murder and the bondsman's death should 'be avenged'. 'Under his hand' indicates that the bonds- man dies while or shortly after being beaten as opposed to dying a few days after the beating. A 'rod' in this context is an instrument designed to inflict pain rather than death, the kind of rod used for punishing children (Prov. 13.24) or for the back of one lacking understanding (Prov. 10.13). If a bondsman dies on the spot by such an instrument, it would most probably be via continual, unmitigated beating rather than the more limited punishment legitimate if for making the bondsman work. On the other hand, if the bondsman lives for a few days before he dies, this would be evidence that the master had intended to punish the bondsman to make him work (which is his right) rather than to abuse or kill him (which is not his right), and therefore under this condition the master does not deserve to be the object of 'vengeance'.

The interpretation of Case C* (vv. 22-25, injury to a pregnant woman in a brawl) is difficult, though its structure is fairly clear. Case C* is organized around the concept of אָסוֹן, though the meaning of this term is debated. If there is not אָסוֹן, then a man pays a fine. If there is אָסוֹן, then 'you' are to give 'life for life, eye for eye...' There is an unusual change in person and number within the passage. Men (3rd person masc. pl.) brawl. Men (3rd person masc. pl.) run into the pregnant woman. But only one man (3rd person masc. sing.) pays her husband a fine. And if there is אָסוֹן, then it is not 'he' but 'you' (2nd person masc. sing.) who render 'life for life...' As for the formulation 'life for life, eye for eye, tooth for tooth...', which has a poetic ring to it, there is clear organization in three sections: (1) 'life for life' representing the most serious, i.e., deadly injury, (2) 'eye for eye, tooth for tooth, hand for hand, foot for foot' representing various parts of the body injured, working progressively from the head down to the foot, (3) 'burning for burning, wound for wound, stripe for stripe' representing various types of injuries.[1] In this regard, categories (2) and (3) overlap: one can have a 'wound' to a 'foot' or 'hand'. It can also be noted that at least one element of this formula, that is, 'burning for burning', is an unlikely injury in the context of a blow to a pregnant woman. This leads to the conclusion that this formula is broader than the present context, expressing a general principle in a poetic/proverbial manner, a conclusion supported by the partial repeating of the formulation in Lev. 24.18b and 20 (where 'breaking for breaking' is added before 'eye for eye' and the formula ends with 'tooth for tooth'), and Deut. 19.21 (where only 'life for life' through 'foot for foot' is quoted, and preposition בְּ replaces תַּחַת 'for').

I adopt the following interpretation of 21.22-25, the full defense of which has been published elsewhere.[2] I take אָסוֹן here to mean, not 'deadly injury' but 'serious injury/medical calamity', in this case including serious injuries up to and including death. אָסוֹן seems to be related to the noun אָסֵי that means 'physician' in Talmudic Aramaic and Syriac, itself derived from Akkadian *asû*, a loanword from Sumerian A.ZU (traditionally 'knower of the waters').[3] Denominative

1. Boecker, *Law*, p. 173.

2. J.M. Sprinkle, 'The Interpretation of Exodus 21.22-25 (*Lex Talionis*) and Abortion', *WTJ* 55 (1993), pp. 233-53.

3. S.A. Kaufman, *The Akkadian Influences on Aramaic* (Assyriological Studies 19; Chicago: University of Chicago Press, 1974), p. 37, though he rejects association of *asû* with אָסוֹן. Cf. *CAD*, Vol. A II, p. 347.

verbs have been derived secondarily from this non-Semitic noun in Aramaic (Aphel 'to cure', Ithpaal 'be cured, recover'), and it seems likely the noun אסון in biblical Hebrew is also a secondary development from this word. Hence, אסון would be expected to be a medical, not a legal term, meaning something like, 'injury requiring attention of a physician, serious injury'. That less than fatal injuries are included may be deduced from the talionic formula which does not end with 'life for life', but contemplates various lesser injuries.

I take אסון to apply solely to the woman, the plural ילדיה implying an abstract, 'child-product, fruit of the womb', or the like, an apt term for a stillborn baby.[1] Most premature births before modern medical science would result in the death of the fetus,[2] and the many parallel cuneiform laws which have influenced biblical formulations all assume the death of the fetus.[3] Hence the death of the child at the premature birth is presumed.

The purpose of the plurals (men brawl, men strike a pregnant woman) is to point out the accidental nature of the injury—they are fighting each other, not the woman, and are out of control. (Deut. 25.11, in which a woman intervenes in a fight involving her husband, is an entirely different case, and is irrelevant to the present context.) The switch to singular, 'he pays', reflects an indefinite use of the singular.[4] That is, 'someone' pays, whether the most negligent party in the brawl, or a representative of the men who brawled. The point is that the accidental, negligent taking of the life of an embryo has resulted in a great loss for the woman's family, and someone should compensate monetarily for the damage done by paying a fine to

---

1. Keil (*Pentateuch*, p. 135) argues that the plural ילדיה occurs 'because there might possibly be more than one child in the womb'. This seems far-fetched, however, since the possibility of twins is irrelevant to the point of this case.

2. R.N. Congdon, 'Exodus 21.22-25 and the Abortion Debate', *BSac* 146 (1989), pp. 140-42.

3. Hittite Laws §17; Sumerian Laws §§1-2; LH §§209-14; MAL A §§21, 50-52; what has been identified as part of the Laws of Lipit Ishtar (translated by M. Civil, 'New Sumerian Law Fragments', in *Studies in Honor of Benno Landsberger* [Assyriological Studies 16; Chicago: University of Chicago Press, 1965], pp. 4-6).

4. Cf. F.E. König, *Historisch-kritisches Lehrgebäude der hebräischen Sprache*. III. 2.2. *Historisch-Comparative Syntax* (Leipzig: Hinrichs, 1897), pp. 354-55, §§324d-324dß, for this use of the singular verb. Examples: Gen. 19.17; 38.28; 48.1; 50.26; Exod. 10.5, 21b; Lev. 2.8.

the father as the head of the family.

Someone pays בפללים. בפללים does not mean 'by judges' but, 'by assessment' or 'according to the amount to which he is culpable',[1] probably in the sense of a payment made proportional to the stage of development of the fetus (cf. Hittite Laws §17). The rationale for this is that the later the stage of pregnancy, the more time has been lost to the woman, the greater the grief for the loss of a child, and the more difficult the miscarriage. Although the stage of development is a factor to be considered, the exact price is not legislated, being a matter of tort between the husband and the offending party.

As for the other half of the regulation, if there is serious injury (אסון) to the woman up to and including death, then the so-called *lex talionis* applies which states that the punishment should correspond to the injury caused. This formula expresses a principle that is more general than the present context, applying to both unintentional injury as well as intentional injury of one person against another: to wit, that the punishment should be proportional with the damages caused by the offense.

The *lex talionis* is not to be taken literally, but assumes a system of ransom in which monetary composition can serve to substitute for the literal talion as in Exod. 21.29-30 and 1 Kgs 20.39.[2] Literal application of the *lex talionis* is inconsistent with Exod. 21.18-19 where a deliberate injury does not result in a punishment of injuring the offender to the exact same degree he injured the man he struck—which, by the way would be absurdly impractical—but instead the offender pays money. The verb נ.ת.ן used in 'you will pay out' (v. 23) is used of monetary payments in the immediate context (vv. 19b, 22b, 30, 32), and the word תחת translated 'for' in the terms 'life *for* life, eye *for* eye...' is used in the expression 'ox *for* ox' (21.36) in the sense of giving the value of an ox for the ox killed, whether that be by substituting a live animal or its monetary equivalent. This, incidentally, makes the so-called talionic formula a more general application of the principle already applied to the fetus in the expression בפללים that also

---

1. See E.A. Speiser, 'The Stem פלל in Hebrew', *JBL* 82 (1963), pp. 301-306; and A. Berlin, 'On the Meaning of פלל in the Bible', *RB* 96 (1989), pp. 345-51.

2. This is an old rabbinic interpretation: *b. Sanh.* 79a, *B. Qam* 83b, *b. Ket* 33b; Rashi on Exod. 21.24; *m. B.Qam* 8.1. It is defended by P. Doron, 'A New Look at an Old Lex', *JANESCU* 1.2 (1968–69), pp. 21-27.

requires proportional payment for damages.[1]

The 'you' (sing.) who pays according to this principle is Israel represented by an individual. Israel is not a different entity from the one who pays the fine בפללים to the husband, but is an example of 'you' (sing.) meaning Israel standing by metonymy for an appropriate party within a case (cf. 21.2 and 21.13).[2] This passage may be paraphrased: 'This is what you, O Israel(ite), should do in so far as you find yourself to be the negligent party in similar circumstances, you should pay in accord with the principle life for life...'[3] This usage of the second person again reminds the reader that this is not an impersonal law-code, but YHWH's address to Israel.

Case D* (injury of a bondsman's or bondwoman's eye or tooth, Exod. 21.26-27) returns to the subject of bondsmen. The main clause introduced by וכי states that the damage of a eye of a bondsman or bondwoman results in the bondsman's freedom. Likewise, in the related ואם clause the destruction of a tooth results in the bondsman's freedom. Why is the damaging of an eye rewarded in the same way as the knocking out of a tooth, since an eye is obviously more valuable than a tooth?[4] The point of this word pair is perhaps to be understood

---

1. A similar system of ransom probably also operated in Mesopotamia. Scholars have noted the contrast between LH §196 'If a free man has injured the eye of a patrician, his own eye shall be injured', and LE §42 that designates one mina payment for the same. This contrast is unexpected since the two collections are from chronologically, geographically, and culturally closely related societies. R. Westbrook (*Studies in Biblical and Cuneiform Law* [Cahiers de la Revue Biblique 26; Paris: Gabalda, 1988], pp. 45, 47-55) resolves this discrepancy on the assumption that the 'ransom' principle operated in Mesopotamia as it did in Israel, so that the statement in LH §196 also allows the possibility of ransom. LE §42 simply specifies the ransom price appropriate to the injury. Cf. MAL B §2 where in the case of murder the 'owner of the life' can either execute the murderer or receive compensation from him.

2. Cf. R. Westbrook, '*Lex Talionis* and Exodus 21.22-25', *RB* 93 (1986), pp. 52-69. Westbrook rightly identifies the 'you' as Israel, but identifies Israel as paying only when there is 'perpetrator unknown', his view of אסון. אסון can hardly bear this meaning, however, since this is not the sort of circumstance where one would expect a 'perpetrator unknown'; surely there would be plenty of witnesses. Moreover, the use of אסון in Sir. 34.22 and 39.1 cannot bear this interpretation.

3. Another possibility is to take נ.ת.ן to mean not 'pay' but 'impose (the penalty according to the rule of)' as in Lev. 17.11; Deut. 26.6, 2 Kgs 18.14; 23.33. Then 'you' would be the Israelite judge.

4. In LE §42, an eye was worth 1 mina (60 shekels), a tooth $\frac{1}{2}$ mina (30 shekels).

as defining upper and lower limits: for as much as an eye, or for as little as a tooth, if you permanently damage him, you must set him free.

Case D* immediately follows the so-called *lex talionis* with its 'eye for (תחת) eye, tooth for (תחת) tooth' and intentionally draws on the language of that formulation, both in the choice of the damaging of a bondsman's 'eye' and 'tooth', and in the use of תחת. Moreover, Case C*, having nothing directly to do with bondsmen, comes in between Cases B* and D* that have to do with killing and injuring bondsmen, respectively. Why does Case C* come in between these two regulations? How are Cases C* and D* related?

According to Patrick, Case D*'s link with Case C* is only superficial: the case of the injured bondsman came to the lawgiver's mind because, like the *lex talionis*, it deals with 'eye' and 'tooth' and uses the term תחת.[1] Jackson offers a source-oriented explanation, that Exod. 21.24-25 (the *lex talionis*) is a later interpolation inserted on the basis of the similar language of the slave law of vv. 26-27, and thus the two were originally unrelated.[2] In fact, most source-oriented scholars think that Case C* is an example of interpolation or else represents some other scribal misadventure.[3] Many see no integral connection between Case D* and C*, and base their reconstructions of the text on the premise that the original reading has been garbled.

It is possible to see a more integral connection between Case C* and D*, however.[4] Case C* on the pregnant woman breaks the sequence between the two bondsman laws (Cases B* and D*) in order to introduce the principle of the so-called *lex talionis*, the best known (made famous by its citation in Mt. 5.38-39), and arguably the least understood line of the whole of Exod. 20.22–23.19. This formula, 'life for

1.   Patrick, *Law*, p. 77.
2.   Jackson, *Essays*, p. 105.
3.   A.S. Diamond, 'An Eye for an Eye', *Iraq* 19 (1957), p. 153; S.E. Loewenstamm, 'Exodus XXI 22-25', *VT* 27 (1977), p. 357, who thinks 'the text of a law dealing with a blow given to a pregnant woman has become mixed up with the text of another law providing for the consequences of blows which men dealt upon one another in a brawl.' Cazelles (*Études*, p. 56) thinks vv. 24-25 belong after vv. 18-19 rather than their present position. McNeile (*Exodus*, pp. liii, 129) would put the whole of vv. 22-25 after v. 19, though he also states that vv. 23b-25 are irrelevant to the case at point. Schwienhorst-Schönberger (*Bundesbuch*, p. 82) remarks that only a few exegetes consider 21.22-25 to be a unity in the strict sense.
4.   The main lines of this interpretation I owe to H.C. Brichto (personal dialogue).

life, eye for eye, tooth for tooth…' with its proverbial ring is not to be taken literally, but (as argued above) reflects a system of monetary composition in which 'life for life' in practice meant 'monetary value of a life in exchange for the life lost', and 'eye for eye' meant 'monetary value of an eye in exchange for the eye lost', etc.

Cases B*, C* and D* as a group are fundamentally about injuries to bondsmen, specifically debt slaves as in 21.2-6, which is a natural progression of the discussion of injury to the full citizen in Case A*. Case C* is parenthetical, though necessary to further the author's discussion of bondsmen.

What Case C* introduces is a principle that one should as a rule pay the exact monetary equivalent for mayhem that one caused even if the mayhem was unintentional, as the striking of a pregnant woman in a brawl among men would be. This principle was introduced, however, to form a contrast with Case D*. D* by using similar language but drawing a quite different conclusion indicates that this principle does not apply in the case of a beating of a bondsman in which the beating is intentional (this is his master's right if for the purpose of making him work), but the maiming was (in all likelihood) unintentional. In this case, and unlike the 'talionic formula', the penalty does not vary according to the degree of injury, but maiming of any sort, as great as the loss of an eye, as little as the loss of a tooth, results in the bonds-man's freedom and the loss of the master's investment, that is, the master loses the time owed by the bondsman in lieu of the bondsman's unpaid debt.

The reason why the talionic formula does not apply, but that any maiming results in the slave's freedom, is that this bondsman (being actually a 'distrainee' or an 'indentured servant' rather than a 'slave'—cf. 21.2-6) must be treated as a human being despite his reduced social status. The master has the right to the bondsman's time and to a limited extent can use force to make him work, but the master has no right to his bondsman's person. If he murders the bondsman, he is subject to 'vengeance' (Case B*) as with the murder of any other human being; if he maims him, he loses all rights as master (Case D*) since he has no right to treat another human being in that way. Hence the biblical author has artfully expressed a philo-sophical concept concerning the humanity of a bondsman by this juxtaposition of the case of the pregnant woman and the case of the maiming of the bondsman.

Excursus: On the Impersonal Style of Exodus 21.18–22.16

A most significant stylistic feature to be observed in Exod. 21.18-27 is its impersonal, third person formulation. Beginning with 21.18 and (with the exception of 21.23) continuing through 22.16 (the central core of Exod. 20.22–23.19) is all impersonally formulated. This is in contrast to the personal character of the prologue (20.22-26), as well as 21.1, 2, 13-14 which all precede the central section. It is even more in contrast with the concluding portion, 22.17–23.19, which is highly personal. It is not at first obvious why this should be so in the literary context of a personal address of YHWH to Israel (20.22; 21.1).

The old-fashioned, source-oriented explanation commonly given is that these regulations were originally part of a collection of Canaanite case laws derived originally from Mesopotamia, a 'law code', which as such is normally stated impersonally. According to this explanation, the material of 21.18–22.16 has been clumsily inserted into the Sinaitic narrative without being fully integrated into the narrative context.[1] This explanation is in direct contradiction with the thesis argued here. Some recent source-oriented scholars have argued for greater Israelite input into these laws, no longer seeing them as a mechanical insertion of a foreign corpus, but derived from Israelite legal practices and scribal traditions merely influenced by Mesopotamia.[2]

Whether or not these regulations existed previously as a code, there certainly are parallels in content between the regulations here and ancient Near East legal collections. The parallels between cuneiform law collections are much greater for 21.2–22.16 than for what goes before or after.

At this point I am compelled to adopt an admittedly source-oriented explanation for this phenomenon, though not the usual one. Our author in this core unit is making religious and ethical comment on judicial matters.[3] Because legal matters are normally expressed impersonally, our author feels a compulsion to express these matters impersonally. However, since the laws are part of a narrative in which God is personally addressing his people, there is also a tendency for the author to formulate this core section personally.

The author has made a compromise between these two compulsions. He has 'personalized' the entire corpus of Exod. 20.22–23.33 by framing it in personal language, but has expressed the more strictly legal regulations more impersonally, as is customary for the genre of 'law'. Having already established the overall context of a dialogue between God and Israel, there is less need for the author to underscore

---

1. Representative proponents of the view that all or most of 21.2–22.16 is a secondary insertion from a law code: Paul, *Studies*, p. 43; Noth, *Exodus*, p. 173; Eissfeldt, *The Old Testament*, pp. 212-19; W. Beyerlin, *Origins and History of the Oldest Sinaitic Traditions* (trans. S. Rudman; Oxford: Oxford University Press, 1965), pp. 4-6. Cf. Alt, 'Origins', pp. 79-132.

2. Schwienhorst-Schönberger, *Bundesbuch*, pp. 254-56, 268; E. Otto, 'Town and Rural Countryside in Ancient Israelite Law: Reception and Redaction in Cuneiform and Israelite Law', *JSOT* 57 (1993), pp. 3-22.

3. Cassuto, *Exodus*, p. 262.

every individual context with 'I-Thou' language. Nevertheless, personal pronouns do occur in 21.2 ('Should you acquire'), 21.13-14 ('*I* will establish a place for *you... you* may take him from *my* altar'), and in Exod. 21.23 ('*you* will pay "life for life"') in order to remind the reader that this is still part of a monologue of YHWH to Israel.

Perhaps an illustration can show how it is reasonable for an impersonal emphasis to occur in the middle of an address of YHWH to Israel. A mother instructing a young son on how to bake a cake might be expected to address her son personally: 'First *you* get the bowl and the cake mix, then *you* get two eggs...' She need not continue to do so, however. The mother could choose to give the bulk of the steps impersonally, being influenced by the genre of 'cake instructions' given on the box of the cake mix: 'the mix goes in the bowl; a cup of milk and two eggs have to be added, and it must be stirred until it is well mixed.' Even so, here and there an occasional personal aside could be expected: 'Now make sure *you* do not get any egg shells in *your* mix.' At the end, the mother could choose to revert back to highly personal language: 'And when it is all done, then *you* put it on the table, and then *you* get plates and forks, and then *you* cut a piece for *your* little sister and one for *me*, and finally you may cut a piece for *yourself.*'

The effect of framing the cake instructions, for the most part given impersonally, with personal language at the beginning and the end is to 'personalize' the address as a whole. So also in Exod. 21.22–23.33, by formulating the regulations at the beginning and end in a highly personal way—you/me/I—the entire address has been personalized despite the impersonal formulation of the middle regulations.

These regulations may or may not have existed as an originally independent collection of laws. If they did, the redactor felt no need to personalize every individual regulation because the whole is personalized by the personal framework. But whether or not the material existed as a previous collection, the impersonal formulation would be the standard way of conveying this kind of legal or semi-legal material. Moreover, impersonal formulation is more concise than personal formulation that tends to be discursive. For these reasons, an author may have chosen the mostly impersonal formulation of 21.18–22.16 regardless of whether he was utilizing a preexisting law code as a source.

Exodus 21.18-27: Law or Morality?

Although the material in Exod. 21.18-27 relates to legal matters, the author is using law as a vehicle for expressing morality rather than giving a detailed law code.

Case A*, striking a fellow citizen, makes no allowance for mitigating circumstances such as 'self-defense', not because the author rejects the possibility of mitigating circumstances, but because these regulations serve as illustrations of certain principles rather than attempting to give a complete law code. Being an illustrative example, there is no need to treat various possible exceptions and mitigating circumstances.

Cases A*, B* and D* give no hint of courts or judges who might administer these regulations. Some have seen a hint in Case C*'s use of בִּפְלִלִים traditionally understood to mean 'by judges',[1] but this is not certain. Speiser argues that the root has to do with 'reckoning, assessing' and that בפללים means 'by assessment/reckoning'; Westbrook argues that the root פ.ל.ל has the sense of 'sole responsibility' and that בפללים means '[he pays] alone', and Berlin, who is specifically modifying Westbrook's conclusion, argues that the root has to do with 'responsibility, accountability' and that בפללים means 'as the culpable party'.[2] There is no certain reference to judges.

In Case B* (the killing of a bondsman) the text states that the bondsman's death is to 'be avenged'. There is some uncertainty over the exact meaning of 'be avenged' (יֻקַם). According to Mendenhall (and with qualified support from Pitard),[3] נ.ק.ם here does not refer to 'vengeance' in the sense of 'malicious retaliation for inflicted wrongs', as do the English terms vengeance/avenge, nor does it imply a 'blood feud' of the type practiced traditionally by bedouin, but normally refers to retributive justice, an exercise of force by a legitimate authority to redress a crime committed by punishing the criminal. This meaning fits Exod. 21.20-21.

Does נ.ק.ם in Exod. 21.20 imply the same result as the מוֹת יוּמַת ('he may be put to death') in vv. 12, 15, 16 and 17 or does it indicate

---

1. The HtD Stem of פ.ל.ל means to pray. Assuming פ.ל.ל means 'to judge' in G, the HtD could be understood to mean 'to seek a judgment for oneself'. Cf. M. Greenberg, *Biblical Prose Prayer* (Berkeley: University of California Press, 1983), pp. 21-22.

2. Speiser, 'פלל in Hebrew', pp. 301-306; Westbrook, *'Lex talionis'*, pp. 52-69; Berlin, 'פלל in the Bible', pp. 345-51.

3. G.E. Mendenhall, 'The "Vengeance of Yahweh"', in *The Tenth Generation* (Baltimore: Johns Hopkins University Press, 1973), pp. 69-104. W.T. Pitard ('Amarna *ekemu* and Hebrew נקם', *Maarav* 3 [1982], pp. 5-25) criticizes Mendenhall's conclusion that נ.ק.ם relates to 'extra-legal executive action by a sovereign'. Pitard agrees, however, that in the 14 times נ.ק.ם is used in 'legal' contexts including Exod. 21.20-21, it means 'punishment given to a wrongdoer upon being found guilty in a trial, or recompense awarded to the victim of the crime' (pp. 16-17) and that נ.ק.ם has the same sense in some 24 other occurrences not in strictly legal contexts. In 12 occurrences in non-legal contexts, however, he thinks the sense is more 'revenge', but this is not relevant to our passage.

some lesser form of punishment? The usage of נ.ק.ם suggests similarity of outcome. נָקַם and its cognate nouns נָקָם and נְקָמָה are strong terms, regularly accomplished by the taking of human life, whether in military battle or by personal action.[1] It is true, as Prov. 6.34 states, that one can be spared on the 'day of vengeance' if the offended party can be persuaded to accept a ransom, but this simply confirms that 'vengeance' normally demands the life of the one on whom vengeance is taken. Moreover, that ransom is possible in the case of 'vengeance' is no argument against identifying the outcome with מוֹת יוּמָת since (as argued above) cases where death is prescribed as a penalty do not necessarily exclude the possibility of ransom. The negligent owner of an ox who gores a man to death is 'condemned' to death but, in view of the circumstances, he is allowed the possibility of saving his life by ransom (Exod. 21.29-30). Similarly, the master in Case B* receives a death sentence using נ.ק.ם, but if this is a case where an intentional and legitimate beating of a bondsman to make him work unintentionally resulted in his death, ransom in all likelihood would be allowed. The conclusion, then, is that נקם ינקם is the same result as מוֹת יוּמָת, but neither of these expressions was necessarily meant always to be carried out literally; in many cases ransom could serve as a substitute.

But who would see to it that 'vengeance' was carried out? The matter has perplexed commentators who assume that what we have is essentially a legal statute.[2] The bondsman's family? This seems the most likely intent. On the premise that the 'slave' is more indentured servant than slave, he might have a family who could avenge his death, and נקמה seems to be a family responsibility (cf. the 'avenger of blood' in Num. 35). However, if a bondsman has no family the case as law becomes unenforceable. Would the enforcement then fall to the state or the community of Israel? The text is silent about these possibilities. However, if (as is supposed here) the regulation is primarily using legal formulation to make a moral statement that condemns the

---

1. Examples where vengeance is accomplished by slaughter in war: Num. 31.2-3; Josh. 10.13; Esth. 8.13; Isa. 34.8; Nah. 1.2; Jer. 51.11; Ps. 149.7. These merge with examples of personal vengeance in military contexts: Judg. 11.36; 1 Sam. 14.24; 18.25; 2 Kgs 9.7. Personal revenge regularly involves killing: Gen. 4.24; Judg. 15.7; 16.28; 1 Sam. 24.13. Although there are some instances that are ambiguous (e.g. Jer. 15.15), there are no clear instances where the taking of human life is not involved in words related to נ.ק.ם.

2. E.g. Westbrook, *Studies*, pp. 89-100.

fatal abuse of bondsmen by masters, then whether the vengeance is carried out by the bondsmen's family, or a civil authority, or God himself is immaterial. The moral condemnation of this act remains the same.

Case B*, by calling for 'vengeance' against the man who kills his bondsman, implies the full humanity of the bondsman. This seems to be in contrast with ancient Babylonia where there is no extent regulation prohibiting the killing of one's own slave, and killing of another man's slave (unlike the formulation for killing another man's son) was punished but by payment of his price to the master,[1] leading some scholars to suppose that the master could kill his slave with impunity. Dandamaev, for example, argues that the master had power of life and death over slaves in Babylonia.[2] In any case it is clear that the slave's life was considered less valuable than a full citizen's life. If the master had the power of life and death over his slave, the only punishment the master would receive in Babylonia if he injured or killed his slave would be the self-inflicted loss of his human property.

In comparison, the concept of slavery envisioned in Case B* is elevated. Here the bondsman is no mere commodity, but a full human being. His servitude in most instances is not permanent, but temporary (cf. 21.2) so that he is more an indentured servant than a slave. In any case, he is a person not a thing. Taking his life comes under the category of Exod. 21.12, 'Whoever strikes someone to death, ought to be put to death.' The taking of his life should be avenged just as the murder of a free citizen should be.

These cases could have served as illustrations to guide a magistrate (who would in practice have to fill in the gaps and make allowances for mitigating circumstances). However, use by a magistrate is in no

1.   LH §116, for example, states that if a slave given as pledge is beaten to death, the offender must pay the slave's owner ⅓ mina of silver and forfeit the balance of the money which the owner owes him. In contrast, the same law states that if a man's son given as a pledge is beaten to death, the offender's son must die. The possibility, and in practice the probability, of ransom serving as a substitute for the owner's son in this law (as argued above) lessens the contrast between slave and full citizen in this case. Nonetheless, even if ransom was the normal outcome for the death sentence on the offender's son in this law, the formulation here implies that killing a man's slave was not even potentially a capital offense.

2.   Dandamaev, *Slavery in Babylonia*, pp. 460-63. Actual documentation for killing a slave with impunity is lacking, however, which raises doubts about this conclusion.

way incompatible with a more general use of these regulations to illustrate certain moral principles. Viewed from that perspective, Case A* expresses the principle that if a man injures someone, he should pay for the financial damages he has caused—courts, by the way, would come into play only if the offender tries to evade his moral obligation. Cases B* and D* offer moral condemnation for the killing and maiming of bondsmen. Case C* asserts the moral principle that the composition paid in the case of accidental mayhem should be proportional to the injury caused rather than punitive (an 'eye for an eye' rather than 'two eyes for an eye'). Without denying the legal nature of this material, the text's intention is only fully grasped by looking at its moral implications.

Chapter 5

GORING OXEN AND DANGEROUS PITS: EXODUS 21.28-36

These regulations have to do with injuries or damages caused by someone's property (ox or pit) to a human being or to another person's (live) property, and the question of the degree of the owner's liability.

Damages Caused by Someone's Property: Oxen and Pits
Exodus 21.28-36
Pericope A. Cases of Oxen Goring Humans

(28) Should an ox gore a man or woman to death, the ox must be stoned and its flesh may not be eaten, but the ox's owner should not be held further accountable. (29) But if the ox had a history as a gorer, that is, its owner had been warned about this and yet he did not keep it under control,[1] so that it killed a man or woman, then the ox must be stoned to death, and the owner too deserves to be killed. (30) If a ransom is assessed against him, then he must pay for redemption of his life as much as is assessed against him. (31) Whether a freeborn male [בֵּן] or female [בַּת], it gores, this regulation shall be applied to him. (32) If, however, the ox gores a slave, male or female, he must pay the owner thirty shekels of silver and the ox must be stoned to death.

1. שׁ.מ.ר ('to keep'). LXX renders with ἀφανίζω ('destroy, make unseen') on which basis Jackson (*Essays*, p. 124) emends the MT to שׁ.מ.ד ('to destroy'), reasoning that an owner must kill an ox inclined to gore or else be liable to capital punishment. Against Jackson is that when the ox gores another ox (vv. 35-36), it is a 'gorer', yet the text is silent about destroying it. Moreover, the parallel in LH §251 requires the habitually goring ox's horns to be screened and it 'kept under control' (Akkadian, *sunnuqu*; cf. *CAD* S, XV, p. 143), the latter being essentially the same sense as שׁ.מ.ר, suggesting that שׁ.מ.ד rather than שׁ.מ.ר is corrupt. M. Greenberg ('More Reflections on Biblical Criminal Law', in *Studies in Bible: 1986* [Scripta Hierosolymitana 31; ed. S. Japhet; Jerusalem: Magnes, 1986], p. 10 n. 19) argues that the LXX reading is a reflection, not of a different *Vorlage*, but of a later Jewish legal interpretation of the law.

Pericope B. *Cases of Injuries to Animals due to Open Pits*

(33) Should someone open up a pit, or if he digs a pit, without covering it so that an ox or donkey falls into it, (34) the owner of the pit must make payment by remitting silver to its owner, but he may keep the carcass.

Pericope A*. *Cases of Oxen Goring Oxen*

(35) If one man's ox fatally attacks another man's ox, then they are to sell the living ox and divide the receipts, and they should also divide up the carcass. (36) On the other hand, if it was known that the ox had a history as a gorer and yet its owner did not keep it under control, then he must render payment '[full value of] ox in exchange for ox', and he may keep the carcass.

Exodus 21.28-36 and Structure

Exod. 21.28-36 can be divided into three parts. The first (Pericope A, vv. 28-32) has to do with an ox goring a human being to death. The second (Pericope B, vv. 33-34) treats the death of an animal due to someone's negligently leaving a pit uncovered. The third (Pericope A*, vv. 35-36) has to do with an ox goring another ox. Combined, these three pericopes form a unit that can be generalized as offenses of one person's property (ox) against a person and one person's property (pit or ox) against another person's property. They follow a group of regulations dealing with offenses of humans against other humans (21.12-27), and precede a group of regulations whose emphasis is offenses of people against other people's property (21.37–22.16). All this represents logical progression in 21.12–22.16: from offenses of humans against humans, to offenses of property against humans, to offenses of property against property, to offenses of humans against property.[1]

Many scholars are troubled by the fact that Pericope B (vv. 33-34) concerning pits disrupts the theme of the goring ox. Childs[2] states that strict logic would require vv. 35-36 to have been placed before v. 33, for the hierarchy of vv. 28-32 becomes complete by moving vv. 35-36 before v. 33, forming a descending order of status: ox gores a man/woman, ox gores a son/daughter, ox gores a male or female slave, ox gores an ox. Jackson, likewise finds disruption in the text,

---

1. Paul, *Studies*, pp. 106-11.
2. Childs, *Exodus*, p. 473.

regarding v. 36, at least, to be secondary.[1] Jepsen viewed vv. 33-34 as secondary.[2] E. Otto explains the disruption as the boundary between two originally independent collections, 21.18-32 and 21.33–22.14.[3]

Daube proposed that this sequence is disrupted because the original collection of laws has been supplemented by an addition at the end of the original legal paragraph:

> Once again, the disorder we have before us is due to the fact that there is an older part and a supplement, and that the supplement has never been combined with the older part but has simply been put at the end. Originally, two offenses only were dealt with: the case where your ox killed a person and the case where your pit caused the death of an animal... it is worth mentioning that the Code of Hammurabi, whilst it has some rules on the case where an ox kills a man, has none on the case where an ox kills an ox... It was not until a later period that a paragraph was appended on the less urgent case (not appearing in the Code of Hammurabi) where the ox killed an ox. It was appended: but it was not introduced where we should introduce it, between the two original paragraphs.[4]

According to Daube, either because of laziness, inertia, or respect for tradition, when a legal code (biblical or ancient non-biblical) was emended, it typically was done by adding the new regulation to the end of an appropriate paragraph in the previously existing one to minimize the disruption. Thus vv. 35-36 represent a secondary insertion.[5]

Daube's view assumes both that a secondary insertion has been made and that it has been made in a mechanical way rather than well-integrating the new material into the structure of the old material. The only evidence for any insertion is the perceived disruption in the text interpreted along the lines of the second assumption, the use of different vocabulary in the 'supplement', and the lack of a parallel in the Laws of Hammurapi of the 'less urgent case'.

Daube wrote before the publication of the Laws of Eshnunna. LE §53 is virtually identical with v. 35, the so-called 'less urgent case', and is the closest parallel known so far between a rule in an ancient Near East legal text and a biblical provision. This eliminates Daube's

1.   Jackson, *Essays*, p. 148.

2.   Jepsen, *Untersuchungen*, p. 36.

3.   Cited by Schwienhorst-Schönberger, *Bundesbuch*, p. 130.

4.   Daube, *Biblical Law*, p. 85.

5.   Daube, *Biblical Law*, pp. 76-77. Similarly, Schwienhorst-Schönberger, *Bundesbuch*, p. 156.

argument from the lack of a cuneiform parallel. The argument from the vocabulary is based on the distinctive terminology in vv. 35-36: אֹו 'or, alternatively' replaces אִם 'if', נ.כ.ף 'smite' replaces נ.ג.ח 'gore', and נֹודַע 'made known' replaces הוּעַד 'warned'.[1] The assumption that insertions are made in a mechanical way requires many instances where this explanation seems preferable to explanations assuming the text's unity. Daube's theory is in direct opposition to the thesis of this book that 20.22–23.19 is a well-edited unity.

Why might an intelligent author deliberately choose the present organization of these regulations in which Pericope B interrupts Pericopes A and A*? The following outline will assist the discussion of this question:

Pericope A (21.28-32)

>Case 1. Ox kills human//Owner not accountable but loses ox
>via execution//No payment for human life. (v. 28)
>Case 2. Ox kills human//Owner accountable due to negligence
>for life and loses ox via execution//Full assessed payment.
>(vv. 29-32)
>>Sub-category A—Victim is freeborn citizen, male or
>>female: assessment on the basis of 'life for life' in
>>which כֹּפֶר is acceptable. (vv. 29-31)
>>Sub-category B—Victim is slave, male or female:
>>assessment based on value of slave. (v. 32)

Pericope B (Exod. 21.33-34)

>Owner digs or opens pit//Owner accountable and bears full
>loss, but no more.

Pericope A* (Exod. 21.35-36)

>Case 1*. Ox kills ox//Owner not accountable but shares loss
>equally with owner of victim//No transcendent life value,
>only commodity.
>Case 2*. Ox kills ox/Owner accountable and bears full loss,
>but no more//No transcendent life value, only commodity.

---

1.   Daube, *Biblical Law*, pp. 85-88. Paul (*Studies*, p. 84 n. 1) agrees that this is 'a possible indication that these sections [28-33 and 35-36] were originally incorporated from different sources'.

The structure above is semi-chiastic in which Pericopes A and A*
are parallel, both having to do with goring oxen and both beginning
with cases without negligence (Cases 1 and 1*), and concluding with
cases in which there is negligence (Cases 2 and 2*). If vv. 35-36 were
removed as secondary as Daube suggests, or if v. 36 were removed as
Jackson suggests, the author's desired parallelism between Cases 1 and
2 and Cases 1* and 2* would be lost.

Case 1 (v. 28) in Pericope A is that of the full citizen where no
negligence on the part of the ox's owner occurs. The basic case ends
up saying that the ox's owner is 'not held responsible'. This means that
he is not responsible for bloodguiltiness rather than that he goes
unpunished, for the loss of his ox's life and the prohibition against the
use of its flesh represents a considerable economic loss for the owner.[1]
What actually occurs is that the owner loses his ox, just as the victim's
family lost the life of one of its members. Here the execution of the ox
is sufficient to atone for the loss of the victim.

The main clause of Pericope A is Case 1, marked by כִּי, which the
other clauses, marked by אִם (vv. 29, 30, 32) modify at some point or
another.[2] Since v. 29 builds on the כִּי clause of v. 28, it can be
elliptical: it does not repeat but assumes 'and its flesh is not to be
eaten' after repeating that the ox is to be stoned. Verse 30, also
introduced by אִם, is grammatically related to v. 29. It does not repeat
the premises (ox gores a person to death, ox previously a gorer,
owner negligent in not restraining it) nor the outcome (ox stoned,
owner deserving of death), but assuming all this, picks up on the last
statement, 'and the owner also will be/deserves to be killed', to make
clear that כֹּפֶר or ransom is allowed in the case of manslaughter due to
negligence.

Verse 31, however, which is introduced by אוֹ ('or') rather than אִם,
need not be understood as a new sub-category. Instead this verse could
be understood as defining more precisely the class for which the just
stated regulation in vv. 28-30 applies. Verse 31 reads: 'Whether a בֵּן
or a בַּת it gores, this regulation shall be applied to him.' In light of the
contrast with v. 32 and continuity with what goes before, בֵּן ('son')

---

1.   Durham, *Exodus*, p. 324.

2.   E. Otto, 'Rechtssystematik im altbabylonischen "Codex Eshnunna" und im
altisraelitischen "Bundesbuch"', *UF* 19 [1987], pp. 175-97) discusses the way in
which biblical regulations repeat or do not repeat premises and conclusions in
associated paragraphs.

and בת ('daughter') are better taken to refer not to minors but to freeborn members of the household regardless of age.[1] If so, v. 31 defines more specifically the ones for whom the regulation applies, that is, who count as members of the איש or אשה class, in order to form a contrast with the case of a slave.[2]

According to this view and in contrast with the common view of Childs and others, Pericope A could be understood as containing but two classes (free and slave), not three (adult, child, slave). If correct, this view weakens the case for the reconstructed hierarchy of adult/ child/slave/ox in the hypothetical 'original' version of the law.

Note also how this understanding of בן and בת as 'freeborn citizens', if adopted, would render irrelevant the debate between Greenberg and Jackson concerning this verse. Greenberg contrasts this regulation with a variety of Mesopotamian ones where a child is punished vicariously for the crime of a parent.[3] Jackson, rejecting Greenberg's view as assuming too much of the original audience—that they would have to know of vicarious punishments in Babylonian law—takes this verse to be a scholastic addition to avoid the blaming of parents for not keeping their children out of the way.[4] If, however, בן and בת refer to citizens regardless of age, both interpretations are undermined.

Verse 32 introduced by אם is a new circumstance that I label Sub-category B. It provides a situation in contrast with vv. 28-31[5] by making the victim not a freeborn member of the household, but a slave. Unlike Sub-category A, there is no mention of 'ransom', but rather the price of a slave (30 shekels) is specified. The problem here

---

1. בן is short for בן־איש. Similarly, *mar awilim* in Akkadian, lit. 'son of a man', means 'freeborn citizen' (*CAD* M, vol. X, part I, p. 315; A, vol. I, part II, p. 56). בתות means 'freeborn daughters' at Exod. 21.9, and בן־אמתך at 23.12 (literally, 'son of your maidservant') means member of the slave class, male or female.

2. Schwienhorst-Schönberger (*Bundesbuch*, p. 141) concludes that the deviating formulation from אם to או in 21.31a betrays the hand of a secondary redactor. But if או is not equivalent to אם here, his basis of argument is undermined.

3. Greenberg, 'Postulates', pp. 20-23; Cassuto, *Exodus*, p. 280.

4. Jackson, *Essays*, p. 150.

5. Verse 32 could be regarded as in contrast in particular with v. 28 (the case without negligence) since there is no mention of the owner's life being put in jeopardy, or it could be regarded as in contrast with vv. 29-30 (the case with negligence) in which the כופר of v. 30 has been set at 30 shekels, or perhaps both simultaneously (with or without negligence one must compensate a slave's owner).

is the ambiguous status of the (permanent?[1]) slave, who is both his master's 'money' (cf. Exod. 21.21) and yet is certainly a human being. The former aspect requires the master to be compensated in accordance with the replacement value of the slave; the latter requires the ox to be stoned.

In this case a monetary value is set, namely 30 shekels, for the life of the slave to be paid to the master. This is but a 'representative' or 'fair value' price, which, at least for a woman would probably be higher than the average value, female slaves being priced lower than males.[2] Paul points out that this is the only place in Exod. 20.22–23.19 where a specific sum of money is recorded, in contrast with cuneiform law where the exact amount is almost always stated.[3] Payment to the master for his slave both compensates the master's economic loss and provides, for a slave without any family, a representative to seek 'justice' for his death.[4]

It is interesting to note that in each case of an ox goring a human, the female member of each social class is mentioned alongside her male counterpart, implying equality of value so far as the regulation is concerned (contrast Lev. 27.2-8). In the Mesopotamian parallels, no

---

1. If an indentured servant were in view (as in Exod. 21.2), the compensation to the master would be expected to vary with the amount of time still owed by the bondsman.

2. Prices varied according to age and sex of the individual slave as can be seen in the differing valuations of redemptive prices of persons given as votive offerings to YHWH in Lev. 27.2-8: from fifty shekels for a prime male to but three shekels for a female aged one month to five years. Paul (*Studies*, p. 83 n. 1) observes that 30 shekels was also the price of slaves in Nuzi. LH §252 records the amount as $\frac{1}{3}$ mina (= 20 shekels), while 30 shekels was the value of a free citizen's life (§251). G. Wenham, ('Leviticus 27.2-8 and the Price of Slaves', *ZAW* 90 [1978], p. 264 n. 2) indicates that the average price of slaves was 40 shekels at Ugarit, 50-60 in neo-Assyrian documents, 50 in neo-Babylonian documents. Dandamaev (*Slavery in Babylonia*, pp. 200-202, 395) notes from actual neo-Babylonian contracts that slave prices vary from as little as 8 shekels for a slave girl to as much as 4 minas (240 shekels) in an unusually high instance, with one mina (60 shekels) being the 'normal' price for that period. The weight of a shekel varies by time and place (W. von Soden, '*šiqlu(m)*', *Akkadisches Handwörterbuch*, III, p. 1248), and the purchasing value of the 'shekel' depreciated over time. Lev. 27.3 specifies the shekel 'by the sanctuary weight' (Tanakh), implying other valuations existed.

3. Paul, *Studies*, p.83.

4. Similarly, Greenberg, 'More Reflections', p. 14.

explicit mention of the female counterparts are made.[1]

With Pericope B (21.33-34) the lawgiver temporarily leaves the realm of goring oxen and goes to that of pits. Someone who negligently forgets to cover a pit and thereby indirectly causes the death of another person's ox or donkey when it falls to its death in the pit must make restitution by giving the value of the animal to its owner. The lawgiver does not require the negligent party to give the animal's owner a windfall by both paying the price of the animal and allowing the animal's owner to keep the carcass, which was of some value for its meat and hide. The animal's owner is due only the exact value of what he lost.

As for the problem of Pericope B, the interruption of regulations by what seems parenthetical or even irrelevant material is a feature that recurs frequently among these laws (20.24b; 21.16; 21.22-25; 22.1-2b; 22.10; 23.4-5; 23.13). Besides whatever 'practical value' this 'sandwiching' of material may have had, the frequent usage of this structuring suggests that this is part of the lawgiver's style.

In this case the structuring is not without practical value. Finkelstein has provided a good explanation for the 'interruption' caused by Pericope B. According to him, the 'logical sequence' as Daube would perceive it is actually disruptive to the author's ideological intention:

> This break in the sequence is very telling. The biblical author is, in effect, warning us that those cases in which the victim of the goring ox was another ox are of an entirely different legal order from those cases in which the victim was human. The sharpest way in which the biblical writer could make this distinction, other than by stating his juristic principles explicitly, was by breaking up the sequence as he did. We may perhaps even be driven to posit that the biblical writer was conscious of a sequence of goring ox laws in a non-Hebraic prototype, such as that illustrated in the Laws of Eshnunna, in which no apparent distinction was made between cases in which the victim was human and those in which

---

1.   LH §§250-52 and LE §§53-55. The lack of explicit mentioning of the female in these Mesopotamian laws does not necessarily imply that the legal principles expressed in them applied only to men. I merely observe that the regulations in Exod. 21.28-32 are uniquely unambiguous. Cf. A. van Selms, 'The Goring Ox in Babylonian and Biblical Law', *ArOr* 18.4 (1950), pp. 321-30; R. Yaron, 'The Goring Ox in Near Eastern Laws', in *Jewish Law in Ancient and Modern Israel* (ed. H.H. Cohn; New York: KTAV, 1971), pp. 50-60 [= *Israel Law Review* 1 (1966), pp. 396-406]; J.J. Finkelstein, *The Ox that Gored* (Philadelphia: American Philosophical Society, 1981), pp. 20-25.

the victim was another ox. We might then be entitled to perceive in the author's rearrangement of the material an implicit rejection of the Mesopotamian classificatory principle: by breaking up the series he reasserts the biblical outlook.[1]

The author, according to Finkelstein, avoids blurring the distinction between human and animal by placing the parenthetical Pericope B between those having to do with goring oxen. He was thereby intentionally avoiding the 'logical' sequence that Daube and others would have liked to have seen to further his ideology of the supremacy of man in the divine hierarchy (cf. the discussion of Gen. 9.5 below).

Pericope B forms the center of the semi-chiastic structure, forming a transition between the other two pericopes. In Pericope B, as in Case 2 of Pericope A, the owner is accountable, but unlike Pericope A no transcendent life value is involved, for only animal rather than human life is lost; hence, there is no question of either executing or ransoming the owner. Like Sub-category B of Case 2, the amount paid corresponds to the value of the 'commodity' lost, but Sub-category B differs in that transcendent life value is involved as indicated by its ordering the stoning of the ox. Pericope B corresponds most closely with Case 2* of Pericope A* in that the owner is accountable and bears full loss but no more and no transcendent life value is involved.

The last pericope, Pericope A* (Exod. 21.35-36), returns to the goring ox, though in this case its offense is against another ox rather than a human. Since it is introduced by כי rather than אם, Pericope A* is grammatically independent of Case A. Were Pericope A* a later supplement to Pericope A as Daube supposes, אם would have been more appropriate.

Pericope A* is similar to Pericope A in that it begins with a case in which there is not negligence (Case 1*, v. 35; parallel with Case 1, v. 28), and then follows with a case in which there is negligence (Case 2*, v. 36; parallel with Case 2, vv. 29-32). As in the case of the uncovered pit the negligent owner of the goring ox is responsible for paying the owner of the dead ox the full price of the ox on the principle of '[full value of] ox in exchange for ox' (cf. 21.23-25 'life for life, eye for eye...' that also implies monetary payment). Again there is no bonus for the dead ox's owner, since the carcass goes to the owner of the goring ox. The dead ox's owner receives the exact full amount of the animal lost while the negligent owner of the goring ox

1. Finkelstein, *Ox*, p. 37.

takes the loss, which is the difference between the value of a live ox and a dead ox.

The point of the last part of v. 36, that the owner of the goring ox keeps the value of the dead ox's hide and flesh, might have been lost were it not for the insertion of vv. 33-34. What Pericope B and Pericope A* have in common is that despite the negligence of the owner of the pit or goring ox, where no human person is physically (maimed or) killed, the owner of the victim is not benefited by the loss. He receives no windfall by receiving both replacement value and keeping the carcass, but in both cases the owner of the victim receives only the replacement value for the loss of his animal while the negligent owner is allowed to keep the carcass.

This is in contrast to Pericope A (the goring of a human) where the ransom (v. 30) for the negligent owner's life may well exceed the value of the life of the victim (as determined by the value of his estate) since the negligent owner could lose his entire fortune if such is the ransom required of him. It is the value of the negligent owner's estate, not the value of the victim that is determinative. It is also true in the case of the slave where 30 shekels might be taken as a 'top dollar' price for a male slave, and is in any case more than the value of a very old or young or infirm slave (cf. Lev. 27.2-8).

Thus in both cases where the victim is human, the case of a free citizen and the case of a slave, the family/owner of the human victim can (in case of negligence) receive a windfall. In contrast, the owner of an animal victim can never receive a windfall. Or to put it differently, in the case where the victim is human, the negligent owner pays in two ways (loss of his ox and loss of his life/ransom); whereas with the animal victim, he pays less than once (exact replacement value alone, less salvage value of the dead animal). Thus the author has again underscored his ideology that places cases where the victim is human on an entirely different level than cases where the victim is animal.

Having observed this, it now becomes clear that Pericope B (vv. 33-34), the seeming insertion, actually forms a bridge between Pericope A, Case 2, Subcategory B (v. 32, the goring of a slave) and Pericope A* (vv. 35-36, the goring of an ox) that follows. The goring of the slave (v. 32) features a victim who is both human and property. Because he is property the master must be compensated for the loss of the slave's services, but because he is human the compensation can be more than one-for-one replacement. Pericope B moves to a case in which the victim is mere (live) property, and accordingly the negligent party pays only the replacement value of the dead animal. Pericope A* (ox gores an ox) continues discussion of cases where the victim is property, distinguishing between the penalty of a case without negligence (Case 1*, v. 35) and one with negligence (Case 2*, v. 36). Case 1* is parallel with Case 1 (v. 28), but the penalty is quite different: loss of a whole ox in the case of a human, loss of less than half of an ox for the non-negligent loss of an ox. Likewise Case 2* is parallel with both Case 2 (vv. 29-32, negligent death of a human) and Pericope B (vv. 34-35, negligence with pits) in that negligence is involved, but in penalty Case 2* corresponds only with Pericope B (payment of one-for-one replacement value only, less salvage value of the dead animal) and not Case 2 (death of ox and ransom [or 30 shekels if slave]).

Thus the transition serves to underscore that a case where an ox gores an ox is like the transitional Pericope B and not like Pericope A where an ox gores a human. Hence Pericope B by its interruption of the cases involving goring oxen and by the differences in penalties involved indicates that the case of an ox goring an ox is an entirely different category from that of an ox goring a man.

Before leaving Pericope A*, some similarities and differences in language between it and Pericope A can be noted. It is not clear on the basis of a discourse-oriented approach rather than source-oriented ones (which can explain these differences on the basis of different sources or textual corruptions) why vv. 35-36 introduces נ.ג.ף ('smite, plague') rather than נ.ג.ח ('push, gore') which was previously used to describe the goring action of the ox,[1] why אוֹ ('or', 'alternatively') is used rather than אם,[2] and why נוֹדע[3] is used for הוּעד.

As for הוּעד 'warned' and נוֹדע 'made known', there is perhaps a difference in nuance. הוּעד could be taken as the stronger term ('warned,

---

1.   Jackson (*Essays*, p. 143) takes יגּף (root נ.ג.ף) of v. 35 to be a corruption for יגּח (root נ.ג.ח). The LXX makes no distinction in its translation of the verbs.

2.   Jackson (*Essays*, pp. 151-152) takes the use of אוֹ to be a shorthand device used to introduce a new condition with a minimum of repetition (cf. Num. 35.18), though, as we have seen, אם clauses can be elliptical as well.

3.   It could be a textual corruption, in which נוֹדע and הוּעד have somehow been confused with metathesis of the final letters. Paul (*Studies*, p. 80 n. 5) records the suggestion of Goetze that v. 29 originally read הוֹדע rather than הוּעד.

testified to' by someone else) and נודע as a weaker term ('known, acquainted with the fact that' whether it was noticed by others or not). If so, it is easier to be held accountable for negligence in the case of an animal where the penalty is less than in the case of a person, where the negligent owner in principle forfeits his life. This slight change in vocabulary may develop the author's ideological purpose in distinguishing cases involving humans from those involving animals.

There may also be a difference in nuance between נ.ג.ח ('gore') and נ.כ.ה ('smite') which also reflects the author's distinction between human and animal, though the philological evidence is not unequivocal.[1] In the case of a human, the immediate cause of death would in every case be the animal's 'goring'. In the case of an animal's 'smiting' another animal, however, death could be indirect. The verb נ.כ.ה can refer both to injuries less serious than death as well as deadly injuries (cf. Exod. 21.22; Ps. 91.12). In the case of an ox smiting another ox, the term 'smite' could include serious maiming or a breaking of the other ox's limb in which case the owner might be compelled to put the miserable creature to death. Since this would ordinarily not be contemplated for a person who is maimed, the change in vocabulary could well again express a distinction between humans and animals.

Of course, differences in language and vocabulary between vv. 28-29 and 35-36 may simply serve to make the style less tedious rather than to provide any real difference in meaning. This is my only discourse-oriented explanation for the use of או rather than אם.

Exodus 21.28-36: Law or Morality?
To what extent can the regulations of the goring ox and the negligent owner of a pit be regarded as law enforced by society as opposed to being statements of morality regardless of their actual enforcement as law?

In favor of interpreting this unit as law is the fact that some of this material is related to, possibly borrowed from, Mesopotamian legal traditions.[2] The formulations are 'legal' and impersonal, and the regu-

---

1. In support of נ.כ.ה simply meaning 'to gore', cf. the Akkadian *nakapu* which seems to be a cognate and is used in the parallel cuneiform laws in LE §§53-54 and LH §§250-51 in the sense of 'gore' and the cognate in Talmudic Aramaic and Hebrew נ.ק.ף I = נ.ג.ח according to M. Jastrow, *A Dictionary of the Targumim* (Brooklyn: P. Shalom, 1967), p. 934.
2. M. David, ('The Codex Hammurabi and its Relation to the Provisions of

lations are very specific rather than giving general moral principles. True law must be enforced by society, and accordingly, the society is involved in stoning the ox that gores a human to death. As a practical matter, judges or arbitrators would need to be involved in setting ransoms and in determining damages and liability. All this suggests that this material should be read as law.

On the other hand, even what Mesopotamian legal traditions record is not necessarily enforced 'law' in the strict sense. Finkelstein argues that legal *forms* sometimes convey something other than a legal *message*:

> Mesopotamian penalty prescriptions... were not *meant* to be complied with literally even when they were first drawn up, any more than the equally offending biblical rules, be it the goring ox laws, the *ius talonis*, or others... we must recognize that both the biblical and Mesopotamian statements serve an admonitory function.[1]

To support this statement he refers to LH §230 and §218. In §230 it is stated that should a builder build a house that collapses and kills the son of the house owner, the son of that builder is to be put to death. What, Finkelstein asks, if the owner does not have a son? Would a daughter do? What if he had no daughter either? It can be readily seen that in some instances this would be an enforceable regulation, yet despite its absurdity in at least some cases, it retains value as an admonitory principle. This admonition could be rephrased, 'Woe to the contractor who undertakes construction and in his greed cuts corners, or is otherwise careless in his work to the point of endangering life and limb.'[2] Even more absurd, if applied literally, is

---

Law in Exodus', *OTS* 7 [1950], pp. 149-78) and van Selms ('The Goring Ox', pp. 328-39) minimize the connections between cuneiform law and biblical regulations. Yaron ('The Goring Ox', p. 53) disagrees with van Selms in divorcing biblical regulations from ancient Near East legal collections, based on LE §53, a text which was unavailable to van Selms. LE §53's being almost identical with Exod. 21.35 demands, in Yaron's view, much greater dependence of biblical laws on cuneiform ones than David and van Selms allow. Schwienhorst-Schönberger (*Bundesbuch*, pp. 267-68) speculates that these laws developed from a combination of received Mesopotamian laws, local legal practice, and the innovations of legal scholars at the Israelite scribal schools. My view is that the biblical author is not merely quoting previous laws, but has freely modified them to reflect his own ideology.

1.   Finkelstein, *Ox*, p. 35.
2.   Finkelstein, *Ox*, pp. 34-35.

the statement in LH §218, that states that a physician whose patient dies in surgery or is blinded by the surgery is to have his hand cut off. If applied literally as law, Finkelstein states, 'it is inconceivable that any sane person in ancient Mesopotamia would ever have been willing to enter the surgeon's profession.'[1] It was, as law, absurd and unenforceable. But if taken as a hyperbolic admonition for physicians to take care in the performance of their duties, it makes a telling, one might say 'cutting', point.

So it is with the goring ox regulation in the Bible. With the negligent owner of an ox who kills a man, a death sentence is passed: 'the ox must be killed and the owner is to die.' There is good reason to suppose that this sentence is given not because the author expects it to be carried out—he expects the ox's owner to ransom himself as v. 30 goes on to suggest—but to say in the strongest possible fashion, 'woe to him who in flagrant disregard of human life allows his dangerous ox to go about unrestrained.' The form may be legal, but the intent is moral.

The conventional view of Exod. 21.29-30 is that this regulation decrees death to the ox owner guilty of negligent homicide unless the family of the victim (perhaps in conjunction with the civil authorities) is willing to accept ransom. Finkelstein even argues that the wording 'if a ransom is imposed upon him' implies that the lawgiver is reluctant to make this exception, that allowing the owner to be ransomed is a resolution that does not totally meet with the lawgiver's approval.[2] But if it did not meet with his approval, why did he not leave it out? It seems better to suppose that at minimum the author considered this provision of a ransom for the owner appropriate in at least some cases.

The 'ransom' (כֹּפֶר) of v. 30 is not a fine for negligence, but rather a substitution of a monetary payment for the 'life' of the negligent owner by which he placates or mollifies the victim's family, thereby settling the grievance between the family and the offending party.[3] On

---

1.   Finkelstein, *Ox*, p. 35.

2.   Finkelstein, *Ox*, pp. 29-30.

3.   כֹּפֶר 'ransom' is related to כָּפַר 'to atone'. A. Schenker ('כֹּפֶר et expiation', *Bib* 63 [1982], pp. 32-46) argues on the basis of Exod. 21.28-32, Gen. 32.21, and Prov. 16.14 that כֹּפֶר means a 'placating' or a 'mollifying', closely related to expiation of cultic terminology where God is expiated. Brichto, ('Slaughter and Sacrifice', pp. 27-28) suggests that כֹּפֶר is most closely approximated by the term 'composition'

the principle of 'life for life' (cf. 21.23) the negligent owner, having allowed his ox to take a human life, had in principle forfeited his own life. Yet because it was not a matter of intentional homicide in which ransom was forbidden (Num. 35.31), he could, with the agreement of the victim's family, be saved from execution by a monetary payment. The amount of payment is left open, possibly due to the lawgiver's reluctance to place a monetary value on human life,[1] for the only thing really commensurate with the life of a victim would be another human life.

The possibility of ransom in v. 30 is not a begrudging exception by the lawgiver but the presumed normal resolution of the situation described. A victim's family would have little to gain by having the negligent owner put to death, whereas if they accepted a ransom, they would both punish the culprit and compensate themselves for the economic loss of one of their members. Even if the owner had no money he could be sold into servitude to gain the price of his life. Killing him would be the waste of a valuable asset.

Moreover, an Israelite would be reluctant to invoke the death penalty in the case of negligent homicide on the moral ground that such a punishment would be excessive for the crime. There is a danger here of reading modern values into an ancient culture, but there is also a danger of an unjustified modern condescension towards the moral thinking of the ancients. It is not just modern people who would find the death penalty in this case objectionable. More than a millennium and a half ago, the rabbis of the Talmudic period sensed that the actual execution of the owner was excessive, and accordingly presumed that the ransom option was the one always taken in a case such as this.[2] The parallel in LH §251 prescribes a monetary penalty of $\frac{1}{2}$ mina of silver rather than death under these circumstances. As for the lawgiver himself, capital punishment is excessive in comparison with the lawgiver's moral/legal system as found in other cases of manslaughter. In the case of accidental manslaughter, the manslayer might well have been regarded as negligent in not looking where he

---

in its legal sense, the settling of differences or an 'imbalance' between two parties, and thus restoring equilibrium. כּוֹפֶר and פִּדְיֹן represents the same payment from different perspectives: the former 'satisfies' the offended party, the latter 'saves' the offending party from distress.

1. Patrick, *Law*, p. 251.
2. Finkelstein, *Ox*, p. 31. Cf. *b. B. Qam.* 40b-c; *m. B. Qam.* 4.5.

threw his stone or not checking to see that his ax head could not slip off the wood (Exod. 21.12-15; Num. 35.9-15; Deut. 19.1-13), yet according to biblical law his life is threatened only if he leaves the city of refuge. Why should the penalty be so much harsher against one guilty of negligent homicide via his animal?

On the basis of objective guilt (he killed another human) he deserves to die, but because he is subjectively innocent (there was no intent to kill), he may ransom his life and live. This whole matter relates to the so-called *lex talionis*. I have already argued in Chapter 4 that 'life for life, eye for eye...' reflects a system of ransom or כּוֹפֶר in which a monetary payment served as a substitute for literal maiming.

In sum, there are good reasons for understanding ransom as the author's expected outcome. But why, in this case, does the author say, 'and its owner will also be killed' if he expects this rarely if ever to be the outcome? First, the mood of the imperfect verb in the death sentence could be rendered, 'and its owner *deserves* to be killed' rather than '*must*'. Second, putting it so starkly is a provocative way of underscoring the seriousness of negligence leading to human death. Merely having the culprit pay a fine would not show the seriousness of his offence. The present formulation makes clear that there is nothing which the guilty party can pay that would make up for the human life lost, for the only thing commensurate with a human life is another human life. Yet the lawgiver knows that capital punishment is excessive in this case. Hence, after condemning the man with the hyperbole of a death sentence, he provides for a ransom so that it is not normally carried out. The pronouncement of capital punishment is more moral admonition than genuine law.

It is interesting that there is no reference to any court or judge in this unit. The expression הוּעַד ('warned, testified to', v. 29) might be interpreted as 'warned by community officials'. This is the usual interpretation of the Akkadian *babtum* 'the ward/quarter of the city', in the parallels in LE §54 and LH §251. There the *babtum* makes known to the owner that his ox was a gorer, *babtum* being generally taken as a metonym for the authorities of the neighborhood. But Exod. 21.29 does not specify the one doing the warning. This is rather vague for a 'law'. The ransom in v. 30 is probably lain on the negligent owner by the victim's family (no doubt with witnesses from the community) rather than being laid down by judges.[1]

1. Paul, *Studies*, p. 82 n. 1. Contrast Phillips, *Criminal Law*, pp. 89-91, who

It is unquestionable that as a practical matter in the real world courts and judges would be necessary in cases such as these. But this passage need not be read as being about effective law. Instead, it can be read as telling the Israelite what is the right thing to do. If he negligently causes the death of his neighbor's animal (Case 2*, Pericope A*), he should take responsibility and pay his neighbor for his loss. There is only need for a court or state enforcement if one or the other party fails to do the moral thing or if there is disagreement over the facts.[1] In the case of the ox goring an ox where responsibility cannot be determined (Case 1*, Pericope A*), there being a presumption of innocence on the part of both owners, the right thing to do is to share in one's neighbor's suffering rather than leaving him to bear the entire loss. The lawgiver requires the owners to split the losses, selling the living ox and dividing its value, and dividing the carcass of the dead ox (or its value) and sharing the loss equally (v. 35).

Finkelstein shrewdly observes that this represents a primitive form of 'shared risk' accident insurance:

> [Rather than 'letting the losses fall where they may'] The principle of 'loss distribution' is invoked instead: An unforeseen accident ought not to be an occasion on which one party is made to bear the entire loss; the loss must be borne by both parties equally. We may legitimately view this resolution of the case as a perception—however simplistic or crude—of the social need for a form of loss equalization or distribution which in modern times has been supplied by the more complex institution of accident insurance.[2]

He goes on to state why this rule is needed:

> In the absence of grounds for imputing fault to either party... the society feels that it would be contrary to its sense of justice to allow the full burden of the loss to be borne by the owner of the dead ox while leaving the owner of the goring ox without any liability at all. To have adopted such a position would surely have engendered resentment and ill will that might very well have led to some overt act on the part of the owner of the

dubiously sees everything as the state intervening, and the ransom's amount determined by assessors (פללים) appointed by the court as in Exod. 21.22.

1.   Jackson (*Essays*, p. 131) suggests that in the case of an ox goring an ox (v. 35), some independent tribunal would be necessary to divide the value of the ox sold and carcass (if sold). But this is true only if one party or the other has reason to doubt the honesty of his neighbor.

2.   Finkelstein, *Ox*, p. 23.

dead ox against the other party and thus have touched off a chain of *socially* harmful consequences. In this instance therefore, the goal of the adjudication, which cannot be divorced from what the society perceived as the ends of justice, is the restoration of communal equilibrium.[1]

If one's animal causes the death of another human being, the right thing to do is to have one's animal stoned to set right this violation of the divine hierarchy that threatens the community with divine wrath (see below). If one's animal causes the death of a human being through one's negligence, the right thing to do is to offer one's own life to the victim's family, to give whatever they think fair, to atone for one's negligence.

This approach assumes that general principles can be derived from these specific regulations, in other words, that the regulations are paradigmatic of a broader reality than the specific cases listed.[2] This is not without some basis in the text. In the case of the pit (21.33-34), the expression 'ox or donkey' is a merismus for domestic animals of whatever sort. Clearly, the same principle would apply if it were a sheep. In other words, the author is saying that this is not to be read as if only this specific case were in view, but broadly. It has been the traditional interpretation of biblical 'law' that this is true everywhere. As Maimonides put it, 'The Scripture speaks not of the ox but as an instance.'[3] Each example is a particular embodiment of principles that are not necessarily stated as such, but are implied, and can be derived from the particular regulations.

Jackson opposes the paradigmatic nature of this and other 'legal' texts.[4] Part of the objection is epistemological: Jackson thinks that scholars who search for principles in law cannot but be influenced by their own legal, theological and other preconceptions, and would thereby derive 'principles' that would never have occurred to the lawgiver. He also questions whether 'principles' can be rightly deduced from particular cases. For example with Exod. 21.35, he notes that principles could be drawn from the case with various degrees of

1. Finkelstein, *Ox*, p. 36.
2. What Westbrook (*Studies*, p. 77 n. 156) says of cuneiform law applies well to biblical: 'Jackson... argues that Babylonian law dealt in cases, not principles. We would argue that it dealt in principles but could only express them as cases. The principles can be extracted, but by applying the *native* cultural and social concepts.'
3. Cited by Bush, *Exodus*, II, p. 22.
4. Jackson, *Essays*, pp. 30-34.

abstraction: one person's ox gores another person's ox to death, one person's ox gores another person's animal to death, one person's animal kills another person's animal, one person's property damages another person's property. Jackson believes it to be impossible to determine the degree of abstraction intended in the assumed 'underlying principle'.

Moreover, Jackson accuses Greenberg and Finkelstein of reading into the laws items that are not there. For example, with Exod. 21.35, where an ox gores an ox, the principle of 'loss distribution' that Finkelstein derives from the outcome requires also an assumption that the two oxen were of equal value to begin with, for if they were not, a literal application of the regulation would result in non-equal cost distribution contrary to the supposed principle.[1] Having derived the 'principle', Finkelstein must come back to Exod. 21.35 and say that it was not intended to be applied literally if the oxen were of unequal value, something about which the text is silent.

Jackson's legal analysis of Exod. 21.35 does show the unsophisticated nature of the biblical regulation, but he draws the wrong conclusion from this. He concludes from the paucity of cases covering various possibilities that occur to him as a lawyer that this one rule must have applied literally as stated even if the oxen were of different value. But his mechanical reading of the regulation is absurd in that it would result in cases where the literal application of the original rule in instances where the oxen differ greatly in value would obviously be grossly unfair. It is true, as Jackson implies, that ancient notions of 'fairness' might be quite different from what modern interpreters might suppose 'fair', but Jackson exaggerates this possibility. The notions of morality or fairness in ancient and modern cultures, and indeed all cultures, do not differ radically, but rather have much more in common than they differ. On that assumption, what seems clearly 'unfair' to us can be assumed likely to have seemed unfair to the ancients as well unless there is clear evidence to the contrary.

The unsophisticated nature of the biblical regulation ought rather to be interpreted as evidence that this was not intended as positive law to be inflexibly applied, but as paradigmatic illustrations of the kinds of resolution of grievances that should take place in Israelite society. Jackson misreads it all as 'law' in the modern, narrow sense of that term. It is more fruitfully read as morality.[2]

---

1. Jackson, *Essays*, p. 133.
2. Westbrook (*Studies*, p. 77) correctly notes that cuneiform law was likewise

Exodus 21.28-32 and the 'Priestly Code'

In order to understand rightly the rationale for 'stoning' the ox in Pericope A (21.28-32), it is necessary to refer to passages in the so-called Priestly Code of the Pentateuch, namely Genesis 1 and 9 that explicitly state the ideology inherent in this regulation. The close relationship between a 'P' source and this passage supports my thesis that Exod. 20.22–23.19 is well integrated into the Pentateuch.

If an ox gores a human being to death, the ox is to be stoned to death (v. 28). The same rule applies whether the victim is a freeborn member of the household (v. 31), or a slave (v. 32), but evidently it does not apply if the victim is another ox since the text on an ox goring another ox (vv. 35-36) is silent about the fate of the offending ox.[1] Mere viciousness is not a sufficient criterion for killing the ox. Moreover, if the motive were simply utilitarian, that is, to remove a dangerous animal, there would be no need to specify the mode of killing ('stoning') nor any purpose in prohibiting the use of its flesh, as van Selms points out.[2] Parallel regulations in LE §54-55 and LH

not read mechanically as inflexible statutes. After a discussion of the relationship of Babylonian law codes and actual legal documents from the period, he concludes: '[The court] looked to the code, not for an exact, mechanical precedent, but for the *principle* [italics mine] that the code indirectly laid down through its examples.' Such a method allows for exceptions from the code's decision based on individual circumstances.

1. Westbrook (*Studies*, p. 86) rightly warns in the context of this passage that arguments from silence are dangerous. Here, however, the lawgiver would be expected to repeat his statement about the fate of the ox because he did so in the case of the slave and because he has gone out of his way to separate the cases of an ox goring a man from those of an ox goring an ox, making ellipsis unlikely.

2. Van Selms, 'The Goring Ox', p. 329. Finkelstein (*Ox*, pp. 56-57) cites T.H. Gaster (*Myth, Legend, and Custom in the Old Testament* [New York: Harper & Row, 1969], p. 250) who presents a utilitarian argument for stoning and not eating the flesh:

> obviously, one could not risk getting too close to a habitual gorer as to be able to dispatch it in the normal way by slitting its throat! The further provision against eating its flesh would then be nothing other than the normal Hebrew prohibition against eating of any animal that had not actually been slaughtered.

Finkelstein counters that this rule applies not only to habitual gorers, but to first-time, even inadvertent gorers who might not be particularly dangerous. Moreover, there would be ways of incapacitating even a habitual gorer to dispatch it in such a way so as not to waste its precious meat. Hence the biblical provision must be more than utilitarian. Westbrook (*Studies*, pp. 86-88) takes a utilitarian approach which sees

§250-52, as van Selms also points out, make no mention of the stoning of the ox, the taboo status of its flesh, or the possible execution of a negligent owner.[1] The concern of the two cuneiform law collections is economic: to compensate the victim's family for their loss. The biblical regulation has more complicated, religious motives: The flesh is not eaten because a murderous ox is 'unclean' and 'laden with guilt'.

It is sometimes said that the stoning of an ox that gores reflects a primitive idea of guilt in which animals are considered 'guilty' of murder and tried and executed for their crimes. According to this view, primitive societies, unlike us moderns, did not discriminate between reasoning beings, that is humans, and other entities.[2] This view of the ancient outlook, however, is far too patronizing.[3] There is no evidence of any trial here. Furthermore, as Finkelstein argues, the rationale is likely more complicated:

> 'Guilt' or 'innocence' of the offending object or animal is immaterial; it offends solely because it has become the source of contamination and hence poses a danger to the well-being of the larger community.[4]

He adds elsewhere,

> The ox is to be executed, not because it committed a crime, but rather because the very act of killing a human being—voluntarily or involuntarily—had rendered it an object of public horror. The horror is engendered by the implications of such a killing: the animal was seen as a living rebuttal of the divinely ordained hierarchy of creation; by an action that itself could not be judged on a moral standard the ox turned into an instrument that undermined the moral foundations of the universe.[5]

the animal killed to subdue a threat to society, but he adds a cultic twist to this to explain the mode: stoning is preferred since the ordinary dispatching of the animal would be considered a sacrifice to deity, but such sacrifice was unacceptable for two possible reasons. Either (1) the ox having killed a man was regarded as unfit for sacrifice, having a moral, if not a physical, blemish, and/or more likely (2) allowing the owner to sacrifice his animal allowed him unfairly to profit (via divine blessing in reciprocation for the sacrifice) from the unfortunate event.

1.   Van Selms, 'The Goring Ox', pp. 328-29.
2.   Driver, *Exodus*, pp. 220-21; J.G. Frazer, *Folklore in the Old Testament* (London, 1918), pp. 415-45, cited by Finkelstein, *Ox*, p. 55; Childs, *Exodus*, p.473.
3.   Finkelstein (*Ox*, pp. 48-85) examines the 'trials' of animals from ancient times through the Middle Ages into modern times, often showing that the ancients had a very sophisticated concept of what they were doing.
4.   Finkelstein, *Ox*, p. 28.
5.   Finkelstein, *Ox*, p. 70.

The ox that gores a man to death disrupts the divinely sanctioned hierarchy in which man in the image of God was to rule over the beasts (cf. Gen. 1.27-28). An animal that violates that hierarchy by homicide is to be killed, as is explicitly stated in Gen. 9.4-5. This is not because it was regarded to be guilty of criminal intent,[1] but because the failure of Israel to enforce the divine hierarchy would make the covenant community subject to divine wrath for allowing the violation of the divine order. A single act bringing the whole community into jeopardy is like the case of Achan, whose sin brought defeat upon the whole nation (Josh. 7).

To understand rightly the reason why the ox is stoned when it gores a human being to death, a reader must be acquainted with Gen. 1.26-30 and 9.1-6 where the hierarchy between man made in the image of God and beast (who is not in the image of God) is established. Permission is given man to take animal life, and death is decreed for man or beast that takes the life of a man. This helps to explain why the ox is stoned to death as a community execution rather than just killed, and why its flesh is not eaten. Greenberg states:

> The establishment of a value hierarchy of man over beast means that man may kill them—for food and sacrifice only (cf. Lev. 17.4)—but they may not kill him. A beast that kills a man destroys the image of God and must give a reckoning for it. Now this is the law of the goring ox in Exodus: it must be stoned to death. The religious evaluation inherent in this law is further evidenced by the prohibition of eating the flesh of the stoned ox. The beast is laden with guilt and is therefore an object of horror.[2]

The stoning of the ox is therefore a reflection of the value of human life vis-à-vis animal as reflected in the theology of Genesis. A vicious ox that gores a man to death is executed, while a vicious ox that gores another ox (vv. 35-36) apparently does not have to be because the

---

1.   Finkelstein goes too far in dispensing with the concept of the ox's guilt. Greenberg ('Asylum', p. 128) distinguishes between 'objective' and 'subjective' guilt: the latter involves criminal intent, the former comes from a criminal act with or without criminal intent. Hence, the accidental manslayer of Num. 35 is objectively guilty, even though he had intended no murder. Objective guilt for manslaughter without subjective guilt meant confinement to the city of refuge until the death of the high priest, while subjective guilt meant execution. The same concept applies in the case of the goring ox, according to Greenberg: 'Here, where there can be no intent since the killer is a brute, the law nonetheless regards the animal as bloodguilty and requires it to be stoned.'

2.   Greenberg, 'Postulates', p. 15.

latter ox has not violated the divine hierarchy.

The interpretation just given provides a rationale for the mode of killing the ox: community stoning. The community is threatened by this violation of the divine order in the universe; consequently, the community is involved in restoring the proper order by stoning the ox. Finkelstein states this well:

> Never is stoning prescribed for someone condemned to death for intentional homicide. Death by stoning, in biblical tradition and elsewhere in the ancient Near East, is reserved for crimes of a special character. In those cases there is no designated 'executioner', for the community assembled is the common executioner of the sentence. Offenses which entail this mode of execution must therefore be of a character that, either in theory or in fact, 'offend' the corporate community or are believed to compromise its most cherished values to the degree that the commission of the offense places the community itself in jeopardy.[1]

Whereas simple homicide is subject to execution by the sword (cf. Num. 35.19 and the use of פ.נ.ע 'strike with an instrument'), stoning is sanctioned for cases of a different sort: worship of a foreign god, a rebellious and disobedient son, a newly wed bride found not to be a virgin, fornicating couples, child sacrifice, sorcery and necromancy, 'blasphemy' against YHWH's name, violation of the Sabbath, and taking something under the 'ban' (Deut. 13.7-10; 21.18-21; 22.20-21; 22.22-24; Lev. 20.2; 20.27; 24.10-12; Num. 15.32-36; Josh. 7.16-26). Finkelstein points out:

> most if not all of these offenses would, in modern juristic terms, be categorized as 'victimless crimes'. They are at the same time crimes of the most serious kind for they are revolts against God, or the world order which is ordained by the divine word.[2]

Also with the goring ox, the offense is not only civil, but of a religious nature. Stoning expresses the community's religious outrage at the ox's usurping of man's rule over nature, perhaps leaving a lasting testimony of that outrage by burying the carcass under a heap of stones (cf. Achan, Josh. 7.26). Indeed, civil regulation here becomes intertwined with religious regulation.

The religious explanation of the stoning also helps to explain why the flesh of the ox could not be eaten. If the expression of outrage

1.   Finkelstein, *Ox*, pp. 26-27.
2.   Finkelstein, *Ox*, p. 28.

were memorialized by a heap of stones over the carcass, this would of course render the consumption of the flesh impossible. However, the mode of the ox's execution (stoning), even if there were no heap of stones, is possibly enough to render the creature unfit for human consumption along the lines of the rules of purity and impurity.[1] Moreover, the nature of the ox's offense would tend to make it unfit either for human consumption or as a sacrifice to God, having 'a moral, if not physical, blemish'.[2] This violation of the divine order by the ox's homicide makes the beast a 'horror' and ladens it with 'blood-guilt' (objective guilt even without subjective intent).[3] Blood-guilt produces pollution that must be expiated to be removed (Num. 35.33). Eating a beast laden with blood-guilt would bring this guilt and horror upon the consumers, and make them subject to divine wrath. By prohibiting the eating of the flesh, the regulation serves to express the lawgiver's outrage at a violation of the divine order and to underscore the value that he places on human life.

Drawing the background to the goring ox regulation from Genesis 1 and 9, and cultic law generally, must be troubling to a source-oriented critic since Genesis 1 and 9.5 belong to the so-called 'Priestly' source that is considered to date long after the 'Covenant Code'. How can the text draw upon material from a source subsequent to the 'Covenant Code'?

Two answers to this question can be given. From within a source-oriented perspective, Greenberg[4] can defend this connection by supposing that the ideology reflected in Gen. 9.1-6 existed before being written in the Priestly strata.

My answer is more radical, however. I assume that the editor(s) of the final form of the Pentateuch were aware of the material of Genesis 1 and 9 which establishes the hierarchy between man and beast and could assume that the reader of the Pentateuch would be aware of this as well. Hence, by the time of the final editing and regardless of what these laws may have looked like in their 'original' sources, the editor(s) of the final form of the Pentateuch, whether by deliberate modification of a cuneiform goring ox law, or by other received

---

1. Contra Finkelstein (*Ox*, p. 57) who argues against the idea that uncleanness is involved.
2. Westbrook, *Studies*, p. 87.
3. Keil, *Pentateuch*, p. 135: Greenberg, 'Postulates', p. 15.
4. Greenberg, 'Postulates', p. 15.

tradition, expressed the regulation on the goring oxen in such a way as to reflect the ideology of Genesis 1 and 9.

I conclude that Exod. 21.28-32 fits into the matrix of thought found in the 'P' source. This is consistent with my thesis that Exod. 20.22–23.19 is well integrated into the Pentateuch of which it is a part, even with regard to those portions considered to be 'late' by source critics.

Chapter 6

THEFT AND DAMAGE OF PROPERTY: EXODUS 21.37–22.16*

The regulations of this section involve offenses against the property of another person. This section follows a pericope treating offenses by the property of one person against that of another (the uncovered pit and the goring ox, Exod. 21.33-36), and shares with that section the characteristic expression 'he is to make [full] restitution' (שַׁלֵּם [שַׁלֵּם]) which does not occur elsewhere in this corpus. This unit can be further sub-divided into five sections:

i.   penalties for theft, especially of animals (21.37–22.3);
ii.   two cases of the destruction of crops (22.4-5);
iii. cases of suspected theft involving the loss or damage of bailments (22.6-12);
iv.   injury to a borrowed or rented animal (22.13-14); and
v.   the seduction of a man's virgin daughter (22.15-16).

The penalties here are generally much greater than for the offenses of culpable negligence against property in the previous section (21.33-36) where the offender was not directly guilty and derived no benefit from the damages.

Punishments for a Thief: Exodus 21.37–22.3
[English 22.1-4]

(21.37) Should (כִּי) a man steal a head of the herd or one of the flock, whether he has slaughtered it or sold it, five head of the herd he is to repay in exchange for the head of the herd, and four of the flock in exchange for one of the flock—(22.1) If the thief is found in the act of breaking in and is struck dead, there is no blood-guiltiness for [killing]

---

*   English Bible 22.1–22.17.

him.[1] But if [this occurs after] the sun has risen on him, then there is blood-guiltiness for [killing] him—He [the thief] must pay in full. If he has nothing to give, then he is to be sold [into servitude] for the amount of his theft. (3) If the theft is found in his possession alive, be it a head of the herd, a donkey, or one of the flock, then he is to repay [but] twofold.

Exodus 21.37–22.3 and Structure

The principle of organization within Exod. 21.37–22.3 is not easy to discern, especially as relates to 22.1-2a. Most source-oriented scholars regard these verses as an obvious interpolation that interrupts the flow of the law between 21.37 and 22.2b-3. Daube, for example, argues that the order is not particularly logical here:

> Surely, the natural order would be: first, compensation from a thief who has killed or sold the animal; next, compensation from a thief who has not, or not yet, killed or sold the animal; and last, the questions when I may slay a thief and what I am to do if the thief cannot pay.[2]

Daube argues that originally there were only two paragraphs: the first about damages that a thief pays when he has killed or sold the animal, and a second about when to slay a thief and what to do with a thief who cannot pay. Later a paragraph was added about damages payable by a thief who had not sold or slaughtered the animal, the new rule being placed, not where it belongs logically, but at the end of the appropriate legal paragraph following the older rulings.[3] This, he claims, reflects a stage of development in which customary restitution has gone from multiple to only twofold, and hence the addition reflects a reduction of penalties and required degree of proof of a later period.

Cazelles reviews various suggested rearrangements: moving the rule about killing a thief to 21.12ff. (Jepsen), moving 22.1-2a after v. 3 (Heinisch), or rearranging to read vv. 3, 2b, 1, 2a (Beer).[4] The NEB follows Heinisch's rearrangement of the text in its translation.

My goal in this section is not to refute the various source-oriented explanations of the arrangement, but to ask whether or not a plausible

---

1. The expression דמים לו in 22.1, 2 ('blood-guilt for him') is often taken in the sense 'blood-guilt for the owner'. But the only possible antecedent in the text is 'the thief'.
2. Daube, *Biblical Law*, p. 89.
3. Daube, *Biblical Law*, pp. 89-90.
4. Cazelles, *Études*, p. 63.

explanation can be given why an author or editor might have chosen the present ordering rather than one or another of those that modern scholars think more logical.

There have been other proposals for the present ordering more along discourse-oriented lines. Cassuto holds that the author is inserting moral and ethical commentary into a pre-existing legal statute that the author is quoting.[1] This thesis is difficult to prove, however. Moreover, there is little reason why an author could not have added his comments at the end of the paragraph rather than disrupting it.

Paul offers a somewhat different explanation. He regards 22.1-2a as a parenthetical remark or footnote. If an ancient author had a parenthetical thought to include in a discussion, he had no better technique than to insert the material in the midst of the text at the point in the discussion where the parenthetical thought was first brought to mind, and then after completing the parenthetical remark, to resume and complete the original discussion.[2] Such could be the case here. Similarly, Finkelstein sees 22.1-2a as an intentional, parenthetical thought. The lawgiver, although well into the laws on things, having left law on persons in 21.32, nonetheless is compelled at this point to recapitulate and emphasize the value of the life of the thief: that he is not to be killed except in self-defense. This digression was deliberate, and after making it he returns to the question of the burglar's liability.[3]

My interpretation builds on this parenthesis idea and attempts to show how this interpretation gives meaning to the MT ordering of the text.

Exod. 21.37–22.3 deals with penalties for theft, animal theft in specific. The general rule is that the thief must pay multiple restitution (four- or fivefold) to (it is implied) the owner as tort if he has disposed of the stolen beast by slaughtering or selling (21.37), but only twofold if the stolen item is found in his possession (21.3). Between these two injunctions are two other statements. The first is an aside on the question of blood-guilt if a thief is killed while breaking in (22.1-2a). This parenthesis is not irrelevant, for the context of a four- or fivefold penalty, severe as it is, prompts the legislator to note that the thief's

---

1. Cassuto, *Exodus*, p. 282.
2. Paul, *Studies*, p. 110 n. 1. He notes that such footnotes also occur in Talmudic regulations.
3. Finkelstein, *Ox*, p. 39.

life itself is not forfeit unless due to a compounding threat to the owner of a break-in by night. The second statement (22.2b) answers the question, 'What is one to do with a thief who cannot afford to pay the fine?' Answer: The several-fold penalty over and above the value of the animal stolen is assessed only against a thief who can afford to pay that fine. If the thief is too poor to afford to pay anything, he is to be sold into 'slavery' for a period of time commensurable with the value of the animal itself, but not necessarily with all of the several-fold fine.

It is natural that theft of animals would be treated first among regulations having to do with theft or damage of property since the several-fold penalty for animal theft is the most severe among the regulations listed. Subsequent sanctions are no greater than twofold.

After stating the ordinary penalty for theft, there follow in 22.1-2 statements that address questions which might be raised against this maximum penalty. First, is this penalty severe enough? Those ancient readers familiar with the legal traditions of Mesopotamia might suppose the penalty of 21.37 to be too light. After all, in Mesopotamia theft of an animal could require up to thirty-fold restitution and the death of the thief if he could not pay (LH §§8, 265; Hittite Laws §§57-59, 63, 67, 69).[1] Moreover, LH §21 requires any housebreaker to be executed and LE §13 requires the execution of the night house-breaker.[2] Is not death sometimes a legitimate punishment for a thief?

The author answers such an implied question in the negative. Whereas in some circumstances, as when a thief is breaking in at night, one might not be held accountable for taking the life of the thief (Exod. 22.1), this is not a matter of punishment but rather of self-defense. In contrast with Mesopotamian laws, the Bible says killing a thief brings blood-guilt on the slayer just as it would if he killed a non-thief (Exod. 22.2a). In other words, God does not sanction capital punishment for theft of property, and here offers legal protection for the thief.

Secondly, what then does one do with someone who cannot pay the

1.   Some Hittite theft laws, however, are more in keeping with biblical law: §70 that has twofold penalty where the animal is recovered as does the biblical regulation, and §128 that has twofold restitution for bricks.

2.   LE §13, 'A man who is caught in the house of a *muškenum*, in the house during the daytime, shall pay ten shekels of silver. He who is caught in the house at night shall die, he shall not get away alive' (*ANET*, p. 162).

fine? If a man is poor, stealing out of desperation, he would not be able to pay even single restitution for an ox, nor multiple restitution for the less expensive sheep; only a rich thief could do so. What is to be done in the case of a destitute thief? In answer, the author sets an alternative penalty for the poor: a thief is obligated to pay in full, but if he cannot do so, he by no means should be executed. Rather, he is to be sold into servitude, but only for the amount of time necessary to pay for that which he stole (Exod. 22.2b).

This interpretation takes בגנבתו in the sense of 'for the amount of the thing he stole', in which the ב is a beth of price. Another interpretation is that he becomes a (permanent?) slave 'for/because of his theft'. The ב in בגנבתו, is in my view, more naturally a beth of price in the context of fines for theft, and so taken, the expression 'for the amount of his theft' forms a striking contrast with the several-fold restitution of 21.37. Multiple restitution is meant to deter the rich man who could afford to pay it; a different rule applies to a poor one who, though not required to make full multiple restitution,[1] is nevertheless deterred by the potential loss of his freedom. Yet every thief, rich or poor, must pay for his theft somehow.

Having dealt with questions that might be raised against his penalty for the theft of livestock given in 21.37, the author then returns to the question of animal theft in which the stolen beast has not been disposed of. In that case, the normal minimum twofold restitution applies, which is the penalty elsewhere for stealing non-livestock.[2]

The analysis just given can be summarized in the following structure for Exod. 21.37–22.3:

1. According to Dandamaev (*Slavery in Babylonia*, pp. 63, 115, 395) the average price in sixth to fourth century BCE Babylonian was: oxen—40 shekels, sheep—two shekels, asses—30 shekels, wages for hired, unskilled workers—3 to 12 shekels per year, slaves—60 shekels. If the relative value of these commodities are close to those current at the time and place of our author, the fivefold penalty for stealing and slaughtering an ox would be much more than the price of a slave (cf. Exod. 21.32) and the penalty for the sheep would be the equivalent of 8 shekels, months of wages for a hied man. For a thief sold into slavery, the servitude probably would be no more than six years (cf. 21.2-6) if he stole an ox, even though this falls well short of the multiple restitution, while in the case of a sheep, a shorter period of servitude is required, just enough to pay the price owed.

2. Paul (*Studies*, p. 85) notes that a similar twofold restitution when an owner finds his stolen animal is found in Hittite Laws §70. For other twofold restitutions see Exod. 22.6, 8 and LH §§120, 124, 126.

A   Penalty for animal theft with disposal of stolen goods: fourfold or fivefold restitution. (21.37)

B   Comment on upper limits of this penalty: a thief can be killed only under special circumstances. Theft itself is not a capital offense. (Irrelevant if livestock involved, but giving principle). (22.1-2a)

B*   Comment on the lower limits of this penalty: if too poor to pay, the thief must at least work as indentured servant to pay off the amount stolen (not necessarily fully multiple). (22.2b)

A*   Penalty for animal theft with no disposal of goods: twofold restitution. (22.3)

Other Problems of Interpretation in Exodus 21.37–22.3

Several things have puzzled commentators in this passage. Why should the theft of an ox require greater restitution (fivefold) than the restitution for a sheep (fourfold)? Why should a stolen animal being found in someone's possession require only twofold restitution whereas once disposed of there is a required fourfold or fivefold; that is, why should disposal of the animal make any difference? Does the breaking in have to do with stealing livestock, or is it more generally the stealing of items from a home? Why does the sun having risen make any difference as to culpability in taking a thief's life during a theft?

It should not be surprising in an agricultural-pastoral economy that multiple restitution would be required in the case of sheep and cattle, for they are not only a herdsman's property, but also his livelihood, his means of production, his capital base or investment, so to speak. To steal these animals would be like stealing a carpenter's saw or a farmer's plough: it deprives the owner of both present and future benefits. Hence there is multiple restitution for this offense, but only twofold for other theft (cf. 22.6).

The reasoning for the difference between penalties for stealing a sheep (שה more properly a member of the צאן or small animal flock, whether a sheep or a goat) and an ox (שׁור more properly a member of the בקר or large cattle herd, regardless of sex or age) has been the subject of some discussion. Ibn Ezra suggests that stealing a sheep, which is smaller and easier to steal, is less serious a crime than stealing a large animal.[1] More convincing, however, is an explanation that is given by Philo. He attributes the fivefold restitution for an ox

---

1. 'The penalty for ox stealing is heavier because the thief cannot hide it as easily as a sheep. Only an expert thief can execute such an operation'. Quoted by Leibowitz, *Studies in Shemot*, II, pp. 367-68.

rather than fourfold for a sheep to the fact that, unlike the sheep, an ox was a beast of burden, capable of plowing and threshing, and so was significantly more valuable in the ancient economy.[1] Perhaps considered in this is the training that a beast of burden requires before it is capable of useful work. Hence stealing an ox, being more serious a crime than that of stealing a sheep, was assigned the greater penalty.

A basic issue in attributing blood-guilt to the slayer of a thief during the day and not doing so if at night seems to be the degree of danger between night- and daytime theft. The location of the situation described is the home.[2] The owner's act of killing such an intruder at night can be defended in principle as self-defense since in the dark the owner would be uncertain of the thief's intentions (whether theft or even murder) and degree of threat (armed or unarmed). The daytime thief, on the other hand, is generally less of a threat. An owner who catches him can more readily see whether the thief is armed, and there is less reason to resist the thief on the spot since the owner, having seen the thief, can later identify him after the community apprehends him. Given the lesser danger, the lawgiver regards the owner as culpable if he kills the thief.

As for why there is but a twofold restitution if the thief is caught

---

1.   Philo, *Spec. Leg.* 4.3. Less convincing is Philo's attempt to allegorize the four and five to four things that a sheep contributes (milk, cheese, wool, and lambs) and five things that a head of cattle does (milk, cheese, offspring, ploughing and threshing). Leibowitz (*Studies in Shemot*, II, pp. 366-67) notes that the rabbinic commentators Ibn Ezra, Saadya Gaon and the *Mekilta* expressed views similar to Philo's.

2.   B.S. Jackson (*Theft in Early Jewish Law* [Oxford: Clarendon Press, 1972], p. 49) takes the place to be a sheepfold rather than a house in order more closely to connect 22.1 with 21.37, but this view is rejected here for several reasons. Making the location a sheepfold completely undermines the moral principle which prohibits the killing of a thief except in self defense, since there would be no threat to the owner's life if the scene were a sheepfold. The connection with 21.37 is in any case a loose one since in 22.1-2a no theft (animal or otherwise) in fact takes place, only attempted theft, and therefore the premises and results of 21.37 could not apply. Even if animal theft were in view, the location can still be the home since livestock were often sheltered in a man's house (cf. 2 Sam. 12.2-3; 1 Sam. 28.24). More likely, however, 22.1-2a is not limited to animal theft, but is rather expressing a principle which applies regardless of the kind of theft. LE §§12-13 discuss day- and night-time theft both in house and barn.

with the stolen item in his possession, interpreters have offered a number of explanations of varying plausibility.

1.   Some say the animal might have sentimental value to its owner, so its actual return rather than its replacement is preferable.[1] This is far-fetched, however, since most sheep and cattle would be a part of a herd and sentiment is, in any case, a dubious category of value.

2.   Daube sees the key in the degree of proof. If the stolen animal were found in someone's possession, he could always claim that he did not steal but that it had wandered astray into his flock or herd, and that he planned to return it to its owner.[2] Since such a claim could not be disproved, the penalty was less. It seems strange, however, if this is the explanation, that the matter would not be dealt with in accordance with Exod. 22.8 in which the dispute over ownership is brought before האלהים.

3.   Westbrook[3] takes the person in whose possession the animal is found to be, not a thief, but an innocent buyer of stolen goods. Though he did not personally steal the item, he was nonetheless punished, though less severely than a thief, since mere possession of stolen goods, innocently or otherwise, was considered a crime. Westbrook's view sees logic in the present ordering of the text on the principle of descending seriousness: first, ordinary theft of an animal in which the penalty is a fixed ransom in lieu of death (21.37); next, attempted burglary in which the penalty is an unlimited ransom in lieu of slavery (22.1-2); and finally, an innocent possessor of a stolen item for whom the penalty is a fixed ransom in lieu of slavery (22.3). Westbrook's view suffers, however, from the antecedent of the 'him' in Exod. 22.3 being הַגַּנָּב ('the thief'). Moreover, Westbrook's version seems unjust: if the possessor is innocent, why is he fined at all?

4.   Another suggestion is that it is a greater crime to steal and dispose of the property than to steal only, because now the

---

1. Jackson (*Theft*, p. 134) mentions but rejects this view.
2. Daube, *Biblical Law*, pp. 91-93.
3. Westbrook, *Studies*, pp. 111-28.

thief has become 'rooted in sin'.[1] He has not only stolen, but disposed. A variation on this suggestion states that the thief, until he disposed of the goods, might possibly repent and return the goods. Perhaps the regulation offers less severe penalties when the goods have not been disposed of in hopes that this might lead the thief to repent.[2]

5.   The last view I shall cite is that of Abravanel.[3] Abravanel observes that the exact value of an animal would vary from individual to individual, depending on its age, sex, and condition. Once sold or slaughtered, its actual value would be impossible to determine. The thief would naturally claim that the animal he sold or slaughtered was of inferior quality. Four- or fivefold restitution would assure that, no matter how valuable the beast had been, its value would be more than covered by the restitution, assuring adequate compensation to the owner. If the actual animal is recovered, its value can be assessed, so only a twofold penalty is required.

These last two views, (4) and (5), seem to me to be the least open to criticism. They further fit in—as none of the others does—with an approach to the text that sees the formulations, for all of their legalistic quality, as pointing to principles for legal and moral concerns rather than as statutory enactments.

Exodus 21.37–22.3: Law or Morality?

To what extent can the regulations of Exod. 21.37–22.3 be regarded as law rather than morality? It can be readily admitted that the formulation is legal. However, that this is the only case in Exod. 20.22–23.33 dealing directly with theft, and that it does not deal with the theft of movables shows how incomplete these laws are. They were never intended to be a complete 'law-code'.

Granting the legal formulation of 21.37–23.4 in no way denies the essentially moral intent of the regulation. As law, the statement is incomplete. For example, even though 22.1-2a discusses house-

---

1.   Rabbi Akiva in *t. B. Qam.* 7, cited by Leibowitz, *Studies in Shemot*, II, p. 365. Cf. Noth, *Exodus*, p. 183.

2.   Ibn Ezra says, 'Perhaps he will be afraid. Whilst they are still alive he pays twofold, since he may change his mind and repent and restore his theft.' Quoted by Leibowitz, *Studies in Shemot*, II, p. 369. Similarly, Keil, *Pentateuch*, p. 137.

3.   Cited by Leibowitz, *Studies in Shemot*, II, p. 364.

breaking, it does not prescribe any penalty for this crime; rather, it makes the moral point about what the penalty should not be: death. The penalty if the thief is caught is not stated.

The moral and ethical intent of this passage can be seen in several places. For one, it underscores and deliberately expands on the statement in the Decalogue, 'You are not to steal.' A thief who is caught, whether rich or poor, should make restitution in accordance with the circumstances of his offense. On the other hand, in a humanitarian gesture to the poor thief, a distinction is made between rich and poor, so that the penalty on a poor thief is actually less than that required for a rich one in terms of the equivalent monetary value of his servitude.

The content of this passage is consistent with, and can be understood to reflect, the following moral principle: property is not commensurate with human life. Even the most serious case of theft of property is not an offense of such a magnitude as to justify capital punishment. This is in contrast with the offenses of 21.12-17 (intentional murder, physical abuse of parents, kidnapping, 'repudiation' of parents) where the offender deserves death. According to the lawgiver, killing a thief for any reason other than self-defense is murder.

Greenberg rightly sees here an ideology that values human life over property to a greater degree than was the case in Mesopotamia where both theft of property and breaking and entering could result in capital punishment,[1] whereas in the Bible crimes of property are generally not punishable with capital punishment, stealing an item under the 'ban' being the exception. The right to defend one's life from a night burglar is granted, but there is no general permission to kill a thief. Childs perceptively remarks: 'To my knowledge no other law code seems to have a similar concern for the life of the thief!'[2]

Other details of the text could be interpreted as having a moral intent, though there is danger here of an overly homiletical exegesis. For example, the twofold punishment here and elsewhere has sometimes been understood on the principle that the same punishment

1.   Greenberg, 'Postulates', p. 18. Paul (*Studies*, p. 86) notes that LE §§12-13, LH §§6-11, 21-22, 25 and MAL A §3 demand capital punishment for such crimes as breaking and entering, looting, trespassing, and theft. Note, however, that Hittite laws have no death penalty for theft except for Hittite Laws §126, for stealing a god's property.

2.   Childs, *Exodus*, p. 474.

which the thief sought to inflict on the owner ought to be inflicted
instead on him.[1] More promising is the view that sees the twofold
penalty if the animal has not been disposed of, rather than a fourfold
or fivefold restitution if it has, as the lawgiver's way of encouraging
the thief to repent rather than be confirmed in his thievery (this view
was discussed above). Jackson[2] correctly notes that a law could not be
expected to allow for such a possibility, for a thief who is caught with
the goods is not less guilty, only less successful. Yet if the regulation
here is not strictly legal but primarily moral in intent, it possibly
could envision such an eventuality.

Not all of these suggested moral purposes are equally probable, but
the general moral thrust seems clear.

Two Cases of Damage to Another's Field
Exodus 22.4-5 [English 22.5-6]

(4) Should (כי) someone graze bare a field or a vineyard; that is, he lets
loose his livestock and they grazed bare another man's field, he must pay
back the highest value of his [the other man's] field or the highest value of
his [the other man's] vineyard.

(5) Should (כי) a fire spread catching thorn bushes resulting in the
consuming of sheave-heaps or standing grain or whatsoever of the field,
then the one responsible for the setting of the blaze must make full
restitution.

The Text of Exodus 22.4-5 and the Meaning of ב.ע.ר
The interpretation of this verse is compounded by the textual variant
in v. 4 in which the LXX version and the Samaritan is considerably
longer than the MT.[3] Textual critics are divided as to whether the LXX

---

1.   Akedat Yizhak, cited by Leibowitz, *Studies in Shemot*, p. 362.
2.   Jackson, *Theft*, p. 134.
3.   Patrick (*Law*, p. 81), gives the following rendering based on the LXX of
22.4:

When a man causes a field or vineyard to be grazed or lets loose his
livestock and they feed on another's field [he shall make full restitution
from his field according to its yield; but if the whole field has been grazed
over] he shall make restitution from the best of his field or the best of his
vineyard.

The brackets show the portion which is in addition to the MT. In this version of the
law, the issue is one of the uncertainty in calculation. If only part of the field were

and Samaritan, or the MT are closer to the original text.[1] I will limit myself to trying to make sense out of the tradition represented by the MT.

In addition, and not unrelated to the textual question, there has been discussion on the meaning of the root ב.ע.ר in these two verses. ב.ע.ר is used in both vv. 4 and 5, but has traditionally been understood to be from two different roots: ב.ע.ר II meaning 'graze' and the related noun בעיר 'animals who graze, livestock, cattle' in v. 4, but ב.ע.ר I meaning 'burn' and its related noun בערה 'burning' in v. 5. A few interpreters have interpreted the root ב.ע.ר and the בעיר of v. 4 as 'burn' and 'burning', as in v. 5, since the meaning 'graze' is poorly attested for the verb ב.ע.ר and the idea of grazing a vineyard seems odd.[2] On the other hand, grapevines were planted far enough apart (eight to ten feet) for a crop to be grown between the vines, so that grazing a vineyard could mean grazing the crop between the rows.[3] Alternatively, the offense could refer to the trampling and killing of the vines while grazing the nearby grass.

The meaning 'graze' for the root ב.ע.ר can be defended. בעיר clearly has to do with livestock in Gen. 45.17; Num. 20.2, 8, 11, and Ps. 78.48. Moreover, in Isa. 3.14 and 5.5 Israel represented as a vineyard is clearly the object of the verb ב.ע.ר, consistent with the sense 'graze, feed on' for ב.ע.ר.[4] Isa. 3.14, 'You have consumed/grazed bare [בער] my vineyard', could represent an allusion to Exod. 22.4. It seems

---

burned, then the part not damaged would indicate the quality of the field. Hence, simple one-for-one restitution could be calculated and required. But if the whole field were destroyed, then it would be impossible to calculate the damage, so the worst case scenario is adopted to make sure the owner of the field is completely compensated.

1. Preferring the LXX and Samaritan are Childs (*Exodus*, p. 449) and Patrick (*Law*, pp. 80-81). Preferring the MT are D. Barthélemy, *et al.*, *Preliminary and Interim Report on the Hebrew Old Testament Text Project* (New York: United Bible Societies, 1979), I, pp. 118-19, though with considerable doubt; J.J. Rabinowitz, 'Exodus 22.4 and the Septuagint Version Thereof', *VT* 9 (1959), pp. 40-46, who argues that the LXX represents Alexandrian translators' doctoring the text to reflect Egyptian agricultural economy under Ptolemy II; and Durham (*Exodus*, p. 325). For earlier opinions, see Cazelles, *Études*, pp. 64-65.

2. Driver, *Exodus*, p. 225; Hyatt, *Exodus*, p. 237. Cf. B.S. Jackson, 'A Note on Exodus 22.4 (MT)', *JJS* 27 (1976), pp. 138-40; Schwienhorst-Schönberger, *Bundesbuch*, pp. 188-91.

3. Jackson, 'Exodus 22.4 (MT)', p. 139.

4. *TDOT*, IV, p. 204.

probable that there are not two roots ב.ע.ר with the meanings 'graze' and 'burn', but that the semantic range of ב.ע.ר is simply large enough to cover both the action of fire on wood and that of cattle on vegetation (cf. א.כ.ל 'eat [food]' that also is used of the 'consuming' by a fire: Exod. 24.17 ['*consuming* fire'], 22.5 ['the *consuming* of sheaveheaps']). In terms of animals, ב.ע.ר may have a sense something like 'pick clean', or 'reduce utterly (to the roots)'. Moreover, Cassuto is possibly on the right track when he identifies the differing shades of meaning of ב.ע.ר and בער(י)רה between these two verses as the literary art of wordplay, perhaps as a mnemonic device.[1]

Analysis of Exodus 22.4-5

Although Exod. 22.4 and 22.5 are separate regulations, as is indicated by the particle כי introducing each regulation rather than אם introducing the second, the two share similar form, vocabulary (שדה, בער), and content, and must be taken together as a unit.

At first glance both regulations seem to have to do with nearly identical instances of negligence that results in an animal or fire destroying another man's field or vineyard. If so, it is odd that the author/editor did not place this material with the regulations on the goring ox and the open pit which similarly involve negligence, and that he should have two cases which are essentially identical. However, the two cases do have differences in principle.

These verses follow a regulation having to do with penalties for theft of an animal (21.37–22.3), and precede a section (22.6-7) in which a bailment is stolen, and the bailee may be suspected of the theft. This positioning suggests that 22.4-5 ought to have something in common with the idea of theft or suspected theft.

In the first case, a man lets loose livestock into a field or vineyard so that they consume it. Was this sending out (שלח) done intentionally or unintentionally? The text states that the man sent them out to graze 'a' field (שדה) but that they ended up grazing another's field (שדה אחר). This variation of language implies that he sent the animals out into his own field or one in which he had obtained the right to בְּעֵר his cattle, but that the cattle wandered into an adjacent field where they did not belong. Hence, the cattle went unintentionally. Nonetheless, their owner was guilty of negligence through inattention. He should have been mindful of the tendency of cattle to wander into an adjacent field

---

1.   Cassuto, *Exodus*, p. 284.

and have been watchful to prevent such from happening.

But if this is a case of simple negligence, why is the restitution from the 'highest value' of the field in v. 4? For one reason, unlike a fire that consumes especially that which is dry, livestock will gravitate towards the best, greenest part of a field.[1] Moreover, even if the livestock unintentionally wandered into the neighbor's field, the owner of the field could well suspect that the matter was done intentionally, that is, that the owner was not just inattentive, but that he actively 'looked the other way' when he realized that his cattle had wandered into his neighbor's field. It is undeniable that this action has benefited the owner's cattle. By insuring that the owner of the land is reimbursed more than adequately, the lawgiver seeks to defuse a potential source of contention.

The owner of the livestock is to make restitution according to the 'highest value' of his field.[2] That is, he must supply the produce of the equivalent area consumed corresponding to the amount to be expected from the most productive portion of the neighbor's field[3] to make up for the loss of production due to the grazing.[4] Consequently, more would be returned as restitution than would reasonably be expected from the land that the animals grazed. Thus the neighbor, by receiving more than he lost, has no basis for any dispute with the owner of the livestock.

The above interpretation fits v. 4, a case of suspected pilfering of goods (the crop), into the context of a case of theft (21.37–22.3) that precedes, and the case of the bailee who may be suspected of theft (vv. 6-7) that follows. Verse 5, on the other hand, is a different sort of case, provided for sake of contrast with the case of v. 4.

1.   P. Heinisch, *Exodus* (1934), p. 176, cited by Schwienhorst-Schönberger, *Bundesbuch*, p. 190.

2.   מיטב has usually been rendered 'best' or similar. Jackson ('Exodus 22.4 [MT]', p. 141) proposes the meaning to be 'goods, produce'. The traditional rendering has the advantage of connecting this penalty more closely with the several-fold penalties which precede and follow, and allows a distinction between the case where the offender benefits from the destruction of the property, and where he does not.

3.   Taking 'his field' to mean 'the neighbor's field' solves the problem of what to do if the offender's land is inferior in quality or his crops of a different sort than the land destroyed.

4.   The view that he must hand over part of his own field, (cf. Jackson, 'Exodus 22.4 [MT]', p. 140) seems unlikely, though in the parallel case in Hittite Laws §106 there seems to have been an exchange of land, the burnt for the unburnt.

In v. 5, the man ignites a fire that spreads using thorn bushes as a bridge to his neighbor's field, destroying his standing or heaped grain or whatever. The expression וּמָצְאָה קֹצִים ('and it [the fire] finds/ignites thorns') points to a difference between this case in v. 5 and that of v. 4; namely, that in this case the fields (cultivated) are not merely adjacent, but separated by an uncultivated field that is grown up in thorns, thorns by metonymy meaning a field of thorns. Similar imagery of a field of thorns as a bridge for a spreading fire is found in the parable of Judg. 10.8-20.

The fire is deliberately set—an accidental fire due, say, to lightning or some other 'act of God' would involve no negligence or penalty. It is set by the man in his own field who, having already harvested and removed his own yield, is engaging in 'slash and burn' farming. His neighbor's field, on the other hand, has not yet been fully harvested, and the intervening thorn-infested field catches fire and bridges it to the neighbor's field.

In this case there is no *prima facie* appearance of intentionality since the igniter of v. 5, unlike the owner of cattle in v. 4, receives no benefit from this act. Moreover, since the fields are not adjacent but separated by another field, it would be understandable if the owner of the field were less cognizant of the danger to a distant field in comparison with the owner of the cattle in v. 4 where the fields are adjacent. Hence, though the one setting the fire is guilty of negligence, his guilt is less, so that the penalty is simply full restitution rather than restitution from the 'highest value' of the field.

Exodus 22.4-5: Law or Morality?

The formulation here is legal, but again the intent is to give principles of equity as the basis for law. A complete law code would be expected to deal with cases where the offender could not pay, how 'the highest value' would be evaluated, and how the ruling was to be enforced. The lack of detail can be explained if the intent of the author is primarily moral rather than legal.

The author's concern is with maintaining harmony within the covenant community by providing complete satisfaction to those wronged by another. In the case of consumption of a neighbor's field by livestock in which the owner of the livestock benefits from the damages caused, it is probable that the owner of the field would suspect the owner of the animals—whether justly or unjustly—of deliberately allowing the animals to graze his field. Such suspicions would make the owner of the field less easily appeased. To assure harmony in society, the lawgiver requires the owner of the livestock in this case to give an amount probably greater than one-for-one restitution, according to the 'maximum yield' that the neighbor's land could produce. Such an act should placate the owner of the field, whatever he suspects.

In the case of the fire, on the other hand, there are no *prima facie* grounds for supposing a deliberate act against the owner of the field, and given the fact that a worthless field of thorns comes between the burner and the damaged field, the burner is less culpable (in comparison with the first case) because the potential danger was less obvious. Since the offense has not been compounded by suspicions of illicit gain and since the burner might reasonably have been less cognizant of the danger, satisfaction can be achieved by mere one-for-one restitution as in the case of negligence against property at Exod. 21.33-36.

Contracts of Bailment: Exodus 22.6-12
[English 22.7-13]

Case A

(6) Should (כי) someone give to his fellow money or items for safe-keeping and it is stolen from the man's house, if the thief is found, he must pay twofold. (7) If no thief is found, then the houseowner (bailee) is to draw near to God (האלהים), swearing that he made no trespass against his fellow's property.

Case B

(8) Regarding any case of trespass involving a head of cattle, a donkey, a member of the flock, a textile, or anything missing in which the one declares, 'This is it [the missing thing]!', the affair of these two [the possessor and the claimer] are to come to God (האלהים). He whom God (אלהים) declares guilty must pay back twofold to his fellow.

Case C

(9) Should (כי) someone give his fellow a donkey, or a head of cattle, or a member of the flock or any animal for keeping, and it dies, or it is maimed, or is rustled,[1] there being no eyewitnesses, (10) then there is to

---

1.   On נשבה: the verb ש.ב.ה normally describes the activity of a military or para-military force when it seizes men, women, children, cattle, and possessions from a subdued foe. Hyatt (*Exodus*, p. 239) suggests the text may be corrupt for נשבר ('destroyed'), or נשבה should be omitted as dittography, especially since v. 10b

be a YHWH-oath between the two of them, that he [the fellow] did not trespass against the property of his fellow, after which its owner must take it [the carcass (if any)][1] and [the fellow] makes no restitution. (11) But if it was stolen from him, then he must make restitution to its owner. (12) If it was torn by predators, then he should bring the torn animal as evidence: he need not make restitution.

The Problem of האלהים in Exodus 22.6-12

My interpretation of Exod. 22.6-12 depends on taking אלהים and האלהים in vv. 7 and 8 as God, and 22.6-8 as referring to taking an oath. Others hold the scene to be a trial before judges, an oracle, or a trial by ordeal.

(ה)אלהים in vv. 7 and 8 has been understood to mean God, the gods, teraphim, and judges. The traditional rendering of אלהים and האלהים in vv. 7 and 8 is 'judges',[2] often understood by those who accept this interpretation in the sense of men, whether secular judges or priests, who function as mediators to render God's judgment.[3] This rendering has the advantage of making intelligible v. 8, where the אלהים render (note the plural verb) judgment. Its disadvantage is that אלהים in the sense of 'judges' is not a clearly attested usage of אלהים (cf. the discussion at 21.6).

Another view is that אלהים means 'gods', a vestige of pre-Israelite usage of this law. However, it is hardly possible that an editor who included prohibitions against idolatry (20.2-3; 20.23; 22.19; 23.13, 24, 33) would have allowed a regulation referring to 'gods' in this way.

The view that אלהים refers to the teraphim fares little better for similar reasons. If these are 'household gods', this view would be eliminated for the reason just stated. If they are taken as images representing the ancestors, a view found plausible for האלהים in Exod. 21.6,

---

perhaps suggests that the carcass of the animal should be returned to its owner, which is impossible for a rustled animal. Cf. Paul, *Studies*, p. 92 n. 5. The text as it stands makes good sense, however.

1. On ולקח in v. 10: the text does not specify what it is that its owner 'takes'. Phillips (*Criminal Law*, pp. 135-36) argues that the owner must accept the 'oath' rather than the 'carcass' since in the case of an animal being 'rustled', there would be no carcass to take. However, it seems certain that if the carcass remained—and in two of the three cases it would—the owner would have the rights to it. Moreover, though the owner can demand no more than an oath, it is not clear that he would have to lay aside all suspicions and accept the oath as proof.

2. *Targum Onqelos*, KJV.

3. Vannoy, 'The Word האלהים in Exodus 21.6 and 22.7-8', pp. 229-30.

this would seem to make the court guilty of necromancy contra 22.17.

By process of elimination, then, the rendering of אלהים as 'God, deity', its most common usage, must be accepted as the probable interpretation. There are two objections that have been raised against this interpretation. The first is the plural verb in v. 8, יַרְשִׁעֻן. Usually אלהים as a title for YHWH is accompanied by singular verbs. The plural could be taken, then, as evidence that YHWH is not in view here. However, there are exceptions to the use of the singular with אלהים in reference to YHWH. אלהים in reference to YHWH can take plural verbs (Gen. 20.13; 31.53; Exod. 32.1, 8), or even pronouns (Gen. 1.26; 11.7). In such cases, the plural of excellence or majesty of the plural noun אלהים[1] has been extended to other parts of speech. The plural verb here can be seen as a sign of the author's respect for God as judge.

The other objection to taking אלהים as 'God, deity' concerns the question of how God can declare someone guilty (v. 8). God could speak through an oracle or by the casting of the sacred lots, the Urim and the Thummim. However, there is not a single instance in the Bible of a prophetic revelation occurring in a trial. Moreover, if either an oracle or lots were in mind, one would expect the same to be used in the parallel case involving ambiguity over a lost or injured animal (Exod. 22.10), but in that case an oath rather than an oracle and/or casting of lots is prescribed. Such considerations make the oracle and/or lots interpretation very questionable.

On the other hand, the statement about God's declaring someone guilty in connection with the taking of an oath is intelligible. The owner of the house (v. 7) comes near to God, that is, he enters into a formal religious setting or assembly, probably at a sanctuary,[2] in which the invisible presence of God is expected. The purpose of drawing near to God is to make an oath, not only in 22.10 where the language is clear, but on the basis of 22.10 also in 22.7, 8. So the LXX interpreted these verses by adding to v. 7 'he may draw near to God', the words 'and is to affirm by oath'. Note the strong parallelism between v. 10 and v. 7 where 'swearing that he made no trespass

---

1.   Cf. *GKC* §124g.

2.   Fensham ('New Light on Exodus 21.6 and 22.7', pp. 160-61) points to a remarkable parallel in LE §§36-37, where the keeper of lost goods given in deposit is to swear at the temple (or door thereof) to the god Tishpak that he committed no fraud.

(literally 'did not stretch out his hand') against his fellow's property' follows 'drawing near to God' in the latter, but a 'YHWH oath' in the former, suggesting that drawing near to God involves taking an oath.

There is a translation problem with אם לא in 22.7b and 22.10b. אם לא in an oath formula normally affirms what follows. If read as an oath one would expect the translation of אם לא שלח ידו to be: 'swearing that he surely made trespass', which is clearly not the intent. Alternatively, אם could be understood as conditional: he may swear 'if he has not trespassed', this being a warning against false oaths. The view tentatively adopted here is that אם לא is an oath formulation, but is to be read as if it were כי לא: 'swearing that he made no trespass'. Perhaps the fact that respective regulations in which אם לא occur are headed by the particle כי has led to the mixing of direct and indirect discourse and the interchanging of אם for כי.

ונקרב could be reflexive/middle '[the owner of the house] is to draw near', or passive, '[the owner of the house] is to be brought near': a purposeful ambiguity that allows equally for an accused man's willingly seeking to clear his name or a man's reluctantly acquiescing to an oath. The oath (cf. Num. 5.11-31) consists of the suspected party making a conditional self curse, calling divine retribution upon oneself if the oath of innocence should be false. The accuser might be required to take an oath as well (cf. v. 10).

Under these circumstances, the thief's guilt could be shown, for instance, when the suspect, facing the prospect of a divine curse being placed upon him, refuses to take the oath. Or under the intense questioning of the oath procedure, he might break down and confess his crime. Or the story of the accused could prove inconsistent under questioning so his guilt becomes obvious to those administering the oath (cf. 1 Kgs 3.16-28, Solomon's questioning of two claimants), as perhaps in LH §126 where the examination of the facts 'in the presence of a god' (= an oath?) shows a claim of lost property to be false. Or he could confess later, if he believes God is actually bringing upon him the stipulations of the curse. Any of these outcomes could be interpreted as God (by means of the oath ceremony) declaring the man guilty.

What is described here, then, is not a trial by ordeal[1] but a means of

---

1. Similarly, H.C. Brichto ('The Case of the שׂטָה and a Reconsideration of Biblical "Law"', *HUCA* 46 [1975], pp. 55-70) denies that Num. 5.11-31 is a trial by ordeal.

dealing with cases that lack sufficient evidence for courts to decide. In such cases, the matter is left by means of an oath in the hands of God to dispose of.

Structure and Interpretation of Exodus 22.6-12

The structure of Exod. 22.6-12 and its relationship with what has gone before can now be considered. This section continues the theme on theft and impairment of property of 21.37–22.5, and is united also with what has preceded in its frequent usage of the expression יְשַׁלֵּם 'he shall (or shall not) make restitution'. In general, this passage can be seen in part as an expansion of the Decalogue's prohibition of theft, and its command not to invoke YHWH's name in vain (20.7, 15). A false oath would be a violation of the latter.

Exod. 22.6-12 can be divided into three units: Case A (vv. 6-7) concerns theft of non-animal items while in another's safekeeping. Case B (v. 8) involves the use of an oath in disputes over ownership, whether animal or not. Case C (vv. 9-12) involves the death or injury of an animal in another's safekeeping. In each case, there is, under certain circumstances, the possibility of an oath.

Some scholars have difficulty seeing how Case B (22.8) fits in with the other material. Jackson, for example, regards v. 8 as a secondary insertion[1] because it differs in content from what surrounds it, and it differs also in form (עַל replaces כִּי). However, this breaking up of the expected sequence occurs at regular intervals in 20.22–23.33, suggesting this kind of structuring is part of the author's style (20.24b; 21.16, 22-25, 33-34, 22.1-2b; 23.4-5; 23.13).

I begin my discussion of the structure of this passage by laying out its premises and prescriptions as follows:

CASE A (Exodus 22.6-7)

Premise:	Theft of inanimate object with contract of bailment.
Sub-premise 1:	Thief caught.
Prescription 1:	Thief pays twofold.
Sub-premise 2:	Thief not caught. [Bailee suspected but proof lacking].
Prescription 2:	Bailee takes an oath.

---

1.   E.g. Jackson, *Theft*, p. 101.

CASE B (Exodus 22.8)

Premise:	Dispute over the ownership of either an animal or an inanimate object. [Inadequate evidence for proof in court. Not necessarily a matter of bailment].
Prescription:	Oath.
Sub-premise:	God shows the guilt of the offending party through the oath.
Sub-prescription:	Guilty party pays twofold.

CASE C (Exodus 22.9-12)

Premise:	Animal bailment in which the animal dies, is injured, rustled, or otherwise lost.
Sub-premise 1:	[Bailee suspected of wrongdoing, which he denies, but this cannot be proven due to] lack of eyewitnesses.
Prescription 1:	Oath. Return of carcass? [No further action].
Sub-premise 2:	Simple theft of animal.
Prescription 2:	Restitution. [No oath].
Sub-premise 3:	Animal torn by predators.
Prescription 3:	Show carcass. No restitution. [No oath].

As laid out above, Case A and Case C have to do with bailment, whereas Case B does not. Cases A and C have to do with things lost (either physically lost or their value lost), whereas Case B has to do with something found that the finder thinks he had previously lost. The change in the form of introducing the regulations from כי (Case A, 22.6) to על (Case B, 22.8), back to כי (Case C, 22.9) is a means of showing that 22.8 is to be set apart from the other two regulations.

Exod. 22.6-7 (Case A) concerns leaving valuables in the safekeeping of another. The general premise is that the valuable which has been left with another was stolen from the bailee's house. If the thief is found out, then it is a matter of simple theft and the thief pays twofold (cf. 22.3).

But the more difficult question in Case A is what to do if the thief is not found (v. 7) and there is suspicion that the bailee sold or hid the item given in bailment.[1] It is assumed that the bailor has no concrete evidence to bolster his suspicions, still less to prove them. The remedy for this problem is a 'drawing near to God' to make an oath (cf. 22.10) in which the bailee swears on pain of divine retribution that he did not 'trespass against his fellow's property', that is, he did not steal it.

The same principle is then applied (in a parenthetic aside) generally to disputes over ownership (22.8, Case B). An animal or item is claimed to have been lost, in all likelihood stolen. The owner of the lost item finds what he believes to be his lost ox, donkey, sheep, textile, or whatever in the possession of someone else, but that man (it is implied) denies that this is the other man's lost item, and the accuser has insufficient evidence to prove his case in court. What is he to do? The solution again is for the two of them to come to God for the purpose of taking an oath. The man accused of unlawful possession swears that he has not stolen the item from the accuser, and possibly also the accuser swears that he is not making a false accusation. As argued above, this procedure might serve to identify the thief, who must then pay twofold.

Case C returns to the matter of bailment, though limited to animals (22.9-12). Here, the animal is left with a bailee, but when the bailor returns for his animal, he learns that the animal has died, or it has been maimed, or it has been rustled, and cannot, therefore, be returned in good health to its owner. The bailor suspects wrongdoing on the part of the bailee—whether negligence in the case of the dead or injured animal, or fraud in the case of the rustled one—but lacking any eyewitnesses, he can prove nothing. The remedy, again, is an oath in which the bailee swears by the life of YHWH that he did not transgress against the property of his fellow.

This regulation implies that a bailee cannot be held responsible for the death, injury or loss of the animal if such was beyond the bailee's control; unexplained death, an animal injuring itself, and rustling being examples of this. Where the bailee gives claim that the loss or

---

1. Cf. LH §124 that treats the case of a bailee seeking to steal the bailment by denying that any bailment had been given to him. LH §125 and LE §36 imply that the bailee must replace bailment in the event of theft if the bailee has suffered no loss, or where there is no evidence of theft. In such cases his 'responsibility' was automatic and he could not exculpate himself by oath-taking. LH §123 indicates that apart from contract and witnesses a case of bailment was not subject to claim in court.

injury of the animal was beyond his control, and the bailor cannot prove otherwise, the bailor may demand an oath, but he has no right to demand restitution.

The next proviso of Case C is that in the case of theft the bailee must make good the loss; there is no question of the exculpation on the strength of an oath. The logic for this is obvious. The contract for the bailment would be absurd if the bailee were not responsible to protect the animal against thievery. Unlike the rustling of an animal,[1] an act of *force majeure*, simple theft bespeaks negligence on the part of the bailee. This is not so in Case A where the bailment is inanimate, and the expected supervision, accordingly, less stringent.[2] In like manner, the *force majeure* intrinsic to the claim of depredation that concludes Case C need only to be supported by some evidence (עֵד), leaving the bailee free either of payment (as in v. 11) or of oath taking.[3]

The LXX reads for עֵד ('witness') עַד ('unto') resulting in the quite plausible reading 'he shall bring him [the owner] to the torn animal'. That this is the original reading is argued by Fensham.[4] In support of this reading, the suffix on the verb יְבִאֵהוּ is masculine, while its antecedent טְרֵפָה is feminine. Cassuto[5] thinks עֵד ('witness') could perhaps be a play on words for עַד ('prey') since the carcass would be both. Whether the owner is brought to the carcass or the carcass to the owner, and whether the carcass is called 'prey' or 'witness', the overall principle involved is the same. Cf. Amos 3.12 where a

---

1.   On the meaning of biblical terms for theft, see Jackson, *Theft*, pp. 1-19, esp. p. 14; and Westbrook, *Studies*, pp. 15-38.

2.   Cassuto (*Exodus*, p. 287) speculates that a bailee for an inanimate object was not normally paid, whereas a bailee for an animal would be. LH §125 and LE §36 hold the bailee of inanimate objects responsible unless he himself has suffered loss or there is evidence of theft. It is possible that this principle would be applicable to biblical law. Case A would then be explained as being more interested in the ambiguous situation rather than the more clear one.

3.   It is strange that the keeper is responsible for human theft, but not for predators. But would not a bailee be responsible for protecting the flock from both? Perhaps the logic is this: a predator kills first, then drags away, whereas a thief does not kill, so that an alert shepherd could chase the thief down and retrieve the animal. A parallel case in LH §266 places in parallel a lion kill with an act of god, a matter beyond human control. Like the case here, the Laws of Hammurapi seem to have required an oath of innocence: 'the shepherd shall prove himself innocent in the presence of a god' (*ANET*, p. 177).

4.   F.C. Fensham, 'עד in Exodus xxii, 12', *VT* 12 (1962), pp. 337-39.

5.   Cassuto, *Exodus*, p. 287.

shepherd rescues from the lion's jaw two shank bones or the tip of an ear, possibly for evidence along the lines of this regulation to prove he did not steal it.

It is interesting that there are in these regulations four possible outcomes in the situations described. I list them in the order of greatest to least penalties:

1. Twofold restitution (return of item + 100% penalty).
     Case A—penalty for theft when thief is found.
     Case B—penalty for theft when oath ceremony proves
          guilt in dispute over ownership.

2. Simple restitution.
     Case C—penalty for bailee allowing bailor's animal to be
          stolen.

3. Oath taking rather than restitution. Potential of divine
     retribution, but no human retribution.
     Case A—Where bailee is suspected in case of theft of
          inanimate item of bailment and no evidence.
     Case B—Where this is a dispute over ownership of
          property of whatever sort and no evidence.
     Case C—Where bailee is suspected of wrongdoing in
          the death, injury, or rustling of an animal of bailment
          and there is no witness.

4. No oath taking, and no restitution.
     Case C—Where the bailee can exonerate himself of the
          the death of a bailee's animal by evidence of predation
          that is beyond his control.

Having looked into the interpretation of the passage, we may now return to the problem of why Case B has been placed between two cases of contracts of bailment. Our author uses Case B to make clear that the use of oath is applicable more generally to situations other than those involving bailments. That Case B is broader in terms of types of property than Cases A and C, including both animate and inanimate property under its scope, also supports the generalizing purpose of the middle section. Further, Case B adds parenthetic information generally applicable to both Cases A and C; namely, that oath taking could be a means of discovering the guilt of someone. Such generally applicable information fits best in the middle section and its generalizing purpose.

Case B, like A and C, presents a case in which an oath is a possible remedy, and like A, contemplates a twofold restitution where the thief is found. Moreover, Case B forms a transition between Cases A (inanimate property) and C (animate property). Case B is a situation that could come up in connection with either Case A or C when an item stolen from a bailee (Case A) or an animal rustled from him (Case C) is found in another's possession. Case B is therefore related to what precedes and to what follows it. It was not inappropriate to place it in between. There is no need to eliminate Case B as a gloss.

Exodus 22.6-12: Law or Religion?

My interpretation of 22.6-12 clarifies that what is described is not law in the normal sense of the term. There are 'legal' elements: a thief must pay twofold, a bailee must make restitution if the bailor's animal is stolen from him, a bailee may exculpate himself by bringing evidence of predation. However, when these regulations call for an oath, they pass from the legal to the supra-legal sphere.

I do not mean to say that biblical 'law' is unique in this. The oath and divine intervention are normal and accepted mechanisms in ancient Near Eastern laws, and indeed, the oath is used (as a vestige of our religious past) in modern American courtrooms. Ancient societies would not distinguish between the sacred and the secular as does modern Western culture, but according to our modern categories, the matter has passed from law to religion.

An exculpatory oath here is used only where there is insufficient evidence. If there is evidence—the thief being caught, a clear breach of contract, remains of predation of an animal—these regulations do not allow an oath as an option. A human court should decide such cases. It is rather in those cases that lack evidence, cases in which a human court would find the matter impossible to decide, that the oath comes into play. An oath, in effect, brings the case to a higher court, to God himself, for whom lack of evidence is not a problem. Thus here the religious and supernatural invade the realm of the legal.

The purpose of this regulation is essentially moral: to bring about harmony among Israelite citizens. If a man thinks his fellow citizen has stolen from him or by negligence damaged his property, or, from the other point of view, an innocent man is accused of wrongdoing, and the evidence is insufficient to prove either guilt or innocence in court, either party or both could become resentful, and the matter could be a source of strife in the covenant community. But as believers in YHWH, they may have recourse to supra-legal means of resolving the problem. Potential resentment can be pacified with the knowledge that YHWH, the righteous and omniscient judge, will decide where human courts cannot. The means of this is the oath.

Injury to a Borrowed Animal: Exodus 22.13-14
[English 22.14-15]

(13) And should however (וכי), someone borrow [an animal] from his fellow, and it is maimed or dies without its owner being present, then the borrower must make restitution. (14) If its owner was present, he need not make restitution. If it was hired, the risk [which eventuated] was already paid for in the value of the rent paid [by the borrower].

Analysis of Exodus 22.13-14

This unit is related to the previous section (22.6-12) and yet is distinct from it. It is distinguished in content (it has nothing to do with theft or suspected theft or oaths; it concerns borrowing rather than bailments) and to a slight degree it is distinguished in form (introduced by וכי rather than כי). Yet it is related in that it continues Exod. 22.9-12's discussion of serious injuries or death to a man's animal while in the possession of another man. It also continues, and concludes, the regulations emphasizing restitution (with the associated expression ישלם 'he will make restitution') occurring throughout Exod. 21.33–22.14 that deal generally with offenses against another man's property.

The structure depends on the interpretation of v. 14b, but it can be anticipated as follows:

> Animal borrowed but owner not present/
> Full restitution (Exod. 22.13)
>
> Animal borrowed with owner present/
> No restitution (22.14a)
>
> Animal not borrowed but hired/
> No restitution (22.14b).

The situation seems to be that an animal has been borrowed to perform some task (an ox to plow or thresh, a donkey to carry a load). The basic principle is that one who borrows is responsible for the animal's safety and health. If it should die or be seriously injured as a result of the borrowing, the borrower is responsible for paying the difference (שַׁלֵּם יְשַׁלֵּם) between the value of the healthy animal and that of the dead or injured one. That rule does not apply if the owner was present, however, presumably because the owner would know if the animal was about to be used in an unsafe or irresponsible way and has therefore by his acquiescence accepted responsibility for any resulting injury to his beast.

The final phrase (22.14b) is terse and difficult to interpret. There are a number of conceivable renderings: (a) If he [the worker] was hired, he is entitled to (lit. 'goes in with') his wages. (b) If it [the animal] was hired, the money paid for the hire covers the loss [lit. 'it comes with its hire').[1] (c) If he [the borrower] was hired [by the owner], he shall make amends up to the amount of his wages (lit. 'it will be set against his hire').[2] (d) If the animal was hired, the owner receives the price of its hire [for the entire period for which it was hired].[3]

I accept view (b) along with most interpreters, taking the animal to be what is hired (שָׂכִיר), and the statement to affirm that one who rents an animal is not at risk for the damage, for the possibility of risk is considered in setting the rent. This view flows well with the previous cases, providing a contrast with the case of simple borrowing, whereas taking it to mean a hired man involves a more abrupt change of subject matter.

Further support for this view can be derived from LH §§244-45, 249 where the owner rather than the renter takes the loss if the hired animal is killed by a lion in the open or by 'an act of god' (though an oath may be required of the renter), whereas the renter is responsible for simple negligence. Hence, the Laws of Hammurapi imply that one who hires out his animal assumes certain risks of business. The Mishnah, *B. Meṣ.* 6.3-5 (a case of hire) and 2.2 (for a borrower) makes the same distinction between borrowing and hire. In American society, a commercial driver who is paid is held to a higher standard than a driver who is merely a friend of the passenger and who is not paid for the service.

---

1.   Cassuto, *Exodus*, p. 288; *NIV*.
2.   Daube, *Biblical Law*, p. 17.
3.   Cf. Paul, *Studies*, pp. 95-96.

Exodus 22.13-14: Moral Implications
Although Exod. 22.13-14 could be instituted as law, it seeks to express
the moral point: if one borrows an animal, he is in general responsible
for its safekeeping. If I have rightly translated it, 14b perhaps
expresses a moral principle of favoring the poor man who must rent
an animal over the rich man who owns it. The regulation as a whole
places the greater burden on the owner.

Seduction of a Man's Virgin Daughter
Exodus 22.15-16 [English 22.16-17]

(15) Should a man entice a maiden who is not betrothed and lie carnally
with her, he for his part must pay for her in full the bride-price for
[acquiring] a wife. (16) If her father absolutely refuses to give her to him
[as wife], nonetheless he must pay silver equal to the bride-price for
maidens.

Exodus 22.15-16: Relationship with the Previous Sections
There is some difficulty in deciding whether Exod. 22.15-16 belongs
more closely with the regulations that precede or with those that
follow. In favor of connecting these verses with the previous sections
pertaining to offenses of men against property are the following: (1)
Exod. 22.15-16 shares with what has gone before a monetary payment
related to the offense. (2) It continues the casuistic formulations of the
previous sections. (3) Virginity had a marketable value for a girl's
father when he gave her in marriage, for a deflowered maiden
brought a lower brideprice. Hence, the regulation might be classified
with the regulations that precede having to do with monetary loss,
what many commentators call (less accurately) 'property law'.[1]

On the other hand, Exod. 22.15-16 is in some ways more closely
related to the social and cultic regulations that follow than what
precedes. One point of discontinuity: the characteristic expression of
the previous sections יְשַׁלֵּם [שלם] is not used to describe the monetary
payment made to the girl's father. Moreover, it is an exaggeration to
describe the status of women in the Bible as mere 'chattel'.[2] The
woman, like the man and unlike all property, is made in the image of

---

1. Keil, *Pentateuch*, p. 141; Paul, *Studies*, pp. 96-98; Gispen, *Exodus*,
p. 221.
2. Patrick, *Law*, p. 83.

God (Gen. 1.27), and is equally protected with men in many of the regulations (Exod. 21.15, 17, 20, 26-27, 28, 31, 32; cf. 21.7-11, 22-25, and Num. 5.11-31[1]). If women are not, strictly speaking, to be categorized as property, then this case is not fully linked with offenses against property.

Given the strong continuity and yet significant discontinuity between 22.15-16 and what precedes, it seems best to see this pericope as concluding the regulations concerning monetary loss, but also introducing the regulations of a social and cultic nature that follow.

Analysis of Exodus 22.15-16

Exod. 22.15-16 is the only discussion of sexual relations in 20.22–23.33 besides the units on the slave-wife and on bestiality (21.7-11; 22.18). It develops the general subject area (marriage law), though not the specific content, of the Decalogue's prohibition of adultery (20.14).

Exod. 22.15-16 states that a man who seduces an unbetrothed maiden[2] must pay her father the brideprice (מהר) for marriage, after which the father may or may not choose to marry his daughter to the man. By affirming the father's right to give consent before a marriage can take place—even if the couple agrees to live together—the regulation develops another principle found in the Decalogue, that is, of showing respect for parents (Exod. 20.12; LE §27 also stresses the need for parental consent in marriage).

Exodus 22.15-16: Law or Morality?

The incompleteness of the category 'marriage law' in Exod. 20.22–23.33 shows that this corpus is not sufficiently comprehensive to be considered a 'law code'. The purpose, as seen both here and throughout, is rather to give a few examples of various kinds of regulations to

1. Num. 5.11-31 protects a wife from a jealous husband. Cf. Brichto, 'The Case of the שׂטה', pp. 55-70.

2. D.H. Weiss ('A Note on אשׁר לא ארשׂה', *JBL* 81 [1962], pp. 67-69) argued that the use of the perfect ארשׂה rather than the participle מארשׂה must indicate stress on the completed action in the past ('had *never* been betrothed'). Hence, the penalty would not apply if a מהר had previously been received by a former suitor who died or forsook her since the father is not entitled to double reimbursement. However, A. Rofé ('Family and Sex Laws in Deuteronomy and the Book of the Covenant', *Henoch* 9 [1987], p. 133 n. 5) rightly criticizes Weiss. The perfect often describes actions or states that continue into the present.

make moral and religious comment. The need for completeness in this area is mitigated in the final form of the Pentateuch (of which the final editor[s] would have been aware) by the existence of other marriage regulations that supplement the present case (Lev. 18.6-23; 20.10-21; Deut. 21.10-17; 22.13-29; 24.1-4; 25.5-12). Deut. 22.28-29, a more serious case (rape), alludes to Exod. 22.15-16, the general structure and peculiarities of style being strikingly similar.

Whether ever instituted as law or not, Exod. 22.15-16 certainly expresses morality. In particular it expresses sexual morality. By specifying that a seducer of a man's daughter can be penalized as much as the brideprice of maidens without even obtaining the maiden as a wife, the regulation discourages irresponsible sexual behavior.

This regulation protects the father financially since a deflowered maiden would be less 'marketable', and protects the girl from shame (and possible pregnancy) by discouraging this behavior altogether. It also protects the maiden financially. From societies in the ancient Near East outside of Israel we may deduce that part of the brideprice (מהר) was customarily returned to the maiden as a dowry that would remain hers in case of divorce.[1] A lower brideprice could mean a lower dowry, and therefore less financial security for the woman. By requiring the man to pay the brideprice, the daughter could be assured of a substantial dowry.

The regulation shrewdly gives the father much leeway as to whether the seducer is allowed to marry the daughter. If the seducer was otherwise a suitable mate for the man's daughter, and the couple were simply 'jumping the gun' sexually, the man's paying the brideprice and subsequent marriage would in essence be no penalty at all. On the other hand, if (as is not unlikely) the father considers the man unsuitable, the maiden is protected against marriage to an unsuitable mate and against loss of dowry, while the man is rightly penalized for his sexual misadventure. Given this law, a man who was unsure whether he was considered suitable, or a man who had no desire for a perma-

---

1. The Bible rarely speaks of the 'dowry' (שלוחים; cf. 1 Kgs 9.16; Mic. 1.14). R. Yaron (*The Laws of Eshnunna* [Jerusalem: Magnes, 1969], pp. 110-15) discusses brideprice and dowry in the Laws of Eshnunna and Hammurapi. For the custom at Nuzi, see K. Grosz, 'Dowry and Brideprice in Nuzi', in *Studies in the Civilization and Culture of Nuzi and the Hurrians* (ed. M.A. Morrison and D.I. Owen; Winona Lake: Eisenbrauns, 1981), pp. 161-82. Grosz argues that at Nuzi the woman lost control of her dowry once children were born.

nent marriage, had best think twice before seducing a maiden.

The Decalogue's moral principle of respect for parents and its promise that such respect results in a longer life may undergird the logic of requiring the father's consent. Just as respect for parents makes a long life for a child more likely (Exod. 20.12), so (one could reason) giving the father right of consent in marriage makes a daughter's happiness more likely. Accordingly, the affirmation of the father's right to consent before the marriage of his daughter seems to be the lawgiver's means of protecting the best interests of the daughter, and is an expression of his moral outlook.

Chapter 7

CULTIC REGULATIONS AND SOCIAL JUSTICE:
EXODUS 22.17–23.19*

Exod. 22.17–23.19, consisting of cultic regulations and regulations on
social justice, displays a pattern of alternation between three paragraphs relating cultic regulations and two paragraphs pertaining to
social justice that emerges as follows:

Cultic Matters I (22.17-19)

    1. Witchcraft
    2. Beastiality
    3. Idolatry

Social Justice I (22.20-27)

    1. Oppression
    2. Loans

Cultic Matters II (22.28-30)

    1. Firstfruits and firstborn
    2. Eating torn flesh

Social Justice II (23.1-9)

1. Justice in court (begins)
2. Enemy's animal
3. Justice in court (concludes)

Cultic Matters III (23.10-19)

    1. Sabbath years/days
    2. No other gods
    3. Holidays

---

*   *English Bible*, Exod. 22.18–23.19.

By such an organization the author indicates, whether consciously or unconsciously, that there is no dichotomy between the secular and sacred, between 'church' and 'state', between justice and religion in Israel, but that these are inextricably intertwined.

Cultic Matters I:
Sorcery, Bestiality, Worship of Other Gods Condemned:
Exodus 22.17-19 [English 22.18-20]

(17) You (sing.) are not to allow a sorceress to live (תחיה). (18) Anyone who lies carnally with an animal deserves to be put to death. (19) Whoever sacrifices to deity deserves to be put under the 'ban' unless it is to YHWH alone.

Exodus 22.17-19 and Structure

There is no obvious link between the regulations of 22.17-19 and those that immediately precede except that v. 18 like vv. 15-16 deals with sexuality (both using the verb ש.כ.ב), though if this were the only principle of organization one would expect the case of bestiality to begin this series rather than being in the middle. More probably, vv. 17-19 should be seen as introducing (or in light of 20.23-26, reintroducing) the topic of cultic regulation. That these should be first among the cultic sections relates to the seriousness of the offenses: in each case the life of the offender is put in jeopardy in the punishment.

The terse, almost poetic[1] regulations of Exod. 22.17-19 resemble in form those of 21.12-17 that also begin with participles and permit death as the punishment. Alt speculated that 22.18-19 was originally part of an independent, participially formulated, 'apodictic' law collection that included 21.12, 15, 16, 17 as well as 22.18-19. Hence, the two regulations of 22.18-19, Alt concluded are now displaced from their original setting.[2]

However, whether or not 22.18-19 was previously grouped with the

---

1. Read as poetry, each case has three stresses except the last which is 3 + 3. Although 19b is missing from the Samaritan which reads 'other gods', it need not be deleted as a later addition (contra M. Fishbane, *Biblical Interpretation in Ancient Israel* [Oxford: Clarendon Press, 1985], pp. 70-71). Rather it serves to bring this series of participial regulations to a conclusion by changing the rhythm of the last case, and it is logically required to clarify in v. 19a that אלהים which can mean 'God' as well as 'gods' is not in this case meant to include YHWH.

2. Alt, 'Origins', p. 144.

participially formulated regulations of 21.12-17, in the present form
of 20.22–23.19 it would have been inappropriate to put them together.
Exod. 21.12-17 begins a series of offenses of men against men (21.12-
17), followed by offenses of property against men and property
(21.28-36), and then offenses of men against property (21.37–22.16),
whereas the offenses of 22.17-19 are to be seen as primarily offenses
against God. To have placed these regulations with 21.12-17 would be
to interrupt cases of men against men with offenses against God
directly. Content rather than form is the primary determining
principle of organization here.

Just as the terse participial forms of Exod. 21.12-17 introduce the
subject of offenses of men against men as being most serious examples
of such cases, having מוֹת יוּמַת in the penalty clause, so this unit contains
the most serious sort of cultic offenses, having penalties which
similarly threaten the 'life' of the offender. Moreover, 21.12-17 and
22.17-19 form an envelope or bracket around the central core of
21.18–22.16 that deals more directly with legal matters—cf. the
concluding chapter on how this bracketing fits into the structure of
20.22–23.33 as a whole.

The first case on the sorceress differs from the other regulations in
Exod. 20.22–23.19 formulated with the participle in its use of the
second person, 'you [sing.]'. The 'you', assuming it to be the correct
vocalization,[1] must be Israel personified as elsewhere in Exod. 20.22–
23.19, reminding the reader that what is said in 20.22–23.19 is
YHWH's address to Israel, not simply a list of regulations.

Unlike the four cases in Exod. 21.12-17 that each conclude with 'he
shall be put to death' (מוֹת יוּמַת), only the second of the three cases in
22.17-19 concludes with that expression. Rather there is variety that
shows a logical progression from least to most severe:[2] the sorceress
is not 'allowed to live' (לֹא תְחַיֶּה),[3] the animal sodomite merits 'to be

---

1.   Patrick (*Law*, p. 84) observes that תחיה could be revocalized to a Pual without changing the consonantal text and translate: 'A sorceress must not be allowed to
live.' This emendation allows the case to be impersonal in style like the other
participial formulations.

2.   N. Lohfink, 'חרם', *TDOT*, V, p. 181.

3.   J. Weingreen ('The PI'EL in Biblical Hebrew: A Suggested New Concept',
Henoch 5 [1983], pp. 21-29) takes מכשפה לא תחיה to mean 'an identified active
witch was to be denied all means of sustaining life—she was to be thrust out of
society away from all human contact' (p. 28). לא תחיה then would mean 'do not
allow to live' in the sense of 'live well' or 'prosper/thrive' rather than specifically

put to death' (מֹות יומת), and the one sacrificing to other gods deserves 'to be put under the ban' (יחרם), that is, utterly destroyed. That there is such a progression undermines the attempt of Alt and others[1] to emend יחרם to מֹות יומת.

Exodus 22.17-19 and Other Passages

In including the case of the sorceress, the author is possibly indirectly condemning the 'sorcerers' of Pharaoh in Egypt who in the narrative had imitated the miracles of Moses (Exod. 7.11) and contributed to Pharaoh's obstinacy.

The fact that a feminine form, 'sorceress', was chosen here has struck interpreters as curious. Phillips speculates that Exod. 22.17 is meant to fill a loophole in existing legislation where the prohibition of sorcery previously applied only to men.[2] That divination of this type— the exact activities of this kind of divination are not well defined—was more commonly practiced by the female than the male in Canaan is likewise speculative: Deut. 18.10 confirms that men practiced this kind of divination. Interestingly, one of the most prominent diviners in the Bible (under the term אוב) is the female medium of Endor (1 Sam. 28.7). It is at least possible that an author/ editor of this regulation, being aware of the story of the medium of Endor to come later in the Bible, condemned her by making the form here feminine.

Other passages repeat or expand on bestiality (Lev. 18.23; 20.15-16; Deut. 27.21). The condemnation of sacrificing to other gods is an expansion of the Decalogue's prohibition of making or serving other gods (Exod. 20.5).

Exodus 22.17-19: Law or Religion?

Each of these injunctions is expressed in legal-like formulation, though they lack the precision of clear law. The exact meanings of

---

being an equivalent of a death penalty. He supports his view with reference to Saul's practice in which he 'removed from the land' and 'cut off...from the land' those who practiced divination arts (1 Sam. 28.3, 9), the former of which is most easily, and the latter is plausibly, interpreted as banishment rather than execution. But compare Lev. 20.27 where spiritualists are explicitly executed by stoning.

1. Alt, 'Origins', p. 144 n. 73 argues that יחרם of 22.19 is a misreading of אחרים ('other [gods]'), and that the original predicate מֹות יומת was then felt to be superfluous and was removed. H. Schulz (*Das Todesrecht im Alten Testament* [Berlin: Töpelmann, 1969], p. 59) has agreed that מֹות יומת was the original verb.

2. Phillips, *Criminal Law*, p. 57.

'sorceress', 'do not allow to live', and 'put under the ban' are not spelled out. The details of how and by whom the sentences are to be carried out are not specified, nor is the question of exceptions or ransoming addressed. Whether or not these regulations were ever instituted as law, they provide clear religious-moral condemnation of these three activities.

The motivation in each case can be understood as being essentially religious. Deuteronomy condemns sorcery and all forms of divination but allows prophets who speak the word of YHWH to serve as a substitute for divination (cf. Deut. 18.9-15). Divination operated out of the assumptions of a polytheistic world view in which the diviner sought the purposes or will of the gods or of impersonal fates which sometimes even had control over the gods.[1] This world-view was seen by the writer of Deuteronomy as incompatible with YHWH religion and a hindrance to listening to YHWH's word through his prophets. It is probable that a similar rationale operates in Exod. 22.17.

It is true that ancient Near East laws (LH §2; MAL A §47) condemn instances of magic, but they seem to do so only in so far as the use of magic was directed towards other people's harm, that is black magic, rather than condemning all magic as such. The motive was essentially secular: given that magic sometimes actually works, it should not be used to harm a fellow citizen.

Taken by itself, Exod. 22.17 could be understood in a similar way. However, taken in the context of the Pentateuch as a literary unit where magical practices as such are condemned as contrary to the religion of YHWH, it is more likely that there is a religious motive primarily at work here. What was essentially 'secular' law in Mesopotamia becomes more specifically 'religious' regulation for Israel.

The motive for the text's condemnation of bestiality probably lies in the perception that bestiality is contrary to God's hierarchy that separates man in the image of God from other creatures (Gen. 1.26-31; cf. on Exod. 21.28 above). Other possible motives are to provide a polemic against pagan mythology where the gods sometimes indulge in bestiality[2] or against non-Israelite fertility cults presumed to prac-

---

1.   W.H.Ph. Römer, 'Religion of Ancient Mesopotamia', in *Historia Religionum: Handbook for the History of Religions*. I. *Religions of the Past* (ed. C.J. Bloeker and G. Widengren; Leiden: Brill, 1969), pp. 171-78.

2.   At Ugarit, Baal mates with a heifer (UT 67, v, 17-25). In the Cretan myth of

tice cohabitation with animals.[1] Lying with a beast brings such ritual defilement according to the rules of purity that the whole nation could be expelled from the land (Lev. 18.23-25), which helps to explain the severity of the penalty. Thus the ideology behind this prohibition is religious, not merely legal.[2]

Finally, sacrificing to other gods is clearly in the realm of religion rather than ordinary jurisprudence. Such sacrifice is contrary to the exclusive claims that YHWH makes on Israel for worship in the Sinaitic covenant. As a direct violation of the essence of that covenant, this case has the strongest of the condemnation formulae.

Social Justice I: Oppression and Loans:
Exodus 22.20-27 [English 22.21-28]

(20) You [sing.] are not to wrong a sojourner nor oppress him for you [pl.] were sojourners in the land of Egypt.

(21) You [pl.] are not to afflict severely a widow or orphan. (22) If you [sing.] severely afflict such a one, it will be [כִּי] if he [or she] cries out passionately to me, I will listen favorably to his cry, (23) become angry, and slay you [pl.] with a sword so that your women will become widows and your children orphans.

(24) If you [sing.] give money in loan to my people, to the poor person living with you, you [sing.] must not be a creditor to him; you [pl.] are not to charge him with interest. (25) If you [sing.] take as collateral the garment of your fellow, you should return it to him before the sun sets

the Minotaur, the bull-man Minotaur resulted from the copulation between a woman and a bull. In the Gilgamesh Epic, Ishtar is depicted as the wanton lover of a bird, a lion, and a stallion (*ANET*, p. 84, lines 48-56). In contrast, YHWH prohibits copulation with animals. Since deities often blur the distinction between human and animal forms, what was considered acceptable behavior for the gods might not have been for humans. Cf. B.L. Eichler, 'Bestiality', *IDBSup*, pp. 96-97, and for the Ugarit and Cretan evidence Gordon, 'Poetic Legends', pp. 108, 121-22.

1.   Schwienhorst-Schönberger, *Bundesbuch*, p. 322. Cf. W. Krebs, 'Zur kultischen Kohabitation mit Tieren im Alten Orient', *Forschungen und Fortschritte* 37 (1963), pp. 19-21.

2.   The only cuneiform legal collection which treats bestiality is the Hittite which also had a religious dimension. Sexual relations between a man and a cow, sheep, pig, or dog were punishable by death (§§187, 188, 199), though sexual relations with a horse or a mule entailed only exclusion from the presence of the king and priest (§200). The religious element is seen in that ritual purification of the town followed such offenses. Cf. Eichler, 'Bestiality'.

(26) if perchance it should be that his garment is his only covering for his skin. In what else can he sleep? So if he should have to cry to me, I will listen to him, for I am gracious.

(27) [In sum,] you [sing.] must not act in disrespect of God nor bring under a ban a leader of your people.

Exodus 22.20-27 and Structure

Exod. 22.20-27 picks up on the conclusion of 22.17-19 that condemns sacrifice to any god except YHWH by treating the case of a sojourner (גר).

A גר could be an Israelite living outside of his own tribe (cf. Judg. 17.7-9; 19.16), but more often as here it refers to a resident, non-Canaanite foreigner. Such a person would likely have at one time worshipped foreign gods in violation of Exod. 22.19, though while he lives among the Israelites he must follow Israel's religious practices: The גר among the Israelites who eats leavened bread at Passover is to be 'cut off', and if he wants to celebrate Passover he and his household must be circumcised (Exod. 12.19, 48-49; cf. Num. 9.14). He must also keep the Sabbath (Exod. 20.10) and the Day of Atonement (Lev. 16.29). He may offer sacrifice but only to YHWH with proper offering of the blood and is unclean if he eats anything torn by animals (Lev. 17.8-15; 22.18; Num. 15.14-18). If he touches anything dead, he must remove his impurity by ritual (Num. 19.10). He can be put to death for offering his children to Molech (Lev. 20.2), or for 'showing disrespect for the Name' (Lev. 24.16). Sacrifices for the 'unwitting' sins of Israel are valid for sojourners (Num. 15.26-30) and he may use cities of refuge (Num. 35.15).

By its placement after the condemnation of sacrifice to other gods (22.19), the present regulation affirms that though the worship of foreign gods is condemned, a foreigner must not be mistreated even if he had an idolatrous past (22.20).[1] This is perhaps why the case of the sojourner begins this series, after which the author continues the theme of protecting other social groups susceptible to exploitation: widows, the fatherless, and poor debtors.

Exod. 22.20-27 falls into three cases and a concluding generalization:

---

1. So *b.B.Meṣ.* 59b, and the *Mekilta ad. loc.* and other rabbinic commentators. Cited by Leibowitz, *Studies in Shemot*, pp. 379-89.

I. *Three Cases of Oppression (Exodus 22.20-26)*

Case A. Oppression of Sojourners (22.20)
    1. Command: No oppression (v. 20a)
    2. Motive clause: empathy (v. 20b)

Case B. The Oppression of Widows and the Fatherless
    (22.21-23)

    1. Command: No affliction (v. 21)
    2. Motive clause: Threat of Divine Wrath (vv. 22-23)

Case C. Oppression of the Poor (22.24-26)

    1. Commands (vv. 24-25)

      a. No taking of Interest from Poor
      b. Return of needed Items taken as Pledge

    2. Motive Clauses (v. 26)

      a. Sympathy
      b. Threat of Punishment

II. *Generalizing Summary (Exodus 22.27)*

A. Do not show disrespect for the moral standards of heaven
    (v. 27a)
B. Do not show disrespect for the moral standards of earth
    (v. 27b).

There is a clear, parallel structure for the three cases: each includes a command or commands, and a motive clause or clauses that gives Israel reasons for obeying the imperatives. Verse 27 in itself shows poetic parallelism,[1] which thereby underscores this principle that underlies all biblical regulations: respect for God and his human agents.

The most controversial aspect of this outline is including v. 27 with precepts demanding humanitarian treatment of disadvantaged classes. I follow H.C. Brichto in this.[2] Verse 27 is usually rendered as an independent precept, 'Do not revile God, nor curse a ruler of your people.' However, Brichto has shown that קלל needs not, and usually does not involve speech,[3] and that א.ר.ר cannot be limited to the meaning '[spoken] curse', but more basically means 'bind with a spell,

---

1. Patrick, *Law*, p. 87.
2. The connection was previously seen by Keil, *Pentateuch*, p. 143.
3. Brichto, *'Curse'*, pp. 118-79.

put under a ban'.[1] He proposed that in Exod. 22.27, אֱלֹהִים לֹא תְקַלֵּל
means not 'do not curse God' (still less 'judges'), but 'do not show disrespect for Deity', that is, do not disregard God's moral standards.
Also וְנָשִׂיא בְעַמְּךָ לֹא תָאֹר is not limited to 'and do not curse a leader of
your people', but is figurative (by metonymy) for contempt for civil
authority. Hence, Brichto can paraphrase: 'Do not do anything which
is an assault on the moral standards of heaven or earth.'[2]

Interpreted in this way, v. 27, rather than being an independent
precept, forms the generalizing conclusion of the humanitarian precepts that precede. In vv. 23 and 26, God warns that he himself will
take up the case of an oppressed orphan, widow, or poor man. Verse
27 forms a conclusion to this thought: 'Do not take me [or my threatened judgment] lightly [especially, in context, by exploiting a
sojourner, widow, orphan, the poor], nor show contempt for a leader
of your people [who as a human agent of my judgment will also exact
punishment for illegal exploitations].

On the Use of Pronouns in Exodus 22.20-27

At this point Exod. 20.22–23.19 passes from the mostly impersonal,
third person formulation of Exod. 21.2–22.19 to a predominantly
personal, second person style, addressing Israel as 'you' (whether
singular or plural). On the use and lack of use of the personal
pronoun throughout Exod. 20.22–23.19, see Chapter 4.

Not immediately obvious is the reason for the changes from second
person singular (you [sing.]) to second person plural (you [pl.]) and
vice versa that occur in these verses: v. 20a is singular but 20b is
plural; vv. 21-23 pass from plural to singular to plural; v. 24 goes
from singular to plural, and v. 25 is only singular. This could be no
more than meaningless stylistic variation. Others, predictably, see the
plural forms as evidence for secondary insertions,[3] though Sonsino
with good reason criticizes the use of the change in number from
second person singular to second person plural as a criterion for
source divisions generally since the phenomenon of interchange
between singular and plural in the second person is quite common in
Deuteronomy 5–24 where it is impossible to remove the 'sources'

---

1.   Brichto, 'Curse', pp. 114-15.
2.   Brichto, 'Curse', p. 158.
3.   E. Neufeld, 'The Prohibitions against Loans at Interest in Ancient Hebrew
Laws', *HUCA* 26 (1955), p. 366, and Fishbane, *Biblical Interpretation*, p. 174.

without doing damage to the sense of the text as a whole.[1] Given the common nature of this phenomenon, a different explanation must be preferred.

Beyerlin suggested that the switch from singular to plural could reflect the practice of cultic settings and serve to intensify the admonitions that were directed to every listener.[2] 'Intensification' perhaps explains the switch to the plural 'you' in v. 20 and v. 24, assuming the plural verb to be the correct text.[3] However, the introduction of a 'cultic setting' seems gratuitous.

The warning in vv. 22-23 suggested to Ibn Ezra a rhetorical-critical explanation for the change in number. His view is tentatively accepted here for this instance of this phenomenon. The text states that if you [sing.] afflict the widow or the fatherless, God will slay you [pl.] with the sword and make your [pl.] wives widows and your [pl.] sons fatherless. The threatened punishment is clearly that of war against the nation rather than retribution directly against the actual oppressors. The point is that if individual Israelites commit this offense (hence the singular), it can bring Israelites not directly involved into peril (hence the plural), following the same principle as the case of Achan's sin causing the nation to suffer in Joshua 7. Ibn Ezra draws the following principle from this phenomenon: if Israelites passively stand aloof and do not succor the afflicted when an Israelite oppresses his fellow, the nation as a whole by merit of its inaction can be held guilty of the offense.[4]

Exodus 22.20-27 and Other Passages
The choice of including a regulation about sojourners (Exod. 22.20b) is related to the narrative. The text clearly alludes back to the sojourn in Egypt: 'for you were גרים in the land of Egypt' (cf. Lev. 19.34). A verb for oppression in v. 20 (ל.ח.ץ) is a root also used to describe Israel's oppression during the sojourn in Egypt (Exod. 3.9; Deut. 26.8-9).

---

1. Sonsino, *Motive Clauses*, pp. 195-98.
2. Cited by Sonsino, *Motive Clauses*, p. 197.
3. The Samaritan, LXX, Syriac and Targum have all the verbs in the plural in v. 20; the LXX, Syriac, and Vulgate read all the verbs as singular in v. 24. Hence the versions avoid some of the changes in number found in the Masoretic Text, which could be used as evidence that the MT is corrupt.
4. Cited by Leibowitz, *Studies in Shemot*, p. 391.

The inclusion of 22.21-23, the case of the widow and the fatherless, and 22.24-26, the case of the poor, may also be related to the Exodus narrative. The verb for oppression in v. 21 (D-stem of ע.נ.ה, 'afflict') is used to describe the harsh treatment of Israel by the Egyptian taskmasters (Exod. 1.11-12). The motive clause of vv. 22-23 warns that if a widow or orphan whom they afflict cries out to God, God will become angry and punish Israel, which is exactly what God did to Egypt when he saw Israel's affliction (עֳנִי) and heard their cry (Exod. 3.7, 9). Similarly in v. 24 God will hear the cry of the poor/afflicted (הֶעָנִי) whose garment is seized as pledge (v. 26b).

Lev. 25.35-38 and Deut. 23.20-21 expand on the prohibition of loans at interest. Deut. 24.13-14 repeats the injunction encouraging lenders to return the poor man's pledged garment (cf. Amos 2.8).

An allusion is made to Exod. 22.27 in 1 Kgs 21.10 where Naboth is falsely accused (according to the usual translation) of 'cursing God and the king' (ב.ר.ך here is used as a euphemism for D-stem of ק.ל.ל). In my view, however, Naboth would be accused, not of blasphemy, but of generally transgressing the laws of God and man, the specific charge not being indicated by the author of Kings. Note also Acts 23.5 where Paul quotes v. 27b in apologizing (in an ironic tone?) for showing contempt for the high priest.

Exodus 22.20-27: Law or Morality?
Upon close examination, it is clear that Exod. 22.20-27 is essentially moral rather than legal in nature. The calls to empathy ('you were sojourners in Egypt', 22.20b) and sympathy ('It is all he has to cover himself', v. 26) appeal to conscience which is more a moral than a legal category. The threatened punishment (vv. 23, 26) comes not from the state to enforce a law, but from God himself to enforce his morality, though a hint of state enforcement is found in v. 27b with mention of a human leader. The use of first person and second person, I/me/you, places these precepts in the category of moral exhortation rather than law.

Several poetic features here are more appropriate as literary art than legal precision: the allusion to the Exodus narrative in v. 20, the irony of the poetic justice in vv. 22-23 in which Israelites who tolerate the oppression of widows and orphans are threatened by divine punishment with having their wives become widows and their sons orphans, a possible word-play in v. 24 among עַמִּי 'my people', עָנִי

'poor', and עִמָּךְ 'with you',[1] and the poetry-like parallelism in v. 27.

The various types of oppression described here, though always immoral, can sometimes be legal. For example, an employer who takes advantage of a desperate poor man by paying extremely low wages would not be acting illegally in a society without a minimum wage law, but the act is condemned morally by these precepts. A seller who charges an exorbitant price to foreigners simply because he thinks them to be ignorant of the fair market value of his commodity would also be acting legally—he can charge whatever he wishes—and yet he falls under the condemnation of these precepts.

The prohibition of loans at interest is directed specifically to loans made to the poor, just as the parallel passage in Lev. 25.35-38 (Deut. 23.20-21 discourages loans at interest to any Israelite, but even there the motive is the avoidance of the economic enslavement of the poor). This precept does not seem to apply to loans for business ventures; rather, it applies to loans to keep a poor person solvent. Likewise, the prohibition against seizing a garment as pledge applies if and only if the garment is his only one.

These precepts are intended to avoid the economic enslavement and affliction of the poor and to prevent the wealthy from profiteering from their plight. It is not just that interest rates were high, though they often were in ancient times.[2] Rather, interest-taking is seen by the lawgiver as a device for trapping the poor into permanent poverty. A wealthy Israelite, according to the text, should give loans to the poor as an act of charity rather than for his own economic gain.

Such a precept would be difficult to enforce as law: a wealthy man could simply refuse to lend at all. Moreover, legal fictions can be devised to avoid the letter of a usury law, as often happened in the Middle Ages when all interest taking was legally prohibited.[3] But even

---

1.   Cassuto, *Exodus*, p. 292.

2.   R.P. Maloney ('Usury and Restrictions on Interest-Taking in the Ancient Near East', *CBQ* 36 [1974], pp. 1-20) shows that ancient Near East legal collections try to limit the amount of interest which could be charged. For various periods the legal limits were: Old Babylonian—20% for money and 33.3% for grain; Middle Assyrian—25% for money and 50% for grain; Neo-Babylonian and Persian—20% for both money and grain. Despite these 'legal' limits, Maloney notes that abundant examples of even more exorbitant interest-taking occur.

3.   Traditionally in the medieval Christendom, talmudic Judaism, and even Islam (through the Koran's version), these regulations have been (in my view) misinterpreted by (1) understanding the regulations as prohibiting all interest-taking

if this requirement is impractical as enforced law, it remains valid as a statement of a moral ideal. After Nehemiah became governor, he used the moral force of this precept to chide lenders to drop the interest on Jews in distress due to sacrifices made for building Nehemiah's wall (Neh. 5.1-13). Nehemiah did not simply enforce the precept as law, even though Ezra had made Jewish law the state law of Judah (Ezra 7.25-26, assuming the priority of Ezra), for this is not law to be enforced by the state, but a moral precept.

The regulation on the sojourner shows an enlightened attitude towards non-Israelites for which there is no parallel in Mesopotamian law.[1] Indeed, according to rabbinic counting, the Torah cautions Israel regarding behavior towards a stranger some 36 times, more than the commandments concerning love of God, keeping the Sabbath, circumcision, uttering falsehood, and theft.[2] The theme of not oppressing a sojourner recurs at Exod. 23.9 (see below).

Cultic Matters II:
Dedication to God, Firstfruits, Firstborn, and Holiness:
Exodus 22.28-30 [English 22.29-31]

(28) You [sing.] are not to hold back your [sing.] abundance and your [sing.] overflowing [of oil/wine].[3] The firstborn of your [sing.] sons you [sing.] are to give to me. (29) You [sing.] must do the same for your cattle [and] for your flock. Seven days it may remain with its mother, but on the eighth day you are to give it over to me. (30) You [pl.] are to be men holy to me. You [pl.] are not to eat flesh torn by beasts in the field. You [pl.] should rather throw it to the dogs.

altogether, and (2) trying to enforce this moral precept as law. This proved impractical from the financial perspective where economic realities have conflicted with the legal ideal, and resulted in all kinds of 'legal fictions' to get around the letter of the usury laws. Cf. *EncJud*, 'Usury', XVI, pp. 30-31 for various evasions, one of which was to lend to a non-Jew (for whom the law did not apply) who would then lend to a Jew.

1. C. van Houten, *The Alien in Israelite Law* (JSOTSup 107; Sheffield: JSOT Press, 1991), p. 34.

2. *B. Meṣ* 59b, cited by Leibowitz, *Studies in Shemot*, p. 380.

3. 'Abundance and overflowing' is probably a hendiadys for 'your abundant [grape/olive] drippings' (Childs, *Exodus*, p. 450). In Num. 18.27 'abundance' (מְלֵאָה) refers specifically to the produce of grapes as opposed to produce of the threshing floor. דָּמַע only occurs here but seems related to דִּמְעָה 'tear'; hence, seems to be some sort of liquid effluent.

Exodus 22.28-30 and Structure

Exod. 22.28-30 is organized, as Patrick notes,[1] around a threefold use
of the expression 'to me' in vv. 28, 29, and 30. It consists of several
cases of dedication to God. Two cases are of firstfruits and firstborn
that are 'given' to God, and in the third case the Israelite people are
'holy/separated' to God in the realm of dietary law:

I. Firstfruits/firstborn dedicated to God

    A. First 'to me':
        1. Firstfruits of drippings given (v. 28a)
        2. Firstborn sons given. (v. 28b)

    B. Second 'to me'
        1. Firstborn ox/flock given after 8 days (v. 29)

II. Israel as a whole consecrated to God

    C. Third 'to me'
        1. All Israelites holy to God (v. 30a)
        2. One example of holiness; torn flesh not to be eaten by men
          (v. 30b)

Exod. 22.28-30 continues the juxtaposition of cultic and social regulations discussed at the beginning of the chapter. One reason why this
cultic unit in particular might come in between the two sections on
social justice is that it develops the Exodus theme of the surrounding
units. The first verse of Exod. 22.20-27 and the last verse of Exod.
23.1-9 form an inclusio around the 'social justice' units, each giving a
motive clause for social justice based on Israel's experience of
oppression in Egypt ('You [pl.] were sojourners in the land of
Egypt'). Meanwhile, the cultic regulations in between, namely Exod.
22.28-30, repeat commands given during the exodus (13.2, 11-13,
consecration of firstborn; 19.6, Israel's call to holiness at Sinai).

The exodus experience, then, motivates compliance with both the
social justice units and the cultic regulations in between. Those who
were slaves to Egypt have been redeemed by God from earthly
bondage, but remain slaves of God, separated to him in holiness,
worship, and obedience.

There seems to be a formal and auditory link between v. 27 of the
last unit and v. 28a. Both display inverted word order (object, nega-
tion, verb), and לֹא תָאֹר ('you will not put under a ban') in 27b has

1. Patrick, *Law*, p. 87.

174   *'The Book of the Covenant': A Literary Approach*

phonetic similarities with לֹא תְאַחֵר of 28a ('you will not delay'), an example of wordplay.[1]

Pronouns and Unity in Exodus 22.28-30
The regulations here are again personally formulated, God the speaker referring to himself as 'me' and to Israel as 'you', either singular or plural. As in Exod. 22.20-27, there is the curious change in number from second person singular (vv. 28-29) to second person plural (v. 30). This has been sometimes taken as evidence of a secondary insertion.[2]

On the other hand, the switch to a plural can just as well be seen as an intensification by the author to underscore the concept of holiness so basic to the covenant (cf. Exod. 19.6). The alleged discrepancy between this 'addition' and Exod. 21.35-36, where an animal killed by an ox (by implication) could be eaten, can also be explained: The author perhaps saw a distinction between killing by an ox, a 'clean' domestic animal, and killing by a 'dog', an 'unclean' scavenger. 'Pet' dogs are not in view.[3] A distinction can also be made between a killing with humans nearby so the blood could be poured out to God and a carcass torn by beasts in the field where this would probably be impossible.

Exodus 22.28-30 and Other Passages
God's claim on the firstborn of humans and animals is a repetition of the claim made, with similar emphasis on 'to me', in Exod. 13.2 in the context of the exodus and the plague of the firstborn in Egypt: 'Consecrate to me every firstborn opening every womb among the Israelites; whether among man or beasts, it belongs to me.' Hence, the dedication of Exod. 22.28-29 is a reminder of the exodus. In the same

1.   Cassuto, *Exodus*, p. 294. Cassuto (p. 295) also sees wordplay in בְּשַׂר בַּשָּׂדֶה (v. 30), though Budd offers the text-critical explanation that בַּשָּׂדֶה is to be omitted as dittography (noted but rejected by Childs, *Exodus*, p. 450).
2.   Cazelles, (*Études*, pp. 84-85) agrees with Menés, Bäntsch, and Gressmann that Exod. 22.30 is secondary.
3.   Although domesticated dogs were common in Egypt and Persia in antiquity, and the burial of a large number of what may have been domesticated dogs was found at Persian period Ashkelon and other Persian and Hellenistic period sites near the coast of Palestine, there is little evidence of pet, or still less of pampered dogs in ancient Israel generally. Cf. P. Wapnish and B. Hesse, 'Pampered Pooches or Plain Pariahs? The Ashkelon Dog Burials', *BA* 56 (1993), pp. 55-80.

context, Exod. 13.13 makes it clear that this consecration need not be carried out by literal sacrifice, but that more expensive animals, and humans could be redeemed by substitution of a lamb (cf. also Exod. 34.19-20 that essentially repeats this instruction). The author could assume that his readers would read the present regulation in light of previous instructions, and not be tempted to see human sacrifice in the demand to give God the firstborn sons. The reader would also be acquainted with the metaphorical usage of Israel as God's firstborn (Exod. 4.22) which the present regulation of dedication of the firstborn to God serves to enrich. Subsequently in the narrative, the Levites were set apart to serve God as a substitute for the firstborn males (Num. 3.12-13; cf. Exod. 32.25-29).

The statement (v. 30) that 'you [pl.] are to be men holy to me' reminds the reader of Exod. 19.6, 'you [pl.] will be to me…a holy nation', holiness being an essential ingredient of the covenant made in Exodus 19–24 between God and Israel. Indeed, the second person plural in Exod. 19.6, to which allusion is here made, could be an additional reason why the second person plural is used in 22.30 (see discussion above). Deut. 14.21 seems to expand on Exod. 22.30, allowing the carcass to be passed on to a sojourner or a foreigner, but not eaten by an Israelite.

The choice of the number 'seven' in which the firstborn may stay with its mother is probably symbolic for 'the period of completeness' or the like. See the use of 'seven' in Exod. 21.2, 23.10-12. In particular, it parallels the rite of circumcision for all Israelite boy babies on the eighth day (Gen. 17.12) which is another kind of dedication to God.

The rules on firstfruits, firstborn, and prohibited foods can be brief here because the author/editor(s) of the Pentateuch was aware that subsequent passages flesh out these subjects.

Exodus 22.28-30: Law, Religion, or Morality?
Exod. 22.28-30 is religious and ethical rather than legal in orientation. The offering of the firstborn and firstfruits is a way of indicating appreciation to God for the blessings of fruitful wombs and crops, acknowledging that only by God's grace do these blessings occur. At the beginning of the wine or olive harvest, a token of juice from the presses could be offered to God for this purpose (cf. Lev. 23.10-11), and the firstborn of the herd or flock are offered for the same purpose. Not to acknowledge God as provider of all blessings would be an act

of ingratitude. It might lead God to withhold his blessing in the future. However, it is not clear that these religious obligations were to receive enforcement by the state; hence, noncompliance would be immoral and invite divine retribution on the individual, but would probably not be illegal (defined in terms of regulations enforced by the state).

Holiness, an essential feature of the covenant (Exod. 19.6), has both moral and ritual significance. Exod. 22.30b, which speaks against eating meat torn by predators (טְרֵפָה), is perhaps motivated by both concerns. Eating meat torn by predators might be interpreted as dehumanizing,[1] reducing man to the level of vulture, or, to use the text's terminology, a scavenger dog. In the Bible, the dog has primarily negative connotations (cf. Eccl. 9.4); comparison of men with dogs was a common means of indicating contempt (1 Sam. 17.43; 2 Kgs 8.13; Job 30.1; Ps. 22.17 [Eng. 16]). Likewise in Mesopotamia comparison with dogs could be used as a disparagement of oneself or as an invective against others.[2]

Problematic for this ethical interpretation is that neither טרפה nor the related term טֶרֶף is condemned absolutely in the Bible. They are only prohibited if one planned to approach the sanctuary. One text grants permission to use the fat for purposes other than eating (Lev. 7.24).[3] A possible response is that *eating* an animal torn by predators is of a different order of magnitude of involvement than mere *use* of its fat.

If the eating of טרפה were condemned because it would be 'dehumanizing', it is also strange that the related term טרף according to some texts was permissible to be eaten. In Ps. 111.5 God gives טרף to those who fear him, and in Prov. 31.15 the ideal wife gives טרף to her house. This permission would be understandable if טרף were only prohibited when one was to approach a holy site. However, Mal. 3.10 is stronger still: God even calls for טרף to be brought into his house (the Temple), problematic not only for the ethical interpretation, but also problematic (on the assumption that the Bible is consistent on this matter) for the cultic interpretation that טרפה is only prohibited in connection with the sanctuary since in Malachi טרף is to be brought into the sanctuary.

---

1. Cf. Milgrom, *Studies*, pp. 104-18. Milgrom interprets the matrix of dietary laws along ethical lines.
2. S.v. '*kalbu*', *CAD* K, VIII, p. 72.
3. Brichto, '*Curse*', p. 105 n. 58.

The probable explanation for these three texts is that the term טרף here has left its etymological sense of 'flesh torn by predators' behind and has developed the secondary sense of 'meat/food' (BDB, p. 383). This view resolves the conflict between the passages that allow טרף in the general sense of 'meat' and Exod. 22.30's prohibition of eating טרפה in the strict sense of 'flesh torn by predators'.[1]

The cultic aspect of Exod. 22.30 seems clear: to eat a torn animal brings uncleanness upon the eater (Lev. 17.15 says the eater of טרפה is unclean till evening after ritual washing) and renders contact with that which is holy (esp. the Tabernacle) dangerous for the person unclean. The uncleanness could possibly be related to the prohibition of 'eating blood' since it would be impossible to drain the blood properly in the case of a torn animal. However, the connection with 'eating blood' is itself not without difficulty since Deut. 14.21 allows the carcass to be eaten by non-Israelites, whereas eating of blood is prohibited to non-Israelites as well as Israelites (Gen. 9.4).[2]

Touching a carcass in general brings 'uncleanness' upon the one touching it (Num. 5.2). More generally, the prohibition of eating meat torn by predators fits into the larger symbolic matrix of cultic laws of holiness that instructs Israel to turn from death and choose life.[3]

Social Justice II:
Testimony in Court and an Enemy's Beast:
Exodus 23.1-9

Testimony/Administration of Justice (begins)

(23.1) You [sing.] must not voice a baseless rumor, you must not join hands with the guilty so that you become a wrongful witness. (2) You [sing.] must not follow the multitude [or 'the great'] so as to bring about

---

1.   Brichto, ('*Curse*', pp. 105-106), however, denies the existence of the simple sense 'meat' for טרף or טרפה, but instead understands it to mean 'unslaughtered meat' or carrion. He argues from Lev. 17.15; 22.28; Ps. 111.5; Ezek. 4.14, and 44.31 that the prohibition of eating טרפה or טרף was limited to priests who by their duties have daily contact with that which is holy. However, Mal. 3.10 where God asks for טרף in his 'house' is problematic for Brichto's denial of the simple sense 'meat' for טרף. For this reason he emends that text by deleting one consonant to avoid it.

2.   Patrick, *Law*, p. 88.

3.   Cf. J. Milgrom, 'The Rationale for Cultic Law: The Case of Impurity', *Semeia* 45 (1989), pp. 103-109.

evil. You [sing.] must not give an answer in a dispute in such a way that you sway after the multitude [or 'the great'] with the result that you pervert [your testimony]. (3) And as for the poor man, you [sing.] are not to show preference in his dispute either.

Excursus: Concerning an Enemy's Animal

(4) Should you [sing.] chance upon the head of cattle of your enemy, or his donkey, gone astray, you ought to return it to him. (5) If you [sing.] see the donkey of one who hates you lying down under its burden, and you would refrain from freeing [it] along with him (וחדלת מעזב לו), you ought nevertheless to free [it] along with him [its owner] (עזב תעזב עמו).

Testimony/Administration of Justice (concludes)

(6) You are not to pervert the justice due to your needy in his dispute. (7) Distance yourself [sing.] from a false charge. Neither the innocent one [if the accused] nor the one in the right [if the plaintiff] slay, for I do not acquit the criminal. (8) You [sing.] are not to accept a present, for a present blinds the clear-sighted and distorts the words of those in the right. (9) You [sing.] are not to oppress a sojourner. You [pl.] yourselves are acquainted with the life of a sojourner, for you [pl.] were sojourners in the land of Egypt.

Exodus 23.1-9 and Structure

Exod. 23.1-9 continues the pattern of alternating sections on social justice and cultic regulations. Exod. 23.1-9 can be divided into three sub-sections on the basis of content and form: vv. 1-3 that contain five commands in 'apodictic' style which emphasize testimony in court, vv. 4-5 that contain two 'casuistic' formulations (כי) concerning one's enemy's animal, and vv. 6-9 that contain five more commands in 'apodictic' style pertaining to justice in court. Hence the two apodictic sections balance each other around the casuistic section with five imperatives each:

A. Five Imperatives concerning Testimony in Court (23.1-3)
1.   On passing along idle rumors
2.   On cooperation with the guilty
3. & 4.   On testimony unduly influenced by others (v. 2, two imperatives)
5.   On testimony unduly influenced by pity for miserable status of the accused (v. 3)

X. Excursus: Illustration of Impartiality—Even Enemies Must Be Treated more than Decently (23.4-5)
1.   Enemy's animal gone astray (v. 4)
2.   Enemy's donkey lying under load (v. 5)

A*. Five Imperatives concerning Justice in Court (23.6-9)
1.   On justice to the needy (v. 6)
2.   On false charges (v. 7a)
3.   On not condemning the innocent (v. 7b)
4.   On not accepting gifts (v. 8)
5.   On justice to sojourners (v. 9)

Most of the commands in the two apodictic sub-sections can be divided into pairs: 23.1a and 1b has to do with baseless testimony that allows the guilty to go unpunished. 23.2a and 2b prohibits allowing one's testimony to be unduly influenced by the 'many' (רַבִּים), a term which might be rendered 'the great' (Tanakh) in contrast with the poor/needy that follows. The end of section A, 23.3, which prohibits giving special preference out of pity to a poor man (דל) in his case is balanced by the first line of section A*, 23.6, which condemns the opposite problem of perverting justice for the needy (אביון). The next two imperatives, 23.7a and 7b, are less clearly linked, but perhaps, given the previous pattern, should be, and hence mean: do not accept false testimony with the result that the innocent are condemned. The final two imperatives, which prohibit gifts/bribes and oppression of the sojourner are not easily linked, but each has an associated explanatory/motive clause which balances each imperative and largely mitigates the need for balancing with parallel imperatives.

Contrast the radical source-oriented approach of McKay[1] who by eliminating v. 9 as secondary (noting the plurals) and by an arbitrary rewriting and reorganizing of both regulations and their motive clauses to fit a hypothetical original 'decalogue' of apodictic formulations is able to maintain pairs of imperatives. Schwienhorst-Schönberger[2] also proposes a very complicated redactional history: The oldest part of 23.1-9 is vv. 1a, 2a, and 6 (without בריבו) to which was added vv. 1b, 2b, 3, 4, 5, and 6 (only בריבו). Still later v. 7b was added by the *Gottesrechtsredaktor*, and at a still later stage the Dtr redactor added vv. 8-9. Such reconstructions are so arbitrary, speculative, and complex that they must almost certainly be wrong.

The most serious problem of structure is the question of why Exod. 23.4-5 interrupts the series of apodictic regulations concerning matters of court. Frequently, source-oriented scholars have regarded

1.   J.W. McKay, 'Exodus XXIII 1-3, 6-8: A Decalogue for the Administration of Justice in the City Gate', *VT* 21 (1971), pp. 311-25.
2.   Schwienhorst-Schönberger, *Bundesbuch*, pp. 379-88.

180   'The Book of the Covenant': A Literary Approach

these verses as a clumsy intrusion into the apodictic regulations or otherwise displaced from its original context.[1] It is possible, however, to read these verses as a parenthetical excursus deliberately placed by the author in the exact middle of the ten imperatives, designed to show the extent to which one is to be impartial as a witness in court.

Exod. 23.3 says that one is not to show favoritism to a poor man. This is surprising, given the many exhortations on behalf of the poor among these regulations (cf. 22.20-27) and elsewhere in the Bible. So surprising, in fact, that a number of scholars (Knobel, Bäntsch, Jepsen, Noth, BHS mg.) emend ודל 'and a poor man' to גדל, 'a great man'.[2]

Having jarred his readers with the statement about a poor man, and wanting to illustrate the need for radical impartiality, the author gives an excursus on the treatment of an enemy's beast: that you must return it if you find it wandering astray, and you must help your enemy with it if you find it lying under its load.

Exod. 23.5 has two important cruxes of translation. The first question is of syntax: is וחדלת מעזב part of the conclusion, hence an imperative, 'then you must cease from עזב', or is it part of the premise expressing an optative mood, 'and if you would wish to refrain from עזב'? The second issue is the meaning of ע.ז.ב in vv. 5b and 5c.

The context (cf. also the parallel in Deut. 22.4) seems to demand an unusual sense for ע.ז.ב that normally means 'leave, abandon, forsake'. Some resolve the difficulty by emendation of עזב to עזר 'help' on the basis of the LXX.[3] Rashi (and recently the RSV) supposed that ע.ז.ב itself could have the secondary sense of 'help'. BDB (p. 737) suggests a secondary sense for עזב, 'let loose, set free, let go', with the translation of v. 5c, 'you will by all means free it with him [its owner]'. Without resorting to different roots, Keil[4] likewise sees two senses in 5b and 5c: 'cease from *leaving* it to him [the enemy]; thou shalt *loosen*

1.   For example, Driver (*Exodus*, p. 237) thinks vv. 4-5 belong after 22.23 or 26.

2.   Childs, *Exodus*, p. 450.

3.   L. Koehler and W. Baumgartner (eds.), *Lexicon in Veteris Testamenti Libros* (Leiden: Brill, 1958), p. 693, emends עזב to עזר 'help' in v. 5c, finding the MT impossible. This finds some support with the LXX's συνεγείρω [variant: συναίρω] ('help to raise/raise up together').

4.   Keil, *Pentateuch*, pp. 144-45.

it with him'. Cassuto[1] takes the meaning of ע.ז.ב in 5c from the alleged Ugaritic cognate 'DB meaning 'make, prepare, set', in the sense here of 'arrange the load'. The resulting combination, according to Cassuto, is a word-play on two roots עזב I and עזב II, the first part meaning 'you shall refrain from leaving (עזב I) him,' with the second part meaning '[rather] you shall arrange (עזב II) [the load on the donkey's back] with him [its owner]'. Like Cassuto, the Tanakh translation assumes עזב II, but in both 5b and 5c render as 'raising/raise' and defend this rendering from Neh. 3.8, 34 and Deut. 22.4 (cf. LXX above and note). However, Dietrich and Loretz[2] argue that the Hebrew עזב would be cognate with Ugaritic 'DB not 'DB, and so 'DB is of no help for Hebrew עזב. Moreover, the existence of עזב II in biblical Hebrew is rejected by Williamson.[3]

My translation of this difficult text assumes that a secondary meaning of עזב I is used, that both v. 5b and v. 5c use the verb in the same sense rather than differing ones, and (to avoid contradiction) v. 5b is part of the premise, 'and you would wish to refrain from freeing it', rather than a command. I take עזב as an antonym of עצר and אסר in the sense of 'loosen'.

I accept the traditional interpretation that, however one translates 23.5, the regulation encourages one to help his enemy with his donkey (cf. Deut. 22.4), there being in the circumstance described need for one person to support the burden while the other loosens the strappings in order to ease the burden off the animal. Once an animal has been brought to its knees due to an overly heavy load, it is impossible to raise it (short of a derrick) without lightening the load. If the load is strapped on, a single person undoing the knot or buckle may cause the total load to fall over, taking the animal with it and doing it harm. Hence the owner needs a helper to support the load while he loosens it, and the text exhorts that one provide this help even for one's enemy. This is not only for the sake of the enemy, but also for the sake of the innocent victim of the enemy's cruelty or greed, namely the donkey.

---

1. Cassuto, *Exodus*, p. 297.
2. M. Dietrich and O. Loretz, ''DB and 'DB im Ugaritischen', *UF* 17 (1986), pp. 105-116.
3. H.G.M. Williamson, 'A Reconsideration of עזב in Biblical Hebrew', *ZAW* 97 (1985), pp. 74-85.

Cooper[1] is dissatisfied with the traditional interpretations of 23.5 that see it as encouraging 'benevolence towards a personal enemy' because in his opinion the general Old Testament attitude towards enemies is otherwise. Consequently, he has proposed to read the verse instead as practical advice: if you see your enemy's loaded donkey recumbent, although you might be tempted to interfere with it in one way or another, you must leave it alone, that is, not harm it or even help it lest your enemy misinterpret your good intentions and a dispute ensue. Cooper's view does not fit so well with the context of Exod. 23.1-9 or 23.4 as the traditional view does, and its morality is less noble. On its principle, one would expect v. 4 to read, 'If you find your enemy's ox or donkey gone astray, you should leave it alone [lest he see you and suppose you to be stealing it]'. His objection to seeing a New Testamental type of love of enemies is somewhat mitigated when one recognizes that the text is concerned not solely with the enemy, but also with his innocent victim, the animal.

I now return to the question of structure. The principle indirectly implied by the location of the parenthesis of 23.4-5 in the context of 23.1-9 is that just as you ought not to allow sympathy for a poor man to distort your treatment of him in court (vv. 3, 6); likewise, you cannot allow your antipathy for one at odds with you to cause you to treat him or someone related to him badly. These two cases on how one should treat an enemy in context speaks concerning *impartiality in court*, that one should never act out of rancor towards the persons involved, but you should help the one in need—metaphorically represented by the donkey—even if in doing so you help your enemy. But it also expresses a more general principle that transcends the courtroom context of the other regulations.

I note that there is a bracketing of the beginning and end of the two 'social justice' units: the first unit of Exod. 22.20-27 begins, while the last unit of Exod. 23.1-9 ends with the sojourner (גֵּר). This inclusio around the 'social justice' units can be taken as evidence of deliberate structuring on the part of the author/editor.

Pronouns and Other Stylistic Matters in Exodus 23.1-9
Exod. 23.1-9 exhibits a personal style in which God in the first person ('I') addresses Israel in the second person ('you'). Except for v. 9, the 'you' is singular, referring to Israel personified as a typical individual.

1.   A. Cooper, 'The Plain Sense of Exodus 23.5', *HUCA* 59 (1988), pp. 1-22.

In vv. 1-3, the 'you' is the typical Israelite in so far as he acts as a witness (עֵד, v. 1). In vv. 6-9 the 'you' is the typical Israelite as he is involved in court, whether as a judge, witness, or plaintiff. In v. 9 there is a switch to the plural, which perhaps can be regarded as an intensification to underscore the need for sympathy in the motive clause and to conclude with a crescendo the section on testimony in court, 23.1-9. Compare the switch to plural in 22.30 above.

The formulations of vv. 1-3 and 6-8 are 'apodictic' or unqualified statements similar in style to the Decalogue. The form chosen corresponds to the content: there is no reason to use casuistic formulation with a protasis of condition followed by apodosis of penalty ('If a man voices an unfounded rumor in court, then the penalty is X') because the author is not giving laws, but making exhortations. There is no need for conditions or qualifications since false or compromised testimony, perversion of justice for the poor, taking a bribe as a witness or judge, and judicially oppressing a sojourner are in all ordinary circumstances wrong. Hence there is no need for casuistic formulation.

On the other hand, vv. 4-5 can be described, but only loosely, as 'casuistic' in formulation. Casuistic formulation normally has a penalty clause in the apodosis; whereas, the regulation here has no penalty clause. This 'casuistic' formulation is demanded by its content. The exhortation to return an animal to an enemy or to assist an enemy with his recumbent donkey is contingent upon these unusual events occurring at a time and place when 'you' can do something about them. Once it is clear that conditions need to be stated, 'casuistic' formulation naturally follows.

The apodosis clauses of 23.4-5 are not, incidentally, contingent upon the animal belonging to an enemy. The specification of 'an enemy' is for emotive effect: a worst case scenario in which one is initially repelled by the idea of helping. The implication is: 'if he is not an enemy, how much the more so should you help him.'

Other matters of style are as follows. Verse 2 perhaps shows wordplay between רַבִּים and רִב. In the same verse, the two senses of root נ.ט.ה. are used in what seems to be wordplay: first the G-stem which means 'to turn after/tend towards' is used in the sense of 'swaying' after the many/great, then the H-stem is used in which the literal meaning is 'to bring about a turning/turn [something]', but the specific sense here is figurative for 'to bend [your testimony]'. The H-stem of this root is normally transitive so an ellipsis can be assumed, 'perverting justice' being another possible way of filling the ellipsis (cf. v. 6: לא תטה משפט). In addition, רבים could be a double entendre for 'the many' and 'the great', the principle being true in both cases. One interpretation of v. 5 sees a wordplay between two senses of ע.ז.ב: 'You must refrain from *leaving* him, rather you must *release* it with him'.[1] נקי וצדיק in v. 7 is either a hendiadys meaning 'the entirely innocent one' or the like, or a merism in which נקי is the wrongly accused, צדיק is a justified plaintiff, and the combination means 'whichever party is in the right, whether the accused or the plaintiff'. 'Slay' in the same verse is metonymy/hyperbole, including all outcomes to the detriment of the party in the right.

Exodus 23.1-9 and Other Passages

Exod. 23.1-9 in general, and especially vv. 1-3 and 7, is an expansion of the Decalogue's 'You [sing.] must not give (תענה, lit. 'answer') a false testimony (עד שקר) against your fellow' (Exod. 20.16). Exod. 23.1-3, 7 uses the same terminology as 20.16: עד 'witness' (23.1), ע.נ.ה 'answer [to a question asked in court]' (23.2), and שקר 'lie' (23.7). Both passages have to do with the administration of justice.

Exod. 23.9 repeats the thought of 22.20, and its allusion to the exodus, using quite similar language: the same verb (ל.ח.ץ), and the same concluding motivation 'for you were sojourners in the land of Egypt'. Why the repetition of the same command? First, 22.20 and 23.9 form an inclusio around regulations having to do with 'social justice', thereby underscoring that Israel's experience of oppression in Egypt should influence the Israelite's attitude and behavior towards those oppressed in his society.

Moreover, in context the two commands are not identical. Exod. 22.20 refers to oppression which may or may not be illegal, and in any case may never come to court; whereas 23.9, as indicated by its position in the context of 23.1-8, specifically addresses oppression through the legal system.

Exod. 23.1-9 is alluded to and expanded upon in a number of subsequent passages. Among them: Lev. 19.15-16 and Deut. 19.15-21 take up the subject of impartial and false testimony found in Exod. 23.1-3. Deut. 22.1-4 clearly expands on Exod. 23.4-5. Deut. 16.19-20 clearly alludes to Exod. 23.6-8.

---

1.   Cassuto, *Exodus*, p. 297.

Exodus 23.1-9: Law or Morality?

Although these regulations have to do with the administration of justice, they are not 'laws' but moral admonitions. These regulations describe social situations that an Israelite would be likely to experience: he hears an idle report and is tempted to give it as factual testimony in court, he is tempted to withhold testimony or take other actions that allow the guilty to be acquitted, he is afraid to testify because the majority (or the great) disagree with his version of the facts, he wants to distort his testimony because he is moved with pity for the poor defendant or rancor for his enemy, he is tempted to take advantage of the needy, or (for whatever reason) to lie in court, or has been offered a 'present' by someone involved in the case to which he is a witness or judge (if the latter, perhaps a fee for being the judge of the case paid by the richer of the parties involved), or is tempted to be biased against a 'foreigner' (גר). In each of these situations, the text says what is the moral thing to do. Appeal to 'law' is altogether irrelevant.

Several features of these regulations confirm their non-legal nature. First, unlike laws, no civil penalties are specified for the violation of these norms. The only penalty for non-compliance described here is divine rather than human: 'I will not acquit the guilty' (v. 7b). Second, the personal, 'apodictic' form of the address (with its I-thou language), the appeal to a sense of fairness ('a gift blinds the eyes', v. 8) or empathy ('you know how it feels to be sojourners', v. 9) are all better suited to admonition than law. Third, the literary artistry through word-play, figurative language, and double entendre observed above is more appropriate for literature than it is for a law code.

Fourth, v. 9 in context denounces oppressing a sojourner by means of the legal system. Such oppression could be 'unlawful', for example, paying off judges, or hiring false witnesses. On the other hand, an oppression could be of such a nature that though it is morally wrong, it is not covered under any legal statute enforceable by the state, and is, therefore, in the narrow sense, 'legal' (e.g., exploiting the sojourner's lack of familiarity with a country's language and customs).

A sojourner could perhaps also be 'oppressed' by a strictly legal, but pitiless, application of a civil law in which there is a callous insensitivity for the sojourner's difficult plight. Exod. 23.9, read this way, could well condemn an Israelite plaintiff even if he has every legal right to his judgment against the sojourner, if, given the circumstances, he ought rather to have shown mercy. Hence, it is possible to read v. 9 as advocating a standard of justice higher than the legal.

Finally, Exod. 23.4-5 goes beyond enforceable law. Huffmon observed in this regard:

> Apart from maritime law, Anglo-American common law tradition does not acknowledge a general duty to rescue or render assistance. Pound [a modern text of jurisprudence] states that 'so long as one has not caused the peril and there is no relation, one who merely fails to come to the aid of another [person] who is even in extreme peril and even if it would involve no danger, incurs no liability'. As otherwise put by Gregory [another modern legal scholar], 'it is clear at common law that nobody has to lift a finger—let alone spend a dime and dial a phone number or actually render aid—to help a stranger in peril or distress'.[1]

Common law did not seek to regulate in this area, at least in part, because it would be impossible to enforce. Neither the law nor even traditional morality in general demands anyone to risk his life for another. Such acts go above and beyond the minimal norms of legal and moral duty. But neither can a demand for kindness to people having 'troubles', as the enemy is having with his animal in Exod. 23.4-5, be legally demanded. There are all kinds of legitimate reasons why a passerby might not stop to help someone: important duties and obligations elsewhere, lack of the requisite skills to help so that trying to help would only compound the problem, lack of perception that help is really needed. To establish a law requiring such kindness would result in an avalanche of litigation between people who had troubles and those passersby whom the people with troubles think should have stopped but, for reasons of their own, did not.

Exod. 23.4-5, then, represents moral admonition rather than law. Its goal, taken by itself apart from context, is to reduce conflict in society. An Israelite is to do everything in his power to end any hostility between himself and his neighbor. He cannot force another man to cease to be hostile towards him, but an act of kindness to his enemy could well become the first step towards reconciliation, and societal harmony. Moreover, in the specific context of 23.1-9, this call for kindness towards enemies finds application in matters of public testimony where the witness is to tell the truth (the right thing to do)

---

1. H.B. Huffmon, 'Exodus 23.4-5: A Comparative Study', in *A Light unto My Path* (ed. H.N. Bream *et al.*; Philadelphia: Temple University Press, 1974), p. 275.

regardless of whether it benefits an enemy, especially if it helps an innocent one in need, symbolized by the donkey.

Cultic Matters III: Sabbaths and Holidays: Exodus 23.10-19

Pericope A: Sabbaths

(10) Six years you [sing.] may sow your land and gather its produce, (11) but on the seventh you [sing.] are to leave it fallow that the needy among your people may eat of it, and what they leave the wild animals may eat. You [sing.] are to do the same with your vineyard and your olive groves. (12) Six days you [sing.] may do your work, but on the seventh day you should cease from labor so that your ox and your donkey can rest and your slave [literally 'your maidservant's son'] and your sojourner may refresh themselves.

Pericope B: Mentioning Name of other Gods Prohibited

(13) You [pl.] must take care to do everything that I have said to you. You [pl.] must not allow the name of other gods to be mentioned. It should not be heard on your [sing.] mouth.

Pericope C: The Three Pilgrim Festivals

(14) Three times per year you [sing.] should celebrate a pilgrim-festival for me. (15) You [sing.] are to observe the Feast of Unleavened Bread: for seven days you [sing.] are to eat unleavened bread just as I commanded you, at the appointed time in the month of Abib, for then you [sing.] went forth from Egypt. Do not appear [2nd per. pl.] before me empty-handed. (16) [Likewise keep][1] the Festival of the Harvest, [having to do with] the firstfruits of your [sing.] produce which you [sing.] have sown in the field, and the Feast of Ingathering at the close of the [agricultural] year when you [sing.] gather your produce from the field. (17) [These] three times per year all of your [sing.] males are to appear before the Lord YHWH. (18) Do not [2nd per. sing.] offer the blood of my sacrifice with that which is leavened nor allow [2nd per. sing.] the fat of my festal offering to spend the night until morning. (19) The choice first fruits of your [sing.] ground you are to bring to the house of YHWH your God. You [sing.] are not to boil a kid in its mother's milk.

---

1. Ellipsis: תשמר 'you are to keep' is implied from v. 15.

Exodus 23.10-19 and Structure

Exod. 23.10-19 concludes the מִשְׁפָּטִים (*mishpaṭim*, Exod. 21.1), the remainder of ch. 23 being an epilogue to the permanent regulations. It is appropriate that 20.22–23.19 concludes, as it began, with cultic regulations specifically pertaining to worship (cf. 20.22-26 and 23.14-19), since the cult pertains directly to Israel's relationship with God which is at the center of the Covenant. Civil laws and humanitarian precepts are important in Israel's relationship with God, and the Israelite's behavior towards others should grow out of that relationship. Nonetheless, cultic regulations deal most directly with Israel's relationship with God.

Exod. 23.10-19 is not unrelated to what has immediately preceded. Exod. 23.6-9 calls for justice for the *needy* (v. 6) and no oppression through courts of *sojourners* (v. 9) with whose life (נֶפֶשׁ) Israel was acquainted. This language is purposefully followed by the cultic yet also humanitarian regulation regarding the sabbath year for the land in which the *needy* may find food (v. 11) and the sabbath day in which the *sojourner* may be refreshed (v. 12, נ.פ.שׁ, same root as נפשׁ in v. 9). This link between Exod. 23.1-9 and 10-19 illustrates, as does the alternation of cultic and matters of social justice already discussed, that there is no dichotomy in Israel between cultic and moral regulation.

I see the following structure within Exod. 23.10-19:

> A. Sabbaths (Exod. 23.10-12)
>> 1. The sabbath year (vv. 10-11)
>> 2. The sabbath day (v. 12)
>
> X. Essence of Israel's Religion (Exod. 23.13)
>> 1. Obedience to what YHWH says
>> 2. No other Gods
>
> A*. Three Pilgrim Festivals (Exod. 23.14-19)
>> 1. Basic Command to Celebrate
>>> a. Introduction: '3 times per year' (v. 14)
>>> b. Feast of Unleavened Bread (v. 15)
>>> c. Feast of Harvest (v. 16a)
>>> d. Feast of Ingathering (v. 16b)
>
>> 2. Comments on the Respective Festivals
>>> a. Introduction: '3 times per year' (v. 17)
>>> b. On the Passover Sacrifice (v. 18)
>>> c. On the Feast of Harvest (v. 19a)
>>> d. On the Feast of Ingathering (19b)

Exod. 23.10-19 consists of two sections dealing with matters of the religious calendar: first, sabbath years and days (vv. 10-12); last, the three pilgrim feasts (vv. 14-19), and in the middle a verse (v. 13) which has no direct connection with the religious calendar. There is, as often in 20.22–23.33, a breaking up of matters with material of a differing nature: 20.24b between altar specifications; 21.16 between parental laws; 21.22-25 between slave laws; 21.33-34 between goring ox laws; 22.1-2a between animal theft laws; 22.10 between bailment laws; 22.28-30 between social justice precepts; 23.4-5 between court-related admonitions.

In this case, v. 13, sometimes excluded as a secondary insertion,[1] is appropriately in the center of the semi-chiastic structure because it deals with the essence of Israel's religion; namely, obedience to what YHWH says and loyalty to YHWH to the exclusion of all other gods. Keeping sabbaths and holidays is simply an application of that principle. Compare Exod. 22.27 which likewise is a general principle that serves as a transitional verse.

One point where this outline might be questioned is in its placement of vv. 17-19. Others have seen v. 17 as forming an inclusio with v. 14, making vv. 18-19 be additional miscellaneous cultic regulations without any close relationship with the festivals.[2] The outline above, in contrast, takes v. 17 as a new introduction, and sees the regulations that follow as having a strict correspondence with the festivals.

Verse 18, which speaks of not offering a sacrifice with leaven, has an obvious conceptual link with the Feast of *Unleavened* Bread (v. 15). In fact the relationship is even closer. The sacrifice whose blood cannot be sacrificed on leaven (v. 18a) is the Passover lamb (cf. Exod. 12–13) which cannot be slaughtered before all leaven is removed from one's house (Rashi).[3] This view removes the contradiction between this passage and other cultic passages which allow leaven to

---

1.   For example, Driver (*Exodus*, p. 241) suggests that v. 13 perhaps formed an original ending of the collection, or that it belongs after v. 19. Cf. Hyatt, *Exodus*, p. 247.

2.   E.g., Driver, *Exodus*, p. 245; Hyatt, *Exodus*, p. 249; R.E. Clements, *Exodus* (Cambridge: Cambridge University Press, 1972), p. 153.

3.   Cited by N. Snaith ('Exodus 23.18 and 34.25', *JTS* 20 [1969], pp. 533-34) who defends Rashi's interpretation. Other arguments for connecting v. 18 with the Passover are found in M. Haran, *Temples and Temple-Service in Ancient Israel* (Winona Lake: Eisenbrauns, 1985), pp. 323-48.

be used in certain sacrifices (Lev. 7.13, 23.17 at Feast of Harvest; cf. Amos 4.5). The fat of the offering that is not to spend the night till morning is that of the Passover lamb in which *nothing* is to remain till morning (Exod. 12.10, cf. the parallel in 34.25b 'do not let the sacrifice of the Passover feast spend the night until morning').

The mention of 'firstfruits' in v. 19a likewise links this verse with the 'firstfruits' of the Feast of the Harvest in v. 16a. The parallel in Exod. 34.22 identifies this as the Feast of Weeks (later called Pentecost).

Only 23.19b, boiling a kid in its mother's milk, is difficult to relate to its appropriate festival. If the pattern holds, this verse—fancifully used by the rabbis as the basis of later Jewish custom of not eating milk and meat together—must be related to the Feast of Ingathering (elsewhere called Tabernacles) at the end of the year. Haran has made a plausible case for connecting the 'kid in its mother's milk' with the fall festival on the basis of the mating pattern of the flock.[1] According to Haran, goats and sheep generally go into heat in June, staying in heat through the summer. Gestation takes about five months, so that most lambs would be born around November. A few lambs would be conceived earlier and be born in time for the fall festival. Hence the act of cooking a kid in its mother's milk can be connected with that and only that festival.

Finally, in terms of structure, some striking parallels between Exod. 22.20-30 and Exod. 23.1-19 have been pointed out by Carmichael.[2] The general structure of these two units is quite similar as the following (after Carmichael with some modification) demonstrates:

> 1. Exod. 22.20-23/23.1-9, esp. v. 9. Both units share a prohibition against oppressing a sojourner with almost identical wording, as well as protection of other classes (widow and orphan in former/needy and innocent in the latter).

> 2. Exod. 22.24-26/23.10-12. Protection of poor from interest on loans and from oppressive pledging in former; seventh year release of the land's produce for the poor and sabbath rest for bondmaid's son and sojourner in latter.

---

1. M. Haran, 'Seething a Kid in its Mother's Milk', *JJS* 30 (1979), pp. 34-35.
2. C.M. Carmichael, 'A Singular Method of Codification of Law in the *Mishpaṭim*', *ZAW* 84 (1972), pp. 19-25.

3. Exod. 22.27/23.13. Do not show disrespect for human or divine authority by violating the norms of God or man in former; obey all that has been said and name no other god in the latter.[1]

4. Exod. 22.28-29/23.14-19a. Offering from harvest and vintage, offering of firstborn son, offering of firstborn oxen and sheep in former; three pilgrim feasts: Unleavened Bread (related to substitution of passover for the firstborn sons in the story of the exodus), Feast of the Harvest (in which firstfruits offered), and Feast of Ingathering (in which offering of firstborn sheep might well take place, cf. above) in latter.

5. Exod. 22.30/23.19b. Be holy men by not eating flesh torn by beasts in former; do not cook a kid in its mother's milk in latter.

Support for connecting these units in this way is found in Deuteronomy.[2] In Deut. 14.21, the precept on torn animal flesh (Exod. 22.30) and the one on cooking a kid in its mother's milk (Exod. 23.19b) have been brought together, perhaps indicating that the author of Deuteronomy recognized the parallel structure in Exod. 22.20–23.19. Likewise, Deut. 15.1-15 brings together rulings on debts (cf. Exod. 22.24-26) and the 'release' of the sabbath year (cf. Exod. 23.10-11) in accordance with this parallel structure.

These parallels observed by Carmichael between Exod. 22.20-30 and 23.1-19 support the thesis that these regulations have been deliberately organized into an integrated whole as opposed to being a loose miscellany.

Pronouns and Other Stylistic Matters in Exodus 23.10-19
These regulations are expressed personally using first person for YHWH as speaker and second person pronouns for Israel. In the central verse of the structure, v. 13, there is a switch from second person singular to plural. This is perhaps a plural of intensification to underscore this the central principle on which the particulars of the surrounding regulations of the cultic calendar are based. Compare Exod. 22.20-24, 22.30, 23.9b for other examples of switching from second person singular to plural.

---

1. I have modified Carmichael ('A Singular Method', pp. 20-21) who admitted, 'I do not know why a law on reviling God and cursing a ruler should follow a law on lending and pledging.' Note that just as 22.20 and 23.9 on oppressing the גר form an inclusio around the social regulations, so 22.19 and 23.10 on worshipping other gods brackets the first and last group of cultic regulations.

2. Carmichael, 'A Singular Method', pp. 22-23.

There is the symbolic use of the number seven for the sabbath year rest for the land (vv. 10-11) and sabbath day rest (v. 12), all going back to God's resting on the seventh day of creation (Gen. 2.1-3, cf. Exod. 20.11). This symbolic use of 'seven' may also somehow influence the choice of seven days for the length of the Feast of Unleavened Bread (v. 15). Verse 12 shows parallelism and can be regarded as semi-poetic (cf. Cassuto). Part of that parallelism is in the word pairs: 'ox and donkey', being merism for beasts of burden, and 'your handmaiden's son and the sojourner' being merism for subordinate workers of whatever sort who apart from the master's permission cannot choose to rest.

The use of bread without leaven in the Feast of Unleavened Bread (v. 15) is symbolic of the story of the exodus in which Israel had to leave in haste without allowing time for the bread to rise (Exod. 12.34, 39). Verse 17a uses repetition to form a new introduction to the second half of the discussion of pilgrim feasts (see above) in a pattern not unlike the resumptive repetition of biblical narrative (cf. Chapter 1). The use of חֵלֶב and חָלָב, and חַגִּי and גְּדִי of vv. 18b and 19b may represent wordplay. On the symbolism of 'cooking a kid in its mother's milk', see below.

Exodus 23.10-19 and Other Passages
There are a number of clear connections to earlier passages in Exod. 23.10-19. First, there is in the sabbath year and day of Exod. 23.10-12 an expansion of the sabbath commandment in the Decalogue (Exod. 20.8-11) which itself alludes to God's rest on the seventh day of creation (Gen. 2.1-3) and expands on the preliminary introduction of the practice of sabbath related to the story of the giving of the manna (Exod. 16.21-23). The opening words of the sabbath year regulations are strikingly similar to the release of the 'Hebrew' bondsman in Exod. 21.2, bracketing these regulations (cf. the concluding chapter for more on this).

Verse 13a, the command to keep everything that YHWH says, is a reminder of the essence of the covenant which, as previously portrayed in the narrative, involves obeying the voice of YHWH and keeping his covenant stipulations (Exod. 19.5), and having a proper fear of God that leads to obedience rather than sin (20.20). The people had already agreed to this in principle before this regulation was given (19.8), and they subsequently reconfirmed their commitment to complete obedience after this and the other regulations were read to them in detail (24.3). Exod. 23.13b also involves the essence of Israel's covenant with YHWH at Sinai: exclusive devotion to YHWH. Verse 13b, which prohibits the use of the name of other gods is reminiscent of the Decalogue's 'You are not to have other gods in my presence' (20.3), and the special place of YHWH's 'name' which is not to be taken 'in vain' (20.7). It also supplements other regulations in 20.22–23.33: 22.19 which prohibit sacrifice to other gods, and 23.20-23 which condemn Canaanite religion.

Exod. 23.15 and 18, which have to do with the Feast of Unleavened Bread and the Passover lamb, explicitly refer back to the exodus narrative, for it is to be kept 'as I commanded you' (v. 15). The earlier instruction has already anticipated most of what is stated here: that unleavened bread would be eaten for seven days (12.15), that the festival was to occur in the month of Abib (13.4), and that none of the Passover sacrifice was to remain until morning (12.10).

There are many regulations elsewhere in the Pentateuch that repeat or expand on these concerning the cultic calendar. The most significant of these for the present passage is Exod. 34.10-26 in which almost every item is drawn from 23.10-33. It would go too far afield to discuss the differences in order and content between these two passages. It is enough to say that Exod. 34.10-26 has its own, differing organizational principles that must be examined in their own context in conjunction with the Golden Calf narrative. For instance, unlike Exodus 23, ch. 34 prohibits idols, a prohibition very relevant to that particular context.[1] The inclusio between Exodus 23 and 34.10-26 which brackets the material in between (consummation of the covenant [narrative], the tabernacle regulations [cultic regulations], the Golden Calf story [narrative]) could in a fuller study be used as evidence of the purposeful structuring of the book of Exodus.

Exodus 23.10-19: Law, Religion, or Morality?
The regulations here are religious and humanitarian in character rather than legal. The subject matter is not that of ordinary jurisprudence. Even as cultic 'law', it is quite incomplete. Insufficient detail is given to specify how to enact these sabbaths and feasts, and how or whether they are to be enforced by the state. It is not clear whether the sabbath year applied to the whole land at once, or whether the land

---

1. Brichto, 'Worship of the Golden Calf', pp. 32-33.

could be rotated so that every part rested every seven years. Unlike 'law', no punishments are specified for non-compliance. This brevity is possible because the author knows that other passages, both previous and subsequent, fill in more of the details on how the sabbaths and pilgrim feasts are to be observed. These observations lead to the conclusion that the present regulations are more exhortations to do homage to deity than laws.

Although they are 'cultic' in nature, these regulations also show interest in morality. The statement on the sabbath year shows a humanitarian concern for providing the needy and even wild animals with food (v. 11), and the sabbath day shows a humanitarian concern that domestic animals, the son of one's maidservant,[1] and sojourners be refreshed (v 12).

As for the three festivals, each of these is meant to bring to mind God's grace to Israel, especially God's gift of agricultural provision but also God's deliverance in the exodus. Failure to keep these festivals would be an act of ingratitude to God for the blessings of his grace.

The statement about a kid in its mother's milk probably has an ethical concern as well, though the precise nature of that concern is veiled by the verse's obscurity. It is often speculated that cooking a kid in its mother's milk was a Canaanite or pagan custom, though there is no concrete evidence to support this notion. The Ugaritic text, UT 52.14 (CTA 23), once taken as proof of this being a Canaanite practice, must now be read otherwise.[2] Even if the Canaanites had such a practice, that would not be a sufficient reason for condemning it. Canaanites offered more ordinary sacrifices to their gods, but Israel is not for that reason prohibited from sacrifice to YHWH. There

---

1.   Probably a member of the 'slave' class, regardless of age or sex. Cf. Fensham, 'The Son of a Handmaid', pp. 312-21.

2.   UT 52.14 (CTA 23) has been read 'Coo[k a ki]d (*ṭb[ḥ g]d*) in milk, a *lamb* (?) in butter' (trans. Gordon, 'Poetic Legends', p. 60). However, the Ugaritic text says nothing about cooking a kid in its *mother's* milk, so cannot be an exact parallel. Moreover, the text is partially broken; the reading *gd* 'kid' is a conjecture by Virolleaud. Others render it 'mint' or some sort of plant. If the reconstruction *ṭbḥ* is accepted for the verb, it more likely means 'slaughter' than 'cook'. For discussions, see R. Ratner and B. Zuckerman, '"A kid in milk"?: New Photographs of KTU 1.23, line 14', *HUCA* 57 (1986), pp. 15-16; Haran, 'Seething a Kid', pp. 25-27; P.C. Craigie, *Ugarit and the Old Testament* (Grand Rapids: Eerdmans, 1983), pp. 74-76; *idem*, 'Deuteronomy and Ugaritic Studies', *TynBul* 28 (1977), pp. 155-69.

must be something else of a religious or moral character involved that makes this practice abhorrent.

Rabbinic tradition beginning with Philo and including Ibn Ezra and Rashbam understood Exod. 23.19b to have a humanitarian concern: to cook a kid in its mother's milk is a heartless, savage act. Its practice would be cruel and dehumanizing.[1] This prohibition was compared in rabbinic tradition with the one excluding the slaughtering of an animal and its young on the same day (Lev. 22.28), and the command to let a mother bird go free (Deut. 22.6-7), both of which were taken by them to be humanitarian in character.

A somewhat different suggestion by O. Keel[2] involves the symbolism of this act. A mother animal and her milk is symbol of the power of life (*Lebensmacht*) and of zest or vitality (*Lebenslust*), and it is unseemly to mix that which is a symbol of lifegiving with death. Elsewhere other 'unseemly' mixtures are prohibited (Lev. 19.19; Deut. 22.9-11): breeding two kinds of cattle; sowing two kinds of seed; wearing a garment of two kinds of material mixed together, and plowing with an ox and a donkey together. Keel's view allows the present regulation to be placed in the matrix of other cultic laws that as a corpus encourage Israel to choose life and to turn from death (cf. on Exod. 22.30 above). I add to his view that this symbolism would be especially inappropriate at a festival [Ingathering] that celebrates the life-bestowing grace of Yahweh.

With either of these interpretations, the moral implication would be: even in the midst of the frivolity of the fall festival, remain so sensitive to propriety that you would not do something so unseemly as cooking a kid in its mother's milk.

---

1. Cassuto, *Exodus*, p. 305; Haran, 'Seething a Kid', pp. 29-30.
2. Cited by E.A. Knauf, 'Zur Herkunft und Sozialgeschichte Israels: 'Das Böckchen in der Milch seiner Mutter'', *Bib* 69 (1988), pp. 153-54.

Chapter 8

EVALUATION, OBSERVATIONS AND CONCLUSION

It is the purpose of this concluding chapter to evaluate the degree to which Exod. 20.22–23.19 has been found to be a well-integrated unity by the detailed analysis given above, and the degree to which my synchronic, discourse-oriented methodology has been vindicated or invalidated as compared with the source-oriented methodologies commonly employed in the past. In the course of this evaluation some additional observations will be made.

Exodus 20.22–23.19 and the Rest of the Pentateuch

On the basis of this study, it may be concluded that Exod. 20.22–23.19 is well integrated into the Pentateuch. Chapter 1 makes the case that 20.22–23.33 (the regulations of 20.22–23.19 plus its epilogue) has been intelligently and purposefully placed into the Sinaitic narrative by means of the synoptic/resumptive storytelling technique. All of Exodus 20–23 represents flashbacks of aspects of the story of the theophany of Exodus 19. By this technique the author/editor has shown the regulations of 20.22–23.19 to have been given simultaneously with the events of ch. 19 and has isolated 20.22–23.19 for separate didactic study.

Moreover, the author/editor(s) has arranged Exodus 19–24 chiastically so that the giving of the covenant (chs. 19 and 24) forms the main theme that envelopes chs. 20–23, while the theme of 'fear of God' is at the center of this chiasm (20.18-21), fear of God being central to the theme of covenant since it motivates obedience. The laws (20.1-17 and 20.22–23.33) are thereby subordinated to the overall theme of covenant within this chiastic structure, teaching what it is that fear of God should motivate the Israelite to do.

In addition, it was suggested that the Decalogue and 20.22–23.19

can be regarded as an instance of resumptive repetition in which YHWH's message to Moses on Sinai is first given in synoptic form in the Decalogue, and is then told again in a resumed and expanded form in 20.22–23.19, as the many parallels between these two units suggest.

Exod. 20.22–23.19 is not only linked to the narratives and other regulations of the Pentateuch formally by transition verses that relate to the narrative (20.22; 21.1; 23.20-33), but it is also connected in more subtle ways. For example, the frequent usage of the first person pronoun for God and the second person for Israel, especially at the beginning and end of 20.22–23.19, emphasizes that these regulations as a whole, even where the personal pronoun is not used, are part of YHWH's address to Israel and related to the narrative rather than simply being a collection of laws. The placement of the regulations sometimes relates to the narrative: 20.22–23.19 begins and ends with the theme of worship because in the context of Israel's covenant with YHWH, worship plays a primary role. The first non-cultic regulation has to do with the release of a 'Hebrew' bondsman because of the exodus narrative whose central theme up until ch. 19 has been the deliverance of the Israelites (called 'Hebrews') from bondage in Egypt. The choice of the seventh year for the release of the bondsman probably relates to 'seven' as the number of rest in the creation account (Gen. 2.1-3) and elsewhere.

The content of other regulations relates to narratives or regulations elsewhere. Exodus 21.13 on establishing a place for the unintentional manslayer to flee anticipates and alludes to the institution of the cities of refuge, which are established at a later point in the narrative. The execution of a homicidal ox (21.28) finds its rationale in the so-called 'priestly' portions of the Pentateuch, especially Gen. 1.26-30 and 9.1-6, where the hierarchy between man (made in the image of God) and beast is established and death is the sanction for the beast who violates that hierarchy. Exodus 22.20 and 23.9 explicitly allude to the exodus narrative by the statement: 'You [pl.] were sojourners in the land of Egypt'. Moreover, 22.20-26 has other similarities of language and theme with the exodus narrative. 22.28-29 draws upon and repeats commands of ch. 13 at an earlier stage of the narrative. 22.30's call to holiness draws upon a similar call in the narrative at 19.6. 23.15 and 18 allude to earlier regulations ('as I commanded you') found in the Passover regulations (12.10, 15; 13.4). There are numerous parallels between 23.10-33 and 34.10-26 so that the former anticipates and provides background for the repetition in the latter.

Consistent with the thesis of Exod. 20.22–23.19 being well integrated into the Pentateuch is the fact that later passages in the Pentateuch, especially Deuteronomy, draw upon the regulations in this unit. Moreover, those later regulations can be interpreted in harmony with Exod. 20.22–23.19, and often aid in the interpretation of this section. The editor(s) of the final form of the Pentateuch probably intended the reader to attempt this sort of holistic reading.

The Golden Calf story's reference to 'a god of gold' (Exod. 32.31) alludes to 20.23's prohibition of 'a god of gold' and suggests by its context that אלהים in both is a plural of majesty. Deut. 27.5-7 which applies the altar law (in conjunction with Deut. 16.21, Josh. 8, Deut. 12 and Exod. 27) helps to explicate that Exod. 20.24-26 does not contradict the concept of a central sanctuary and altar. Deut. 4.15-16 explains Exod. 20.22's relationship with v. 23, that the fact that Israel saw no image at Sinai was a sign that no images of God were to be made.

Deut. 15.12-15 helps confirm that the 'Hebrew' of Exod. 21.2 is an Israelite and suggests that 21.2 is related to the exodus story. Deut. 15.17 helps to locate the piercing of the servant's ear of Exod. 21.5-6 as at the master's house. Numbers 35, Deut. 4.41-43, 19.1-13, and Joshua 20 explain the allusion to the city of refuge in Exod. 21.13. Deut. 21.18-21 perhaps gives an interpretation of 'repudiation' (מקלל) of one's parents in Exod. 21.17. Deut. 24.7 gives some additional data pertinent for Exod. 21.16 (kidnapping) and the two situations described.

Deut. 19.21 by its use of *beth pretii* in its version of the so-called *lex talionis* suggests that תחת in Exod. 21.23-25 refers to monetary equivalents rather than literal Talion. Exod. 34.19-20 (with 13.13) brings out that the firstborn of expensive animals and men to be given to God (22.28-29) could be redeemed rather than sacrificed. In Deut. 14.21 the precept on torn animal flesh (Exod. 22.30) and cooking the kid in its mother's milk (Exod. 23.19) are brought together, and in Deut. 15.1-15 rulings on debts (Exod. 22.24-26) and the 'release' of the sabbath year (Exod. 23.10-11) are brought together. These two cases perhaps indicate that the writer of Deuteronomy was aware of the parallel structure between Exod. 22.20-30 and Exod. 23.1-19. Deut. 22.4 supports the notion that Exod. 23.5 intends for an Israelite to 'help' his enemy with his donkey rather than to abandon it. Exod.

34.25 confirms that Exod. 23.18 refers to the Passover sacrifice specifically.

It would be unreasonable to expect every regulation of Exod. 20.22–23.19 to allude to, or be drawn upon by, some other passage in the Pentateuch. However, the examples above, plus the parallels with the Decalogue *im passim* not listed (related especially to the worship of YHWH, oaths, sabbaths, parents, murder, theft, and false testimony), and the chiastic structure of Exodus 19–24 as a unit, do show 20.22–23.19 to be well integrated into the Pentateuch.

Exodus 20.22–23.19 and Questions of Structure

Exod. 20.22–23.19 is not only well structured vis-à-vis chs. 19–24, as shown above, but individual pericopes within Exod. 20.22–23.19 are well structured within themselves and vis-à-vis one another.

Frequently chiastic or semi-chiastic structuring has been discovered, a feature that bespeaks artful crafting by the author/editor(s). The units that show this stylistic device are 20.23-26; 21.2-11; 21.28-36; 21.37–22.3; 22.6-12; 23.1-9, and 23.10-19. The chiastic or semi-chiastic character of each of these units is shown under the discussion of 'structure' under each unit respectively. In addition, a parallel structure was found in 21.12-27 in which the four regulations of vv. 12-17 have parallels (though not chiastic ones) with the four regulations of vv. 18-27. A parallel structure also links 23.14-16 with 23.17-19.

It is even possible to see Exod. 20.22–23.19 as a whole being part of a chiastic structure:[1]

---

1. Cf. G. Wanke, 'Bundesbuch', *Theologische Realenzyklopädie*, VII (Berlin: de Gruyter, 1981), p. 413 (attributed to Halbe, though 21.1–22.19 is excluded as not original to the collection; Schwienhorst–Schönberger, *Bundesbuch*, pp. 23-37. N. Lohfink in a paper read in 1990, cited by van Houten (*Alien*, p. 45) independently observed the same pattern which I recognize, though with less detail:

    A   (20.22-26) Cult: Idols and Altar
    　　B   (21.1-11) 6 + 1: Liberation of slaves
    　　　　C   (21.12–22.19) Civil Law Collection
    　　　　C´ (22.20–23.9) Collection 'ger'
    　　B´ (23.10-12) 6 + 1: fallow year and sabbath
    A´ (23.13-19) Cult: feasts and sacrifices

A   Moses ascends Mount Sinai (20.21)
  B   Prologue related to Israel's past experience at Sinai (20.22)
    C   Cultic regulation: worship: images and altars with a promise of God's presence and blessing (20.23-26)
      D   Sabbath principle: release of the עבד עברי on the 7th year (overlaps with what follows) (21.2)
        E   Humanitarian admonition to better the lot of bondsmen and bondwomen as a disadvantaged social class [related to Israel's experience of bondage in Egypt] (21.2-11)
          F   Participially formulated, most serious offenses of man against man, structured on a principle of decreasing violence (21.12-17)
            G   Moral comment on legal matters: offenses of men against men (21.18-27)
              H   Moral comment on legal matters: offenses of a man's property against a man (21.28-32)
              H′ Moral comment on legal matters: offenses of a man's property against another man's property (21.33-36)
            G′ Moral comment on legal matters: offenses of man against a man's property (Exod. 21.37–22.16)
          F′ Participially formulated, most serious offenses against YHWH-religion, structured on a principle of increasingly severe penalty clause (22.17-19)
        E′ Humanitarian admonitions with special emphasis on bettering the lot of sojourners and other disadvantaged classes (widows, fatherless, poor) related to Israel's experience as sojourners in Egypt—with an excursus in 22.28-30 on firstfruits/firstborn and holiness (22.20–23.9)
      D′ Sabbath principle: release on sabbath year and day—overlaps with what follows (23.10-12)
    C′ Cultic regulations: worship: sabbaths and pilgrim feasts with an exhortation to worship YHWH alone (23.10-19)
  B′ Epilogue related to Israel's future entrance in the land after leaving Sinai (23.20-33)
A′ Moses descends Mount Sinai (24.1-3)

One justification for taking 22.20–23.9 together as a unit is because it is bracketed by precepts on sojourners having identical motive clauses: 'for you were sojourners in the land of Egypt' (22.20 and 23.9). Moreover, the 'exodus' theme also holds the subunits together.

Note that there is a double structuring principle in Exod. 22.20–23.19, chiastic with respect to 20.21–24.3 as a whole, but also a pattern of simple parallelism between 22.20-30 and 23.1-19 (as observed by Carmichael) in itself:

Secondary Structuring Pattern

a   Prohibition of oppressing sojourners and protection of other
    classes (widows and fatherless) (22.20-23)
  b   Protection of poor from oppressive loans at interest (22.24-26)
    c   Call to respect the morality of God as adminstered by human
        leaders (22.27)
      d   Offering of firstfruits and firstborn sons and animals [related to feasts
          of Harvest (firstfruits) and Passover (firstborn sons) and perhaps
          Tabernacles (firstborn animals?)] (22.28-29)
        e   Cultic prohibition of eating meat torn by beasts—perhaps
            because it is dehumanizing (22.30)
a´ Prohibition of oppressing sojourner and protection of other
    disadvantaged classes especially with regards to courts (23.1-9)
  b´ Protection of the poor from starvation and exhaustion through
      sabbath year and day (23.10-12)
    c´ Call to obey God's word to the exclusion of other gods (23.13)
      d´ The three pilgrim feasts including the offering of firstfruits at the
          feast of the Harvest and the Passover lamb [which served as a
          substitute for firstborn sons and animals] (23.14-19a)
        e´ Cultic prohibition of cooking a kid in its mother's milk—perhaps
            because it is dehumanizing (23.19b)

This secondary pattern creates some discontinuity in the overall
chiasm since to maintain the parallelism there needs to be cultic
material (22.28-30) in the middle of the 'social justice' section (22.20-
23.9). Nonetheless, the overall chiastic pattern of 20.19–23.3 is fairly
consistent and clear.

A most interesting phenomenon that has been observed in 20.22–
23.33 is the frequent 'bracketing' or 'enveloping' of what at first
seems to be material irrelevant to what surrounds it. In most cases,
however, the relevance of the bracketed material can be ascertained.

For example, in 20.23-26 two precepts on altars are 'interrupted'
by a promise of God's presence and blessing at worship. This
promise, it turns out, is at the center of a chiastic structure and by its
position in this structure expresses a central concept in worship: the
purpose of the worship is to meet God and be blessed by him, the altar
being merely a means to that end.

Likewise, Exod. 21.12-27 has two instances of bracketing what at
first seems to be irrelevant material. 21.16 on kidnapping interrupts
two cases on parents, and 21.22-25 on the pregnant woman struck
during a brawl interrupts two cases on the striking of slaves. The
latter through its so-called *lex talionis* introduces the principle that

one should pay the exact monetary equivalent for the mayhem that one has caused in order to form a contrast between this principle and the case where striking the bondsman produces permanent injury. There, the talionic principle does not apply. Instead, regardless of the mayhem caused, the bondsman goes free and the master loses his entire investment. This structuring serves to make an ideological statement concerning the humanity and non-chattel character of bondsmen.

As for Exod. 21.16, it is in a series of four participially formulated cases (21.12-17) that follow a structure of decreasing physical violence in which kidnapping naturally comes between striking a parent and repudiating a parent. Moreover, it is, in an indirect way, an offense against parents, removing the parents' support via the child in the parent's old age. There seems also to be a pleasing parallelism of structure between the four cases of 21.12-17 (murdering a citizen/ striking parents/kidnapping/repudiating parents) and those of 21.18-27 (striking a citizen/killing a slave/striking a pregnant woman/maiming a slave).

In Exod. 21.28-36 two pericopes on goring oxen (goring men and goring other oxen respectively) are interrupted by one on injuries to animals due to open pits. Again, this interruption is not random but has a purpose: both the interrruption itself as well as the differences in penalties in which the case an ox goring an ox is more like the case of the open pit rather than the case of an ox goring a man indicates to the reader that cases of an ox goring a man are of a completely different legal order than the case of an ox goring a beast, thus serving to make an ideological statement concerning the transcendent value of human life.

Exod. 22.1-2 likewise interrupts the case of animal theft, but it is not irrelevant. Rather, it forms a parenthetical aside on the question of appropriate penalties for theft: namely, to indicate that only under very special circumstance does killing a thief not bring blood-guilt upon the killer (22.1-2a). Before leaving the aside, the author also comments on the minimum penalty: that a destitute thief must at least pay back what he took even if that means his being sold into bondage (22.26). Having completed the aside, which produces a chiastic structure for Exod. 21.37–22.3 as a whole, the author concludes his case on animal theft.

Exod. 22.8 is another case of 'sandwiching' in which a law on taking oaths in disputes over ownership comes in between pericopes having to do with bailment. 22.8 shows that the sort of oaths prescribed for bailments are more widely applicable, and thus has a generalizing purpose in promoting oaths as a remedy for circumstances where there is insufficient evidence for a court to decide. 22.8 forms a transition between the case of inanimate bailment and that of animate bailments since it explicitly refers to both animal and non-animal items, and is a case that could result after a bailment has been stolen (theft or rustling being mentioned by both cases of bailment). Moreover, it produces a pleasing, chiastic structure for 22.6-12 as a whole.

In Exod. 22.28-30, cultic regulations on firstfruits, firstborn, and eating torn flesh come in between two units on social justice. Here the purpose perhaps has to do with larger structuring patterns: the juxtaposition of cultic and non-cultic regulations for 22.17–23.19 serves to show that there is no dichotomy between justice and religion for Israel, and the placement of 22.28-30 produces a parallel structure between 22.20-30 and 23.1-19 as noted above.

Exod. 23.4-5, having to do with an enemy's animal gone astray or recumbent under its load, interrupts a series of apodictic regulations concerning matters of court. 23.4-5 is a parenthesis which, following the surprising statement that one should not show favoritism to the poor man (23.3), serves to illustrate the need for radical impartiality in court, even if it helps one's enemy. Again, this 'interruption' produces a chiastic structure.

Finally Exod. 23.13, on obeying YHWH and not mentioning the names of other gods, interrupts pericopes on sabbaths (23.10-12) and pilgrim feasts (23.14-19). In this case—similar to the case of 20.24b—23.13 forms the center of a chiastic structure to express a concept central to the surrounding regulations; namely, that YHWH's word is to be obeyed and no other god is even to be acknowledged.

In each of these cases of bracketing, some source-oriented critics have posited secondary insertions, textual disorder, or other scribal misadventure to explain the present form of the text. I have offered discourse-oriented explanations for the present ordering that require no positing of sources. These proposals are sufficiently plausible as to show this approach to be a fruitful alternative to the source-oriented explanations.

The Alleged Insertion of a Law Code in Exodus 20.22–23.19

Because source-oriented scholars have posited the inclusion into Exod. 20.22–23.19 of a portion of pre-existing, perhaps Canaanite law-code similar to the collections of cuneiform laws extant in the ancient Near East which they identify with the original meaning of the מִשְׁפָּטִים of Exod. 21.1, attention has been focused on the degree of each pericope's legal as opposed to essentially moral or religious character, in order to evaluate this source-oriented theory.

Given that extant cuneiform law collections devote little attention to cultic matters, the essentially cultic regulations (as most source-critics who hold to this theory agree) would not be part of this inserted code. Hence, the cultic regulations of 20.22-26, 22.28-30, and 23.10-19 would not be expected to be part of this hypothesized source. Nor would 22.17-19, the participially formulated regulations on witchcraft, bestiality, and offering sacrifice to other gods, be expected to be part of any earlier non-Israelite 'law' code, for even though, like law, it has penalty clauses, unlike cuneiform laws the subject matter is of an essentially religious character, and the regulations prohibit matters that non-Israelites would not be expected to prohibit.

There are also regulations that are essentially admonitions rather than laws. The מִשְׁפָּטִים (21.1) do not identify all that follows as 'laws', but refer to 'norms' of both a legal and a non-legal character, including the moral and cultic regulations of 21.2–23.19. There is insufficient reason to end the מִשְׁפָּטִים at 22.16 as some source critics suggest. Exod. 21.2-11 on the bondsman and bondwoman is not 'law' for it lacks any penalty for non-compliance, it uses the second person pronoun (v. 2) which is more fitting for the genre of exhortation than that of law, and it exhibits elaborate symbolism in the ear-piercing ceremony that is more appropriate for literature than a law.

Exod. 22.20-27 on oppression and loans, like 21.2-11, consists of humanitarian precepts rather than laws, as evidenced again by its use of second person formulation, the appeal to empathy and sympathy, and the fact that the punishments for non-compliance come not from the state, but directly from God. 23.1-9, though pertaining to testimony given in court, is presented not as law but as moral admonition: vv. 1-3 and 6-9 are second person, apodictic exhortations; they lack human penalties for non-compliance, and their appeal to a sense of fairness and empathy to motivate compliance are not normally associated with laws. In addition, vv. 4-5's admonition to help with an enemy's animal if it goes astray or lies under its load not only lacks any penalty clause for non-compliance, but would be impractical as a law to be enforced by the state.

The מֹת יוּמַת cases of Exod. 21.12-17 are closer to being laws than any of the cases mentioned above, but even here this categorization is problematic. The penalty clause is permission ('he may be killed') or desert ('he is worthy of being killed') rather than legal dictate ('he must be killed'). These cases lack the precision normally expected of law by not spelling out exceptions. For example in the case of a child striking a parent, the age of the child and degree of the blow would surely be mitigating factors. Nor do they state how and by whom the sentence is to be administered, nor whether ransom could be accepted. However, if the intent is to express moral outrage at certain offenses rather than to establish statutory law, this lack of precision becomes understandable and acceptable given the author's purposes.

Some of the remaining regulations lack elements expected of a law code. There is a general lack of reference to courts or judges (אלהים and פללים have been misunderstood in this regard). Often there is not the specificity expected of clear law: the case of vengeance on the master killing a bondsman (21.20-21) does not specify who takes the vengeance. The case of the ox goring an ox (21.35-36) does not deal with cases where the oxen are of unequal value. 22.1-2a on house-breaking fails to prescribe any penalty for this offense. The cases of grazing or burning a neighbor's field (22.4-5) do not specify how to determine the 'highest value' of the loss. 22.6-12 with its emphasis on oaths gives a remedy for cases where human law fails; that is, through the oath an appeal is made to a supra-human, divine court of justice. In general, 21.28–22.16 is hardly comprehensive enough to be in any case a 'code'.

There are also literary features in Exod. 21.18–22.16 that are unusual for a legal corpus. The juxtaposition of the case of the pregnant woman with the case of maiming the bondsman to make an ideological statement concerning the humanity of bondsmen points to literary artistry rather than legal precision. So does the separation of the cases where an ox gores a man from those where an ox gores another ox to make a philosophical statement about man in creation's hierarchy.

Figurative language and wordplay support the literary view: the *lex talionis* is metaphorical for monetary substitutes. The death sentence on the negligent owner in 21.29 is a hyperbole rather than a rigid legal dictate since the culprit normally escapes death by means of a ransom (21.30). Hence, a legal form is used for something other than a legal purpose: to say in the strongest of possible terms 'woe to him who allows a dangerous ox to roam about unrestrained.' Possible poetic devices observed included poetry (20.23 with enjambment; 21.23b-25, proverbial; 22.17-19; 22.27), double entendre (21.8, Qere/Ketiv; 22.7, וקרב; 23.2, רבים), wordplay (22.4-5, ב.ע.ר; 22.12, עד; 22.24, עמך/עני/עמי; 23.2, רב/רבים), stylistic variation (21.35-36) and irony (22.22-23), as well as chiasmus (21.28-36, 21.37–22.3, 22.6-12, and 20.22–23.33 as a whole). Such devices are not typically associated with laws.

The data above suggests that what we have here is not a law code, but moral comments on some legal and non-legal subjects conveyed in a manner more appropriate for literary art than for adjudication. There were no doubt laws in existence that treated the kinds of subjects that Exod. 21.18–22.16 treats which the author/editor(s) in all probability drew upon in composing these laws; the strong parallel between LE §53 and Exod. 21.35, for example, gives support of this. But it is doubtful that any law code that the author/editor(s) had at his disposal would have had the literary characteristics manifested by the biblical corpus. At the very least, such material has been thoroughly reworked for the author's particular purposes.

Many of the so-called laws of Exod. 20.22–23.19 are not laws at all. The משפטים seem to include non-legal as well as legal regulations. Those regulations of a legal character are not at all comprehensive in subject matter, and show features more appropriate to literary art than law. Therefore, the source-oriented theory of the insertion of a largely intact law code called משפטים into 20.22–23.19 fails to account satisfactorily for the text as we have it.

Conclusion

Exod. 20.22–23.19 has been found to be an artfully crafted unity, being well integrated internally and in relation to the Pentateuch of which it is a part regardless of the hypothetical or even demonstrable sources used by its author(s)/editor(s).

Although the discourse-oriented explanations of the text as it stands may in a few cases be no better than the source-oriented ones (e.g., there is good text-critical evidence that Exod. 21.16 originally followed the two cases on parents), while occasionally a discourse-oriented explanation seems inferior to the source-critical alternative (e.g. the use of אֹו rather than the expected אִם at 21.36 is most easily explained as a corruption of אִם), the discourse-oriented approach to the various problems in the text has generally been shown to be in no way inferior to source-oriented approaches to these sorts of problems, and in most cases it seems superior.

This study has found a purposeful placement of Exod. 20.22–23.19 within the Sinaitic narrative, connections between these regulations and similar texts and themes in the Pentateuch into which these regulations have been integrated, intelligent principles of organization of the regulations vis-à-vis one another, an ideology expressed by the text which is coherent with itself and consistent with the ideology expressed by other texts of the Pentateuch, and literary purpose—both ideological and aesthetic—in the particular formulations of these regulations. Moreover, the exegetical solutions to problems presented by the text along discourse-oriented lines generally seem in no way inferior to those along source-oriented lines, and in many cases it provides exegetical solutions that are better than the source-oriented alternatives. Hence, the 'literary approach' has, on the whole, been vindicated rather than denied by the attempt here to apply it to the text of Exod. 20.22–23.19.

BIBLIOGRAPHY

Alt, A., 'The Origins of Israelite Law', in *Essays on Old Testament History and Religion* (trans. R.A. Wilson; Garden City, NY: Doubleday, 1967), pp. 101-71.

Alter, R., *The Art of Biblical Narrative* (New York: Basic Books, 1981).

Arichea, D.C., 'The Ups and Downs of Moses: Locating Moses in Exodus 19–33', *BT* 40.2 (1989), pp. 244-46.

Bäntsch, B., *Das Bundesbuch: Ex. xx 22–xxiii 33* (Halle: Max Niemeyer, 1892).

Barthélemy, D., *et al.* (eds.), *Preliminary and Interim Report on the Hebrew Old Testament Text Project* (5 vols.; New York: United Bible Societies, 1977–80).

Bayliss, M., 'The Cult of Dead Kin in Assyria and Babylon', *Iraq* 35 (1973), pp. 115-25.

Beer, G., *Exodus* (HAT; Tübingen: Mohr, 1939).

Bentzen, A., *Introduction to the Old Testament*, I (Copenhagen: Gad, 1952).

Berlin, A., 'On the meaning of פלל in the Bible', *RB* 96 (1989), pp. 345-51.

—*Poetics and Interpretation of Biblical Narrative* (Bible and Literature Series 9; ed. D.M. Gunn; Sheffield: Almond, 1983).

Beyerlin, W., *Origins and History of the Oldest Sinaitic Traditions* (trans. S. Rudman; Oxford: Oxford University Press, 1965).

Boecker, H.J., *Law and the Administration of Justice in the Old Testament and Ancient East* (trans. J. Moiser; Minneapolis: Augsburg, 1980).

Brichto, H.C., 'The Case of the שטה and a Reconsideration of Biblical "Law"', *HUCA* 46 (1975), pp. 55-70.

—'Kin, Cult, Land and Afterlife—A Biblical Complex', *HUCA* 44 (1973), pp. 1-54.

—'Law and Law-Codes in the Bible—Exploding a Myth' (paper read at World Congress of Jewish Studies, Jerusalem, 1977).

—'On Slaughter and Sacrifice, Blood and Atonement', *HUCA* 47 (1976), pp. 19-55.

—*The Problem of 'Curse' in the Hebrew Bible* (JBL Monograph Series 13; Philadelphia: SBL, 1963).

—*Toward a Grammar of Biblical Poetics* (New York: Oxford University Press, 1992).

—'The Worship of the Golden Calf: A Literary Analysis of a Fable on Idolatry', *HUCA* 54 (1983), pp. 1-44.

Briggs, C.A., *The Higher Criticism of the Hexateuch* (New York: Charles Scribner's Sons, 1897).

Bush, G., *Notes on the Book of Exodus* (2 vols.; New York: Newman & Ivison, 1852).

Buss, M.J., 'The Distinction between Civil and Criminal Law in Ancient Israel', in *Proceedings of the Sixth World Congress of Jewish Studies 1973*, I (ed. A. Shinan; Jerusalem: World Union of Jewish Studies, 1977), pp. 51-62.

Carmichael, C.M., *The Origins of Biblical Law* (Ithaca: Cornell University Press, 1992).

—'A Singular Method of Codification of Law in the *Mishpaṭim* (Exodus 23.9-19)', *ZAW* 84 (1972), pp. 19-25.

Cassuto, U., *A Commentary on the Book of Exodus* (trans. I. Abrahams; Jerusalem: Magnes, 1967).

Cazelles, H., *Études sur le code de l'alliance* (Paris: Letouzey & Ané, 1946).

Childs, B.S., *The Book of Exodus: A Critical, Theological Commentary* (OTL; Philadelphia: Westminster, 1974).

Chirichigno, G.C., 'The Narrative Structure of Exodus 19–24', *Bib* 68 (1987), pp. 457-79.

Civil, M., 'New Sumerian Law Fragments', in *Studies in Honor of Benno Landsberger on His Seventy-Fifth Birthday, April 21, 1965* (Assyriological Studies 16; ed. H.G. Güterbock and T. Jacobsen; Chicago: University of Chicago Press, 1965), pp. 1-12.

Clements, R.E., *Exodus* (Cambridge Commentary on the New English Bible; Cambridge: Cambridge University Press, 1972).

—*Isaiah 1–39* (NCB; Grand Rapids: Eerdmans, 1980).

Cole, R.A., *Exodus* (TOTC; Downers Grove: Inter-Varsity, 1973).

Congdon, R.N., 'Exodus 21.22-25 and the Abortion Debate', *BSac* 146 (1989), pp. 132-47.

Conrad, D., *Studien zum Altargesetz: Ex 20.24-26* (Marburg: H. Kombächer, 1968).

Cooper, A., 'The Plain Sense of Exodus 23.5', *HUCA* 59 (1988), pp. 1-22.

Cowan, J.M., *Arabic-English Dictionary* (Wiesbaden: Otto Harrassowitz, 3rd edn, 1971).

Craigie, P.C., *The Book of Deuteronomy* (NICOT; Grand Rapids: Eerdmans, 1976).

—'Deuteronomy and Ugarit Studies', *TynBul* 28 (1977), pp. 155-69.

—*Ugarit and the Old Testament* (Grand Rapids: Eerdmans, 1983).

Dandamaev, M.A., *Slavery in Babylonia: From Nabopolassar to Alexander the Great (626–331 BC)* (trans. V.A. Powell; ed. M.A. Powell and D.B. Weisberg; DeKalb: Northern Illinois University Press, 1984).

Daube, D., *Studies in Biblical Law* (London: Cambridge University Press, 1947).

David, M., 'The Codex Hammurabi and its Relation to the Provision of Law in Exodus', *OTS* 7 (1950), pp. 149-78.

—'התעמר' (Deut. XXI 14; XXIV 7)', *VT* 1 (1951), pp. 219-21.

Deem, A., 'The Goddess Anath and Some Hebrew Cruces', *JSS* 23 (1978), pp. 25-30.

Diamond, A.S., 'An Eye for an Eye', *Iraq* 19 (1957), pp. 151-55.

Dietrich, M., and O. Loretz, ''DB and 'DB im Ugaritischen', *UF* 17 (1986), pp. 105-116.

Doron, P., 'A New Look at an Old Lex [*Lex Talionis*]', *JANESCU* 1.2 (1968–69), pp. 21-27.

Draffkorn, A.E., '*ILÂNI*/ELOHIM', *JBL* 76 (1957), pp. 216-24.

Driver, S.R., *The Book of Exodus* (Cambridge Bible for Schools and Colleges; Cambridge: Cambridge University Press, 1911).

Durham, J.I., *Exodus* (WBC; Waco, TX: Word, 1987).

Eichler, B.L., 'Bestiality', *IDBSup*, pp. 96-97.

—*Indenture at Nuzi: The Personal Tidennûtu Contract and its Mesopotamian Analogues* (Yale Near Eastern Researches 5; New Haven: Yale University Press, 1973).

Eissfeldt, O., *The Old Testament: An Introduction* (trans. P.R. Ackroyd; New York: Harper & Row, 1965).

Fensham, F.C., 'עד' in Exodus xxii, 12', *VT* 12 (1962), pp. 337-39.

—'Exodus xxi, 18-19 in the Light of Hittite Law §10', *VT* 10 (1960), pp. 333-35.

—'New Light on Exodus 21.6 and 22.7 from the Laws of Eshnunna', *JBL* 78 (1959), pp. 160-61.

—'The Son of a Handmaid in Northwest Semitic', *VT* 19 (1969), pp. 312-21.

Fewell, D.N., and D. Gunn, 'Tipping the Balance: Sternberg's Reader and the Rape of Dinah', *JBL* 110 (1991), pp. 193-212.

Finkelstein, J.J., *The Ox that Gored* (Philadelphia: American Philosophical Society, 1981).

Fishbane, M., *Biblical Interpretation in Ancient Israel* (Oxford: Oxford University Press, 1985).

Fokkelman, J.P., 'Genesis', in *The Literary Guide to the Bible* (ed. R. Alter and F. Kermode; Cambridge, MA: Harvard University Press, 1987).

Galling, K., 'Altar', *IDB*, I, pp. 96-100.

Gilmer, H.W., *The If-You Form in Israelite Law* (SBLDS, 15; Missoula, MT: Scholars Press, 1975).

Gispen, W.H., *Exodus* (trans. E. van der Maas; Bible Student's Commentary; Grand Rapids: Zondervan, 1982).

Gordon, C.H., 'אלהים' in its Reputed Meaning of "Rulers, Judges"', *JBL* 54 (1935), pp. 139-44.

—'Poetic Legends and Myths from Ugarit', *Berytus* 25 (1977), pp. 3-133.

—*Ugaritic Textbook* (AnOr 38; Rome: Pontificium Institutum Biblicum, 1965).

Gray, M.P., 'The Habiru-Hebrew Problem in the Light of the Source Material Available at Present', *HUCA* 29 (1958), pp. 135-202.

Greenberg, M., 'The Biblical Conception of Asylum', *JBL* 78 (1959), pp. 125-32.

—*Biblical Prose Prayer* (Berkeley: University of California Press, 1983).

—*The Hab/piru* (AOS 39; New Haven: American Oriental Society, 1955).

—'More Reflections on Biblical Criminal Law', in *Studies in Bible: 1986* (Scripta Hierosolymitana 31; ed. S. Japhet; Jerusalem: Magnes, 1986), pp. 1-17.

—'Some Postulates of Biblical Criminal Law', in *Yehezkel Kaufmann Jubilee Volume* (ed. M. Haran; Jerusalem: Detus Goldberg, 1960), pp. 3-28.

Greenfield, J.C., 'Adi Baltu—Care for the Elderly and its Rewards', *AfO* 19 (1982), pp. 309-316.

Greengus, S., 'Law in the Old Testament', *IDBSup*, pp. 532-37.

Grosz, K., 'Dowery and Brideprice in Nuzi', in *Studies in the Civilization and Culture of Nuzi and the Hurrians* (ed. M.A. Morrison and D.I. Owen; Winona Lake: Eisenbrauns, 1981), pp. 151-82.

Gunn, D.M., 'New Directions in the Study of Biblical Hebrew Narrative', *JSOT* 39 (1987), pp. 65-75.

Halbe, J., *Das Privilegrecht Jahwes Ex 34, 10-26: Gestalt und Wesen, Herkunft und Wirken in vordeuteronomischer Zeit* (Göttingen: Vandenhoeck & Ruprecht, 1975).

Haran, M., 'Seething a Kid in its Mother's Milk', *JJS* 30 (1979), pp. 22-35.

—*Temple and Temple-Service in Ancient Israel* (Winona Lake: Eisenbrauns, 1985).

Heinisch, P., 'Das Sklavenrecht in Israel und im Alten Orient', *Studia Catholica* 11 (1934/35), pp. 201-218.

Herzog, Z., M. Aharoni, A. Rainey, 'Arad—Ancient Israelite Fortress with a Temple to Yahweh', *BARev* 13.2 (Mar./Apr. 1987), pp. 16-35.

Hess, R., 'The Structure of the Covenant Code: Exodus 20.22–23.33' (ThM thesis, Trinity Evangelical Divinity School [Deerfield, IL], 1980).

Hoftijzer, J., 'Ex. xxi 8', *VT* 7 (1957), pp. 388-91.

Huffmon, H.B., 'Exodus 23.4-5: A Comparative Study', in *A Light unto My Path: Old Testament Studies in Honor of Jacob M. Myers* (ed. H.N. Bream *et al.*; Philadelphia: Temple University Press, 1974), pp. 271-78.

Hyatt, J.P., *Exodus* (NCB; London: Oliphants, 1971).

Jackson, B.S., *Essays in Jewish and Comparative Legal History* (Studies in Judaism in Late Antiquity 10; ed. J. Neusner; Leiden: Brill, 1975).

—'Note on Exodus 22.4 (MT)', *JJS* 27 (1976), pp. 138-41.

—*Theft in Early Jewish Law* (Oxford: Oxford University Press, 1972).

Jastrow, M., *A Dictionary of the Targumim, the Talmud Babli and Jerushalmi, and the Midrashic Literature* (2 vols.; Brooklyn: P. Shalom, 1967 [reprint of 1903 edn]).

Jepsen, A., *Untersuchungen zur Bundesbuch* (BWANT 5; Stuttgart: W. Kohlhammer, 1927).

—'אמה and שפחה', *VT* 8 (1958), pp. 293-97.

Kaufman, S.A., *The Akkadian Influences on Aramaic* (Assyriological Studies 19; Chicago: University of Chicago Press, 1974).

Keil, C.F., *The Pentateuch* (Biblical Commentary by C.F. Keil and F. Delitzsch; trans. J. Martin; Grand Rapids: Eerdmans, 1978 [1864]).

Kessler, M., 'A Methodological Setting for Rhetorical Criticism', in *Art and Meaning: Rhetoric in Biblical Literature* (JSOTSup 19; ed. D.J.A. Clines *et al.*; Sheffield: JSOT Press, 1982), pp. 1-19.

Kilian, R., 'Apodiktisches und kasuistisches Recht im Licht ägyptischer Analogien', *BZ* 7 (1963), pp. 185-202.

Knauf, E.A., 'Zur Herkunft und Sozialgeschichte Israels: "Das Böckchen in der Milch seiner Mutter"', *Bib* 69 (1988), pp. 153-69.

König, F.E., *Historisch-kritisches Lehrgebäude der hebräischen Sprache. III. 2.2. Historische-Comparative Syntax* (Leipzig: Hinrichs, 1897).

Kornfeld, W., *Studien zum Heiligkeitgesetz* (Vienna: Herder, 1952).

Krebs, W., 'Zur kultischen Kohabitation mit Tieren im Alten Orient', *Forschungen und Fortschritte* 37 (1963), pp. 19-21.

Leibowitz, N., *Studies in Shemot* (2 vols.; trans. A. Newman; Jerusalem: World Zionist Organization, 1976).

Lemche, N.P., 'The "Hebrew Slave"', *VT* 25 (1975), pp. 129-44.

Liedke, G., *Gestalt formgeschichtlich-terminologische Studie* (WMANT 39; Neukirchen–Vluyn: Neukirchener, 1971).

Lipiński, E., 'L'"Esclave Hébreu"', *VT* 26 (1976), pp. 120-24.

Loewenstamm, S.E., 'Exodus XXI 22-25', *VT* 27 (1977), pp. 352-60.

—'נשך and מ/תרבית', *JBL* 88 (1969), pp. 78-80.

Lohfink, N., 'חרם', *TDOT*, V, pp. 180-99.

Loretz, O., 'Ex 21,6; 22,8 und angebliche Nuzi-Parallelen', *Bib* 41 (1960), pp. 167-75.

McCarter, P.K., Jr., *I Samuel* (Anchor Bible; Garden City, NY: Doubleday, 1980).

McConville, J.G., *Law and Theology in Deuteronomy* (JSOTSup 33; Sheffield: JSOT Press, 1984).

McKay, J.W., 'Exodus XXIII 1-3, 6-8: A Decalogue for the Administration of Justice in the City Gate', *VT* 21 (1971), pp. 311-25.

McNeile, A.H., *The Book of Exodus: With Introduction and Notes* (Westminster Commentaries; London: Methuen, 3rd edn, 1931).

Maloney, R.P., 'Usury and Restrictions on Interest-Taking in the Ancient Near East', *CBQ* 36 (1974), pp. 1-20.

Meek, T.J., 'The Origin of Hebrew Law', in *Hebrew Origins* (New York: Harper & Row, 3rd edn, 1960), pp. 49-81.

Mendelsohn, I., *Slavery in the Ancient Near East* (London: Oxford University Press, 1949).

—'Slavery in the Ancient Near East', *BA* 9.4 (1946), pp. 74-88.

Mendenhall, G.E., *The Tenth Generation: The Origins of Biblical Tradition* (Baltimore: Johns Hopkins University Press, 1973).

Milgrom, J., 'Profane Slaughter and a Formulaic Key to the Composition of Deuteronomy', *HUCA* 47 (1976), pp. 1-17.

—'The Rationale for Cultic Law: The Case of Impurity', *Semeia* 45 (1989), pp. 103-109.

—*Studies in Cultic Theology and Terminology* (Studies in Judaism in Late Antiquity 36; ed. J. Neusner; Leiden: Brill, 1983).

Morgenstern, J., 'The Book of the Covenant, Part II', *HUCA* 7 (1930), pp. 19-258.

Muilenberg, J., 'Form Criticism and Beyond', *JBL* 88 (1969), pp. 1-18.

Neufeld, E., *Ancient Hebrew Marriage Laws* (London: Longmans, Green, 1944).

—'The Prohibitions against Loans at Interest in Ancient Hebrew Laws', *HUCA* 26 (1955), pp. 355-412.

North, R., 'Flesh, Covering, and Repose, Ex. xxi 10', *VT* 5 (1955), pp. 204-206.

—'דרור', *TDOT*, III, pp. 265-69.

Noth, M., *Exodus: A Commentary* (OTL; Philadelphia: Westminister, 1962).

Otto, E., 'Rechtssystematik im altbabylonischen "Codex Eshnunna" und im altisraelitischen "Bundesbuch"', *UF* 19 (1987), pp. 175-97.

—'Town and Rural Countryside in Ancient Israelite Law: Reception and Redaction in Cuneiform and Israelite Law', *JSOT* 57 (1993), pp. 3-22.

Patrick, D., 'I and Thou in the Covenant Code', in *SBL Seminar Papers 1978* (Missoula, MT: Scholars Press, 1978), pp. 71-86.

—*Old Testament Law* (Atlanta: John Knox Press, 1985).

—'Studying Biblical Law as a Humanities', *Semeia* 45 (1989), pp. 27-47.

Paul, S.M., 'Exod. 21,10: A Threefold Maintenance Clause', *JNES* 28 (1969), pp. 48-53.

—*Studies in the Book of the Covenant in the Light of Cuneiform and Biblical Law* (VTSup 18; Leiden: Brill, 1970).

Phillips, A.C.J., *Ancient Israel's Criminal Law: A New Approach to the Decalogue* (Oxford: Basil Blackwell, 1970).

—'The Laws of Slavery: Exodus 21.2-11', *JSOT* 30 (1984), pp. 51-66.

Philo, *Works*, VII, VIII (Loeb Classical Library; trans. F.H. Colson; London: Heinemann, 1937, 1939), pp. 97-607, 1-155.

Pitard, W.T., 'Amarna *ekemu* and Hebrew נקם', *Maarav* 3 (1982), pp. 5-25.

Pope, M.H., 'The Cult of the Dead at Ugarit', in *Ugarit in Retrospect* (ed. G.D. Young; Winona Lake: Eisenbrauns, 1981), pp. 159-79.

Rabinowitz, J.J., 'Exodus XXII 4 and the Septuagint Version Thereof', *VT* 9 (1959), pp. 40-46.

Ratner, R., and B. Zuckerman, '"A kid in milk"?: New Photographs of KTU 1.23, Line 14', *HUCA* 57 (1986), pp. 15-16.

Ringgren, H., 'אלהים', *TDOT*, I, pp. 267-84.

—'חקק', *TDOT*, V, pp. 139-47.

Robertson, E., 'The Altar of Earth (Exodus xx, 24-26)', *JJS* 1 (1948), pp. 12-21.

Rofé, A., 'Family and Sex Laws in Deuteronomy and the Book of the Covenant', *Henoch* 9 (1987), pp. 131-59.

Römer, W.H.Ph., 'Religion of Ancient Mesopotamia', in *Historia Religionum: Handbook for the History of Religions. I. Religions of the Past* (ed. C.J. Bloeker and G. Widengren; Leiden: Brill, 1969), pp. 115-94.

Schenker, A., 'Affranchisement d'une esclave selon Ex 21,7-11', *Bib* 69 (1988), pp. 547-56.

—'כֹּפֶר et expiation', *Bib* 63 (1982), pp. 32-46.

Schulz, H., *Das Todesrecht im Alten Testament* (Berlin: Töpelmann, 1969).

Schwienhorst-Schönberger, L., *Das Bundesbuch (Ex 20,22–23,33)* (BZAW 188; Berlin: de Gruyter, 1990).

Skaist, A., 'The Ancestor Cult and Succession in Mesopotamia', in *Death in Mesopotamia* [= *RAI* 26 = *Mesopotamia* 8 (1980)], pp. 123-28.

Smick, E.B., 'גוּ֫ח', *Theological Wordbook of the Old Testament* (gen. ed. R.L. Harris; Chicago: Moody, 1980).

Snaith, N., 'Exodus 23.18 and 34.25', *JTS* 20 (1969), pp. 533-34.

Sonsino, R., *Motive Clauses in Hebrew Law: Biblical Forms and Near Eastern Parallels* (SBLDS 45; Chico, CA: Scholars Press, 1980).

Speiser, E.A., 'The Stem פלל in Hebrew', *JBL* 82 (1963), pp. 301-306.

Sprinkle, J.M., 'The Interpretation of Exodus 21.22-25 (*Lex Talionis*) and Abortion', *WTJ* 55 (1993), pp. 233-53.

—'Literary Approaches to the Old Testament: A Survey of Recent Scholarship', *JETS* 32 (1989), pp. 299-310.

Stamm, J.J., 'Zum Altargesetz im Bundesbuch', *TZ* 1 (1945), pp. 304-306.

Sternberg, M., 'Biblical Poetics and Sexual Politics: From Reading to Counterreading', *JBL* 111 (1992), pp. 463-88.

—*Poetics of Biblical Narrative: Ideological Literature and the Drama of Reading* (Bloomington: Indiana University Press, 1985).

Turnbam, T.J., 'Male and Female Slaves in the Sabbath Year Laws of Exodus 21.1-11', in *SBL Seminar Papers 1987* (Decatur: Scholars Press, 1987), pp. 545-59.

van der Ploeg, J.P.M., 'Studies in Hebrew Law: III. Systematic Analysis of the Contents of the Collections of Law in the Pentateuch', *CBQ* 13 (1951), pp. 28-43.

van der Toorn, K., 'The Nature of the Biblical Teraphim in the Light of the Cuneiform Evidence', *CBQ* 52 (1990), pp. 203-22.

—*Sin and Sanction in Israel and Mesopotamia* (Studia Semitica Neerlandica 22; Assen//Maastricht: Van Gorcum, 1985).

van Houten, C., *The Alien in Israelite Law* (JSOTSup 107; Sheffield: JSOT Press, 1991).

Van Selms, A., 'The Goring Ox in Babylonian and Biblical Law', *ArOR* 18.4 (1950), pp. 321-30.

Vannoy, J.R., 'The Use of the Word האלהים in Ex. 21.6 and 22.7, 8', in *The Law and the Prophets: Old Testament Studies Prepared in Honor of Oswald Thompson Allis* (ed. J.H. Skilton; Nutley, NJ: Presbyterian and Reformed, 1974), pp. 225-41.

Vaux, R. de, *Ancient Israel. I. Social Institutions. II. Religious Institutions* (New York: McGraw-Hill, 1965).

—*The Early History of Israel* (trans. D. Smith; Philadelphia: Westminster, 1978).

Von Soden, W., *Akkadisches Handwörterbuch* (3 vols; Wiesbaden: Otto Harrassowitz, 1965–1981).

Wanke, G., 'Bundesbuch', *Theologische Realenzyklopädie*, VII (Berlin: de Gruyter, 1981), pp. 412-15.

Wapnish, P., and B. Hesse, 'Pampered Pooches or Plain Pariahs? The Ashkelon Dog Burials', *BA* 56 (1993), pp. 55-80.

Weingreen, J., 'The PI'EL in Biblical Hebrew: A Suggested New Concept', *Henoch* 5 (1983), pp. 21-29.

Weiss, D.H., 'A Note on אשר לא ארשה [Exod. 22.15]', *JBL* 81 (1962), pp. 67-69.

Wellhausen, J., *Prolegomena to the History of Ancient Israel* (Gloucester, MA: Peter Smith, 1983).

Wenham, G.J., 'Legal Forms in the Book of the Covenant', *TynBul* 22 (1971), pp. 95-102.

—'Leviticus 27.2-8 and the Price of Slaves', *ZAW* 90 (1978), pp. 264-65.

—*Numbers: An Introduction and Commentary* (TOTC; Downers Grove: Inter-Varsity, 1981).

Westbrook, R., '*Lex Talionis* and Exodus 21.22-25', *RB* 93 (1986), pp. 52-69.

—*Studies in Biblical and Cuneiform Law* (Cahiers de la Revue Biblique 26; Paris: Gabalda, 1988).

Williams, J.G., 'Addenda to "Concerning One of the Apodictic Formulas"', *VT* 15 (1965), pp. 113-15.

Williams, R.J., *Hebrew Syntax: An Outline* (Toronto: University of Toronto Press, 2nd edn, 1976).

Williamson, H.G.M., 'A Reconsideration of עוז in Biblical Hebrew', *ZAW* 97 (1985), pp. 74-85.

Woudstra, M.H., *The Book of Joshua* (NICOT; Grand Rapids: Eerdmans, 1981).

Yaron, R., 'The Goring Ox in Near Eastern Laws', in *Jewish Law in Ancient and Modern Israel* (ed. H.H. Cohn; New York: KTAV, 1971), pp. 50-60 [= *Israel Law Review* 1 (1966), pp. 396-406].

—*The Laws of Eshnunna* (Jerusalem: Magnes, 1969).

INDEXES

INDEX OF REFERENCES

OLD TESTAMENT

ANCIENT LEGAL MATERIAL

INDEX OF AUTHORS